THE POSTAL EXAM PREPARATION BOOK

GUARANTEED
METHODS TO SCORE
90% TO 100%
OR YOUR MONEY BACK

EVERYTHING YOU NEED TO KNOW

ALL MAJOR EXAMS
THOROUGHLY COVERED IN ONE BOOK

CLERKS • CARRIERS • RURAL CARRIERS
DISTRIBUTION CLERKS • MAIL HANDLERS

NORMAN HALL

BOB ADAMS, INC.
PUBLISHERS

Holbrook, Massachusetts

Copyright ©1984, 1985, 1988, 1990, Norman Hall. All rights reserved. No portion of this work may be reproduced in any form, or by any means, without the permission of the publisher.

ISBN: 1-55850-998-4

Published by Bob Adams, Inc., 260 Center St., Holbrook, MA 02343.

Printed in the United States of America.

TABLE OF CONTENTS

Introduction/5

Rural Carrier Exam/7

Clerk Carrier Exam/77

Distribution Clerk Machine Exam Supplement/183

Mail Handler Exam/197

INTRODUCTION

The Postal Service hires a substantial number of people every year in accordance with its labor needs, but there are more applicants than there are positions available. Consequently, to gain a fair overview of those who do apply, the Postal Service has developed an entrance qualification exam. Employment consideration is determined by how well the applicant scores on the exam; the higher your score, the better are your chances for a prospective interview. Now that you have purchased this material and intend to study it in you spare time, you are well on the road to being prepared!

This book parallels what will be expected on the actual exams and demonstrates techniques that can simplify the contents, particularly the memorization section of the Clerk Carrier exam. Excercises for each exam are provided to allow you to implement what you have studied; not only will you gain a sense of familiarity with the test material, but you will also approach the real exam with confidence and a feeling of ease.

A Special Note to Veterans:

If you have an honorable discharge from any branch of the service, you may qualify for a five point preference on your examination, providing you obtain a score of 70 percent of better on your exam. That would mean if a veteran were to score a 90 percent on the exam, five points would be added, giving him or her a 95 percent. Wounded/disabled veterans have ten point preference. Be sure you have a copy of your DD Form 214 and proof of disability to substantiate your claim. Contact your Postal Personnel Office for more details.

GENERAL INFORMATION ABOUT POSTAL EXAMS

Postal Service exams are neither long nor complicated, and all tests with exception of the Distribution Clerk Machine (DCM) exam, are multiple choice. A set number of possible answers are provided and you must decide which one of them correctly applies to the question that you are working on. Once you have determined that, then it is only a matter of recording your choices on an answer sheet. The answer sheet is basically comprised of answer blanks similar to the example shown.

Ⓐ Ⓑ Ⓒ Ⓓ Ⓔ

For purpose of illustation, let's say the answer to this particular question is B. Answer Ⓑ would be completely darkened in with soft lead (2B) pencil such that the answer blank would appear like the next example.

Ⓐ ● Ⓒ Ⓓ Ⓔ

It is important to exercise a little neatness when filling in your answers because your answer sheet will be electronically scored. The scoring machine subsequently lacks any kind of personality and could care less about what your intentions were concerning the answer; that is, if any of your answers look like those shown below, rather than following the previous example, they may be assessed as wrong even if you did know the correct answer! These machines are very objective and if an individual gets a little sloppy filling in answers and other information, not only will things get misconstrued, but worse, that individual's test score will suffer.

Now that the point about neatness has been clarified, one other twist in taking these exams must be considered. The Clerk Carrier and Mail Handler tests are quite limited on time, so it is important to find an effective balance between the speed with which you complete as many answers as you can, and neatness and accuracy. You would not want to find yourself only half finished with the exam when time ran out, just because you spent an excessive amount of time being too neat. Nor, would it be desirable to rush through the test and in the end do poorly because of a large share of mis-marked answers. The practice exercises that are included in this book will allow you ample opportunity to acquire that comforable and effective median, but the key word here is PRACTICE. You will find that the more you do work with the practice exercises, the better you will become at taking these kinds of exams and the higher your score will be.

When taking the actual examination, be sure to bring with you your test admission card (otherwise you will not be allowed to take the exam), your completed job application forms (all of this sent to you when notified as to when and where the exam will be given), a form of I.D, (i.e., a driver's license), and two Number Two pencils, in case they are not provided. Confront your exam with a feeling of confidence and optimism, and do your best.

A Comprehensive Guide

For The

Postal Service
RURAL CARRIER
EXAM

TEST CONTENT

There are essentially two parts to this exam. The first section involves the math used in basic postal transactions. The second section is divided into reader's comprehension and vocabulary exercises. Unlike other postal exams, this test allows more than enough time for completion. You will have 75 minutes to complete the 40 math questions and 90 minutes to complete the 60 reader's comprehension and vocabulary questions. So, you should not feel as hurried as you may taking other postal tests.

As far as preparing for this exam, let's examine it section by section. First, we will take a look at the math portion of the exam. The best hedge you can have on any math test is to practice up on your basic math skills (i.e., addition, subtraction, multiplication and division) well in advance of the test. Calculators would simplify these exercise considerably, but their use is not allowed in the exam room. Therefore, the sharper you can become at working with figures, the more confident you will feel at working this type of exercise. You will be asked to figure the total cost of a postal transaction which may include several items. Rate charts will be provided as a basis for your figures. It is important to read the entire question carefully and determine how many different items are being purchased to determine the total cost of the transaction. Each item will need to be figured separately and then collectively added together to find the correct answer. Be particularly careful when searching for figures on the rate charts. One misinterpretation will throw your calculations off and as a consequence, the answer you come up with will be incorrect. Again, the time appropriated for this part of the exam is not necessarily a constraint. If you take your time and carefully utilize the rate charts for each question, you will do very well.

The second half of the exam consists of a mix of reader's comprehension and vocabulary questions. Specifically, the first 25 questions are reader's comprehension and the 35 remaining questions are vocabulary oriented (60 questions total). Ninety minutes is more than sufficient for completion of this section. Do not skim these questions as a means of saving time because it will prove to be detrimental to your test score. There are many questions that have very similar choices provided. If you do not have a complete grasp of what the question is about, the first alternative that seems appropriate may very well be the wrong answer.

Reader's comprehension questions on the Rural Carrier exam are purely inferential, not literal. Literal comprehension specifically focuses on the content of what one particular sentence in a paragraph has to say. On the other hand, inferential comprehension requires that the reader read a paragraph and surmise the author's underlying statement. Simply skimming a paragraph is fine for finding information contained in a particular sentence, but it is largely ineffectual in inferential comprehension. When you are finished reading a paragraph, first ask yourself, "What exactly is the author trying to say?" What kind of an overall picture do you come up with? Usually, the first sentence of a paragraph should tip you off as to the meaning of the paragraph. Once you have drawn a conclusion as to what you believe the article is about, then proceed to the answers provided. Examine all the options provided and see if any one particular answer draws similar conclusions to your own. Chances are that is the correct answer. As a word of caution, since this test is comprised of inferential comprehension test questions, do not be misled by seeing one or more answers that are basically sentences taken out of the paragraph text. Remember, that is literal comprehension and it has no place in this kind of exam. Also, if you find yourself torn between deciding whether a general answer or a specific answer is the appropriate response, always choose the general answer. If, while working this exercise, you should become tired, take a short break of 30 seconds to 1 minute. Mental fatigue can inhibit your ability to comprehend readings, so taking a break somewhere in the middle is beneficial.

The vocabulary section is the end section of the exam, and comprises 35 questions. A key word highlighted by quotation marks will appear within the text of a sentence or stand by itself. You must select from five alternative answers that one which most clearly means the same thing as the key word (i.e., synonym). This is a fairly straightforward exercise and if you have a strong vocabulary, this will be the easiest part of the Rural Carrier test. There is, however, a guide at the end of this section that may be of considerable assistance to you in your preparations for this section of the exam. Use it as you deem necessary.

There are three Rural Carrier practice exams in this book. Treat each of these as if it were the real exam to get a true idea as to the pace of the test. This way, you will feel much more prepared and hence, confident when you do take the "real" test.

Before you go any further in this book, it is suggested that you find a place that is completely free of any distractions, has adequate overhead lighting, and a comfortable desk and chair. It is not important where you go to satisfy these requirements; what is important is that you simulate examination room conditions as closely as possible. Thus, you will have a reasonable idea of what to expect when taking the actual test, and become comfortable with that atmosphere.

MATH EXAM I
POSTAGE RATES FOR MAILING PARCELS

Various rates are provided below for determination of the cost of sending parcels weighing 2 to 20 pounds to Areas 1 through 6 and locally.

Wt in exact lbs & not exceeding	Local Area	Areas 1&2	Area 3	Area 4	Area 5	Area 6
2	.25	.29	.34	.41	.49	.59
3	.27	.31	.36	.43	.51	.61
4	.31	.35	.40	.47	.55	.65
5	.39	.43	.48	.55	.63	.73
6	.40	.44	.49	.56	.64	.74
7	.41	.45	.50	.57	.65	.75
8	.42	.46	.51	.58	.66	.76
9	.43	.47	.52	.59	.67	.77
10	.49	.53	.58	.65	.73	.83
11	.53	.57	.62	.69	.77	.87
12	.57	.61	.66	.73	.81	.91
13	.64	.68	.73	.80	.88	.98
14	.67	.71	.76	.83	.91	1.01
15	.70	.74	.79	.86	.94	1.04
16	.75	.79	.84	.91	.99	1.09
17	.78	.82	.87	.94	1.02	1.12
18	.84	.88	.93	1.00	1.08	1.18
19	.87	.91	.96	1.03	1.11	1.21
20	.92	.96	1.01	1.08	1.16	1.26

(Note: These particular postage and wrapping charges are not included unless the customer specifically requests their use. The weights shown below are only applicable up to 2 pounds and not including 2 pounds. Parcels weighing 2 or more pounds are shown above.)

(Hint: Fractional weights over 2 pounds should be rounded to the next hightest figure (i.e., 10-1/4 pounds = 11 pounds on the chart)).

GROUP A

Parcel No.	Price
1 or 2	0.30/oz
3	0.40/oz
4	0.45/oz
5	0.50/oz

PADDED ENVELOPE CHARGE
all sizes=0.75

GROUP B

All parcels cost 0.20 for the first 2 ounces and 0.08 for each additional ounce.

PACKAGE WRAPPING CHARGES

Pkg size	Cost
1-3	0.15
4-6	0.25
7-10	0.35

TIME: 75 MINUTES
40 QUESTIONS

MATH SECTION EXAM I

1. How much is the cost of five 22-cent postage stamps?

    A. $0.98   B. $1.00   C. $1.10   D. $2.20

2. What would it cost a customer that wanted three 3-cent stamps, five 10-cent stamps, and twelve 18-cent stamps?

    A. $3.00   B. $2.75   C. $2.55   D. none of these

3. How much would four 22-cent stamps, five $1.00 stamps, and three padded envelopes cost (refer to Table A for the padded envelopes charge)?

    A. $8.13   B. $8.15   C. $8.23   D. $7.13

4. If a customer wanted to send a package that weighed 17 pounds to a local destination, how much would it cost?

    A. $0.75   B. $0.82   C. $0.84   D. none of these

5. Suppose that a customer desired to send a parcel that weighed 9 pounds. The zip code shown would be considered Area 6. How much would it cost to send the parcel?

    A. $0.67   B. $0.76   C. $0.77   D. $0.83

6. What would it cost to send two packages each weighing 12 pounds; one parcel destined for Area 4 and the other for Area 6?

    A. $1.64   B. $1.53   C. $1.74   D. none of these

7. How much would it cost to send a Group B parcel weighing 1-1/2 pounds?

    A. $1.80   B. $1.96   C. $2.00   D. $4.13

8. How much would it cost to mail a 14 ounce parcel if it were considered a No. 5 parcel under a Group A classification?

    A. $7.00   B. $7.50   C. $6.50   D. none of these

9. If a Size 7 package weighing 8 pounds was destined to Area 2 and the customer also wanted it wrapped, what would it cost?

    A. $0.63   B. $0.70   C. $0.75   D. $0.81

10. Three parcels weighing 12, 14, and 6 pounds respectively, are to be sent to local area addresses. How much would it cost to send them?

    A. $1.65   B. $1.70   C. $1.63   D. none of these

11. Collectively, how much would it cost to send the following: two parcels each weighing 10 pounds and destined for Areas 1 and 2, one Size 4 parcel weighing 4 pounds to be wrapped prior to sending to Area 3, and a dozen padded envelopes?

    A. $9.68   B. $12.85   C. $10.63   D. $10.71

12. What would it cost to order a roll of 100 22-cent stamps, 12 3-cent stamps, 2 padded envelopes, and send an 11 ounce parcel that qualifies as a Group B article?

    A. $24.78   B. $22.15   C. $29.71   D. $24.98

13. What is the cost of sending 33 parcels all weighing 10-pounds each and destined for Area 6?

    A. $7.70   B. $8.30   C. $27.39   D. none of these

14. Look at Question 13 again; this time, everything is the same, except the customer wants the packages individually wrapped prior to shipping. Assume all parcels qualify as Size 8. How much would it cost now?

    A. $20.05   B. 19.85   C. $17.65   D. none of these

10 The Postal Exam Preparation Book

15. What is the cost of sending a Group A, No. 4 parcel weighing 17-3/4 ounces? (Hint: always round off to the next highest weight when dealing with fractional ounces).

    A. $7.30   B. $7.65   C. $7.13   D. $8.10

16. How much would it cost to send 17 items to the same local destination that all together weighed 16 pounds and needed to be wrapped in a Size 2 box prior to shipping?

    A. $0.90   B. $1.30   C. $0.75   D. none of these

17. What would it cost to send a Group A, No. 2 parcel weighing 20 ounces in a padded envelope?

    A. $6.00   B. $5.75   C. $6.75   D. $7.00

18. If 4 pound and 6 pound articles were both placed in a Size 3 wrapped package (actual weight 10-1/4 pounds) and sent to Area 3, how much would it cost to send this particular package?

    A. $0.62   B. $0.77   C. $0.70   D. none of these

19. What is the total cost to send 27 Group B parcels each weighing 10 ounces?

    A. $0.84   B. $27.00   C. $22.68   D. $23.68

20. How much would it cost to purchase 33 17-cent stamps, 40 padded envelopes, and 14 2-cent stamps?

    A. $35.00   B. $27.00   C. $35.80   D. none of these

21. A Group A, No. 4 parcel weighing 1 pound and wrapped in a Size 9 package would cost how much to send?

    A. $7.50   B. $7.55   C. $7.05   D. $12.00

22. A Group A, No. 5 parcel weighing 1 pound and wrapped in a Size 2 package would cost how much to send?

    A. $9.00   B. $10.00   C. $8.15   D. none of these

23. What would be the expense of sending 14 parcels each weighing 19 pounds to Area 2, 17 parcels each weighing 12 pounds to Area 6, and 6 parcels each weighing 4 pounds to Area 3?

    A. $29.76   B. $29.61   C. $30.16   D. $30.61

24. Suppose a customer just wanted 225 padded envelopes for his business. Providing you had that many on hand, how much would you have to charge this customer?

    A. $168.75   B. $168.25   C. $168.00   D. $168.57

25. How many 3-pound packages could a person send to Areas 1 and 2 if that person only had $10.00?

    A. 32   B. 31   C. 30   D. 29

26. What is the cost to send 24 parcels, each weighing 4 pounds to Areas 1 and 2, with half of them wrapped in Size 7 packages and the other half wrapped in Size 6 packages?

    A. $8.40   B. $4.20   C. $15.60   D. $3.00

27. If a customer only had $5.00, how many 2-ounce, Group A, No. 5 parcels wrapped in Size 2 packaging could he send?

    A. 2   B. 3   C. 4   D. none of these

28. What is the cost of sending a package locally in a padded envelope that weighs 2 pounds?

    A. $1.05   B. $1.00   C. $0.95   D. $1.15

29. What is the expense of sending a 14 ounce, Group B parcel?

    A. $1.16   B. $1.20   C. $1.61   D. $1.02

30. How much would it cost to send 5, 6 and 7 pound parcels to Areas 3, 5 and 6 respectively?

    A. $1.58   B. $1.67   C. $1.78   D. $1.87

The Postal Exam Preparation Book 11

31. How much would it cost to send a 17, 5 and 12 pound parcel to Areas 3, 2, and 4 respectively?

   A. $1.92 　　　　B. $2.03 　　　　C. $2.00 　　　　D. none of these

32. Suppose a customer wanted to buy 60 22-cent stamps, 35 15-cent stamps, 27 5-cent stamps, and 49 2-cent stamps. How much would all this cost?

   A. $20.78 　　　　B. $20.87 　　　　C. $21.78 　　　　D. $20.07

33. How much would it cost to send three 11 pound packages to Area 4 and seven 16 pound packages to Area 6?

   A. $9.70 　　　　B. $9.69 　　　　C. $9.71 　　　　D. $12.83

34. Assuming you only had $2.40 in pocket change, how many 1 ounce Group A, No. 4 parcels in padded envelopes could be sent for that amount?

   A. 4 　　　　B. 3 　　　　C. 2 　　　　D. none of these

35. If a customer had $15.00, what would be the maximum number of 22-cent stamps that could be purchased?

   A. 67 　　　　B. 68 　　　　C. 69 　　　　D. 70

36. What would it cost to send thirteen 13 pound packages to Area 4, five 20 pound packages to Area 1, and twelve 17 ounce Group B parcels locally?

   A. $10.40 　　　　B. $29.76 　　　　C. $32.75 　　　　D. $32.00

37. What would it cost to send a Size 5 wrapped 18 pound parcel to Area 6, a Size 9, wrapped 9 pound parcel to Area 2, and 15 Group A, No. 4 19 ounce parcels?

   A. $129.20 　　　　B. $131.76 　　　　C. $132.82 　　　　D. $130.50

38. What would it cost to send a Size 2, wrapped 4 pound package to Area 1, 60 Size 7, wrapped 3 pound parcels to Area 5, and 13 Group B, 13 ounce parcels to New York City?

   A. $53.33 　　　　B. $52.33 　　　　C. $54.33 　　　　D. $66.14

39. How much would 675 50-cent stamps, 300 22-cent stamps, 475 18-cent stamps and 700 5-cent stamps cost?

   A. $524.00 　　　　B. $337.50 　　　　C. $504.00 　　　　D. none of these

40. What would be the expense of sending a Size 8, wrapped 14 pound package to Area 3, and in addition, purchase 45 padded envelopes for future use?

   A. $35.46 　　　　B. $38.46 　　　　C. $34.86 　　　　D. $35.00

- END OF TEST -

12 The Postal Exam Preparation Book

ANSWER SHEET TO MATH EXAM I

1. Ⓐ Ⓑ Ⓒ Ⓓ Ⓔ
2. Ⓐ Ⓑ Ⓒ Ⓓ Ⓔ
3. Ⓐ Ⓑ Ⓒ Ⓓ Ⓔ
4. Ⓐ Ⓑ Ⓒ Ⓓ Ⓔ
5. Ⓐ Ⓑ Ⓒ Ⓓ Ⓔ
6. Ⓐ Ⓑ Ⓒ Ⓓ Ⓔ
7. Ⓐ Ⓑ Ⓒ Ⓓ Ⓔ
8. Ⓐ Ⓑ Ⓒ Ⓓ Ⓔ
9. Ⓐ Ⓑ Ⓒ Ⓓ Ⓔ
10. Ⓐ Ⓑ Ⓒ Ⓓ Ⓔ
11. Ⓐ Ⓑ Ⓒ Ⓓ Ⓔ
12. Ⓐ Ⓑ Ⓒ Ⓓ Ⓔ
13. Ⓐ Ⓑ Ⓒ Ⓓ Ⓔ
14. Ⓐ Ⓑ Ⓒ Ⓓ Ⓔ
15. Ⓐ Ⓑ Ⓒ Ⓓ Ⓔ
16. Ⓐ Ⓑ Ⓒ Ⓓ Ⓔ
17. Ⓐ Ⓑ Ⓒ Ⓓ Ⓔ
18. Ⓐ Ⓑ Ⓒ Ⓓ Ⓔ
19. Ⓐ Ⓑ Ⓒ Ⓓ Ⓔ
20. Ⓐ Ⓑ Ⓒ Ⓓ Ⓔ

21. Ⓐ Ⓑ Ⓒ Ⓓ Ⓔ
22. Ⓐ Ⓑ Ⓒ Ⓓ Ⓔ
23. Ⓐ Ⓑ Ⓒ Ⓓ Ⓔ
24. Ⓐ Ⓑ Ⓒ Ⓓ Ⓔ
25. Ⓐ Ⓑ Ⓒ Ⓓ Ⓔ
26. Ⓐ Ⓑ Ⓒ Ⓓ Ⓔ
27. Ⓐ Ⓑ Ⓒ Ⓓ Ⓔ
28. Ⓐ Ⓑ Ⓒ Ⓓ Ⓔ
29. Ⓐ Ⓑ Ⓒ Ⓓ Ⓔ
30. Ⓐ Ⓑ Ⓒ Ⓓ Ⓔ
31. Ⓐ Ⓑ Ⓒ Ⓓ Ⓔ
32. Ⓐ Ⓑ Ⓒ Ⓓ Ⓔ
33. Ⓐ Ⓑ Ⓒ Ⓓ Ⓔ
34. Ⓐ Ⓑ Ⓒ Ⓓ Ⓔ
35. Ⓐ Ⓑ Ⓒ Ⓓ Ⓔ
36. Ⓐ Ⓑ Ⓒ Ⓓ Ⓔ
37. Ⓐ Ⓑ Ⓒ Ⓓ Ⓔ
38. Ⓐ Ⓑ Ⓒ Ⓓ Ⓔ
39. Ⓐ Ⓑ Ⓒ Ⓓ Ⓔ
40. Ⓐ Ⓑ Ⓒ Ⓓ Ⓔ

(This page may be removed to mark answers.)

TIME: 90 MINUTES
60 QUESTIONS

READERS COMPREHENSION SECTION EXAM I

1. In the early 1900's, little consideration was given to land and timber management. It was common practice to consume our natural resources and assume nature, with time, would take care of whatever environmental damage was done. It didn't take an expert to point out that our national forests were disappearing at an alarming rate, or that precious top soils were eroding at levels never before witnessed. Consequently, laws were enacted to promote conservation, and measures were adopted to better manage our natural resources for the present as well as for the future.

   The statement that best supports the above paragraph is:
   A. Conservation is and always has been a first and foremost consideration in managing our natural resources.
   B. It took a long time for anyone to realize the degree of environmental damage being done by current land practices.
   C. Throughout the 19th century, land management took on a whole new meaning.
   D. Despite the lack of human concern about conservation in the early 1900's, nature did take care of itself.

2. Unfortunately, people devote more time and consideration to purchasing their next car than they do planning their retirement. Were it not for the innovation of Social Security, our system of welfare would be inundated with senior citizens. Lately, tax laws have been implemented to promote additional retirement savings over and above that which is already taken out for Social Security. Despite the federal retirement plans, people must give more consideration to financial planning if they are to enjoy their retirement.

   The statement that best supports this paragraph is:
   A. Without financial planning, retirement may be considered more of a burden than the anticipation of living a fulfilled life during the golden years.
   B. As a consensus, people have always planned their retirement.
   C. If your financial planning does not work out, you can always resort to welfare.
   D. Social Security is more than adequate to get along on.

3. Not everyone was pleased when the speed limit on our highways was reduced to 55 miles per hour. To some people, it was an inconvenience to drive slower through less aesthetic areas. While others simply believed that the Department of Transportation (DOT) had nothing better to do. Contrary to their beliefs, some very positive results were realized. National oil and gas consumptions were reduced, and more importantly, there was a sizable reduction in traffic fatalities. The reduction of speed was relatively insignificant in view of the lives saved.

   The statement that best supports this paragraph is:
   A. The DOT is without a doubt a beauracratic institution.
   B. It will only be a matter of time before they'll have us driving 45 miles per hour.
   C. If a person can't drive above 55 mph without getting into an accident, they have no business driving in the first place.
   D. Regardless of some people's misgivings on the 55 mph speed limit issue, the benefits achieved by driving slower overshadowed those gained by driving faster.

4. People are becoming increasingly more health conscious and careful of the types of food they eat. Restaurants are reacting to this new trend by offering extravagant salad bars and low fat meals. Some establishments even disclose the nutritional values of various meals they serve. With the public more informed on what is good and bad nutritionally, there is bound to be a reflection of it in their food expediters.

   The statement that best supports this paragraph is:
   A. By having a more educated outlook on health, more attention is given to what we eat and how we spend our food dollars.
   B. People have become dependent on eating out since restaurants are the only places offering balanced diets.
   C. You are assured of getting your money's worth when you see a salad bar in a restaurant.
   D. If a restaurant does not post the nutritional information pertaining to their meals, they may be covering something up.

5. Great strides have recently been made in the field of genetics. Genetic scientists now have a much better understanding of genes and inherent DNA than in years past. Genetics is an incredibly complex field of study, but ongoing progress

in the area of DNA decoding and gene splicing may unlock the mysteries surrounding such diseases as cancer, Downes Syndrome and Cystic Fibrosis. The beneficial implications of genetic research is overwhelming.

The statement that best supports the above paragraph is:
- A. DNA is too complicated to be studied, therefore the study of genetics could be considered a waste of research dollars.
- B. Genetics cannot be studied without delving into the question of medical ethics surrounding gene splicing.
- C. The continued research into the field of genetics poses a wide array of potential benefits to society.
- D. There is currently very little hope that cures will ever be found for genetically related diseases.

6. The sport of scuba diving can be considered an adventure unmatched by any other sport. It is similar to visiting an entirely different world. The sense of weightlessness, and the colors and sounds exhibited by various sea creatures are incredible. However, diving is not without its dangers. A diver who does not exercise what he or she learned in diver certification safety training can very easily put his or her life in jeopardy. Diving, when conducted in a safe manner, is almost guaranteed to be an experience unequaled by any other.

The statement that best supports this paragraph is:
- A. Diving is a sport meant to be enjoyed by adults only.
- B. This is not a sport for the physically unfit.
- C. Diving, when done safely, can be a sport that offers unparalleled entertainment.
- D. Scuba diving is essentially like any other sport; there are hazards that we must be aware of.

7. It is always easy to just say that a person has a green thumb, not to mention a good deal of luck, when gardens or indoor plants thrive. Actually, the attribution of luck isn't too far from being the truth. Most plants do not have stringent or narrow range requirements in order to proliferate. When we consider the synchrony of ideal soil moisture, nutrient levels, temperatures, humidity, and light, it can all become complicated. In essence, gardening can become something of a juggling act.

The statement that best supports this paragraph is:
- A. Gardening is an adventure not recommended for those with weak hearts.
- B. We would like to believe that we have mastered the techniques of gardening when our plants do well despite the fact that luck plays a significant role.
- C. Most plants have a wide range tolerance and consequently, no amount of abuse will reflect any difference.
- D. Gardening can be extraordinarily complicated.

8. Although people spend large amounts of money these days to purchase a new car or truck, it is surprising how few of them give consideration to general vehicle maintenance. One of the most overlooked yet critical maintenance jobs is to change the engine oil and oil filter regularly. This is relatively inexpensive and easy to do. This particular maintenance job alone can extend the life of your vehicle and reduce the chances of future trouble and costly repair work.

The statement that best supports the above paragraph is:
- A. New vehicles require little, if any, maintenance.
- B. Maintenance is just a continued waste of money.
- C. A car buyer is guaranteed not to have any breakdown if a rigorous maintenance schedule is followed.
- D. Considering the kind of an investment that a new vehicle is, the consumer should give some attention to basic maintenance to get the most longevity and repair-free operation out of that vehicle.

9. The National trade deficit has gained a great deal of public attention lately, and for good reason. A staggering loss of jobs domestically and the potential for rampant inflation are the consequences of our preference for imported goods. Our government is desperately trying to correct this situation by devaluing the dollar. The end result of such a policy has been to make imports more expensive and domestically produced goods cheaper. Hopefully, over the next year or so, our trade balance will begin to show equalization.

The statement that best supports this paragraph is:
- A. The National trade balance has direct bearing on our economy.
- B. The trade imbalance only concerns those who serve in public office.
- C. The only way to restore a trade balance is to devaluate world currencies.
- D. If our country had a policy of not trading with other countries, we would not be in this mess in the first place.

10. The presence and use of laser light was, at one point, considered a horrifying, imaginary power that belonged in a low-grade science fiction film. From the stages of a harmless beam of light to its current refinements, laser technology has demonstrated remarkable application. Lasers are being used in surgery, communications, guidance systems, art, and stereo electronics, to name just a few. It is hard to imagine what the future holds for this area of research.
The statement that best supports this paragraph is:
    A. Laser technology belongs in a science fiction movie.
    B. Laser technology offers too little to warrant further research time.
    C. People still remain skeptical about lasers and their uses.
    D. What emerged as a grossly undervalued science, laser technology has shown viable and versatile applications.

11. Dog obedience for puppies is not a bad idea. In fact, it can establish much better understanding between the dog and owner. Unacceptable behaviors, such as chewing, barking and housesoiling can be curtailed before they turn into long-standing bad habits. Early training can only improve the family-pet relationship.
The statement that best supports this paragraph is:
    A. Adult dogs are virtually untrainable.
    B. Early dog obedience training holds the prospect of improving compatibility with the family.
    C. Dog obedience should only be considered when bad behavior is exhibited.
    D. Obedience training is a lengthy and costly experience that most people will try to avoid.

12. A person swimming on the surface of an ocean and wearing dark-colored trunks or a wetsuit is asking for open invitation to a shark attack. The vibrations caused by the splashing of the swimmer combined with the swimmer's striking similarity to the size and color of a seal (a shark's basic diet) is all too tempting for a shark to pass up. Extreme caution should be exercised when swimming where sharks are prevalent.
The statement that best supports this paragraph is:
    A. Sharks are indiscriminate feeders.
    B. You need not be concerned about sharks when swimming in fresh water.
    C. An awareness of shark behavior would portend anyone swimming in saltwater to exercise a good degree of caution.
    D. Sharks view any swimmer as a juicy morsel.

13. Gun safety is not something to be taken for granted if you are a gun owner. A substantial number of accidents that occur within the home are the direct result of carelessness. Improperly stored guns and ammunition combined with unattended children is an accident waiting to happen. Cleaning a loaded gun can be equally as dangerous. By exercising a little common sense when dealing with guns, gun owners can avoid dangerous accidents.
The statement that best supports this paragraph is:
    A. Guns should be treated responsibly to alleviate accidents.
    B. Guns are outright dangerous and have no business within the household.
    C. Children have an affinity for firearms.
    D. A small number of accidents stem from improperly stored guns and ammunition.

14. Fireplaces or wood burning stoves can significantly save money on a family's heating bill. However, attention should be given to the kind and quality of wood being burned. Green or unseasoned wood can lead to excessive creosote buildup in chimneys. Not only is the heating efficiency of a woodstove or fireplace impaired, but chimney fires caused by creosote build-up are known for their intensity and inherent potential to burn down a home.
The statement that best supports this paragraph is:
    A. Burning wood for home heating has its economic advantages, but an awareness of the properties of the fuel you burn is a important safety advantage.
    B. Creosote buildup becomes dangerous.
    C. It's recommended to only burn green wood in a woodstove or fireplace.
    D. Home heating is by no means a simple consideration.

15. The American badger is particularly well adapted for digging and burrowing. Its short, compact, muscular stature is coupled with an exceptionally well-defined set of claws. This unique combination allows it to easily prey on rodents and other animals that live underground. Badgers are rarely seen in daylight because most of their foraging occurs during the early evening hours.

The statement that best supports this paragraph is:

The Postal Exam Preparation Book 17

A. Badger holes can pose a hazard to livestock such as cattle and horses.
B. Badgers could be considered very versatile animals.
C. A general description of the American badger is given.
D. Badgers are strictly nocturnal animals.

16. Swimming is touted by many experts as being the best form of physical exercise available. It strengthens the cardio-pulmonary system, and unlike running or aerobics, stress on delicate joints and heat exhaustion is avoided. Thus, swimming can be enjoyed by virtually anyone of any age.
The statement that best supports this paragraph is:
A. Swimming should always be done under adult supervision.
B. The premise of unrestricted participation with young and old alike and the medical benefits gained make swimming an enticing form of exercise.
C. Swimming is recommended only for those people that are in reasonable shape.
D. The highlight of swimming is the strengthening of the cardio-pulmonary system.

17. It is often tempting for people camping high in the mountains to drink water directly out of a scenic stream or creek. What may appear as clean and refreshing can very well be cause extreme nausea or sickness. Micro-organisms that can't be seen by the naked eye are the responsible culprits. The simple practice of boiling the water before you drink it will alleviate any ill effects.
The statement that best supports this paragraph is:
A. Avoid camping altogether.
B. Freshwater microorganisms have the capacity to ruin family vacations.
C. Be sure to always bring along the proper utensils to boil your drinking water in.
D. Regardless of where people camp out, it is always suggested to boil your drinking water.

18. Many linguistics (the study of language) experts think that English is one of the most difficult languages to learn. Many spoken words sound essentially the same, however, the spelling and application of those words can radically change the meaning of a statement. That, complimented with a good proportion of slang, can render fluency in English a very difficult challenge.
The statement that best supports this paragraph is:
A. The English language is almost as difficult to learn as Russian.
B. The English language plays host to some tricky variations that make it difficult to learn.
C. English is now considered the international language.
D. English proficiency is largely determined by how well students comprehend its slang.

19. It is very important for people to vote if they desire to have their views known in government policies. Those who choose not to participate in our polling really have no business criticizing future or current policies. Our democracy was founded on the principle of the voice of the people, not by the silence of the unconcerned.

The statement that best supports this paragraph is:
A. A democracy doesn't work for minorities.
B. If you really don't care about a certain public issue, then just don't vote.
C. All views are important in a democracy.
D. Voter participation is mandated for an effective democracy.

20. Since its inception, the typewriter has been dramatically improved upon over the years. The manual typewriters of earlier years were rather slow and required a good degree of finger effort to operate effectively. The lowest priced electric typewriter available today is distinctly superior in efficiency compared to the manuals of yesteryear. If purchase price is of no concern, high-speed typewriters integrated with computer word processing and correction are now available. It's hard to believe, but some typewriters will even automatically correct a typist's misspellings.
The statement that best supports this paragraph is:
A. Typewriter technology has demonstrated significant improvements over the years.
B. Typewriters of this day and age are high tech and sophisticated.
C. You can virtually be illiterate and yet have the capacity to type near perfect prose.
D. Despite their expense, high tech typewriters are seen as an invaluable aid for secretaries.

21. Volunteer fire departments serve a very important role in small towns and rural areas. Typically, there are too few people living in these particular areas to support a large enough tax base to employ a fully manned fire department. Only through the sacrifices of personal time by a dedicated few can rural areas hope to have adequate fire protection.
The statement that best supports this paragraph is:

A. Fire departments outside the larger metropolitan areas are too expensive to maintain.
B. People that live in the country can't afford the same kind of fire protection that is enjoyed by the smaller towns.
C. The lack of volunteers can critically impair the operation of a small town fire department.
D. Volunteer fire departments are really the only means that people living in the rurals or small towns can obtain adequate fire protection.

22. It's a pretty common practice for grocery retailers to put perishables such as bread, meat and dairy products toward the back of the store. This philosophy is founded on the hope that as a customer shops for these basic necessities, he or she will have to pass by lots of other merchandise first. Usually, one of two situations will happen; either the shopper will buy something impulsively that he wasn't intending to purchase or some item that he sees will serve as a reminder of something else that he does, in fact, need. This particular type of store arrangement is a time proven technique to boost the profitability of a grocery store.
The statement that best supports this paragraph is:
A. Grocery stores are set up to take advantage of a customer's impulsiveness.
B. Grocery stores are out to price gouge their customers.
C. The location of basic necessities such as milk, eggs, bread, and meat can always be found at the rear of the store.
D. Grocery retailing strategy is used to capitalize on buyer psychology.

23. There is an old adage that some of the best medical remedies for humans come from the most toxic substances. It sounds ironic, but poisons have been and are now used regularly in the field of medicine. Currently, an interesting study is being conducted in Egypt involving the use of deadly spitting cobra venom. The venom has been fractionated into three separate compounds, one of which the toxicity level is so extreme it has been shown that it can actually attack and destroy cancer cells. Uses such as this, lend further credence to use of toxins as medicinal remedies.
The statement that best supports this paragraph is:
A. The utilization of poisons in medicine can be extremely dangerous if not applied in the right dosage.
B. When people are sick, the last thing on earth they need is poison.
C. Egypt is the foremost leader of studying the benefits of medicinal toxins.
D. Strangely enough, poisonous/toxic substances have and do play an important role in the field of medicine, and can potentially avail new cures for certain modern diseases.

24. To a coffee consumer, the type of bean, freshness, and degree of roast can dramatically affect the flavor of coffee. Those with a trained palate can determine the kind of coffee bean used and the country it originated from just by tasting a small amount of the coffee. For the rest of us coffee drinkers with non-discerning tastes, nothing can beat a freshly brewed pot of coffee in the morning to accompany a breakfast. The aroma and taste of coffee is a refreshing way to start to start the day.
The statement that best supports this paragraph is:
A. Coffee is an addictive substance that should be avoided altogether.
B. Most everybody that drinks coffee can discriminate the origin of coffee bean involved.
C. To some people, brewed coffee has a very distinctive flavor.
D. As any coffee merchant will attest, there is nothing better than a freshly brewed pot of coffee in the morning.

25. Traveling by means of a train can be exciting as well as relatively inexpensive. Passenger rail service usually goes through isolated places that typically cannot be seen from a vehicle traveling the highway. The scenery offered is breathtaking, especially when traveling west through the Rocky Mountain wilderness. Another advantage of riding the rail is that since you are not inconvenienced with the task of driving you may more fully appreciate the scenery.
The statement that best supports this paragraph is:
A. The benefits of riding a passenger train are expounded upon.
B. Rail service is an expensive way to view America.
C. The safety record of passenger rail service is something less than desired.
D. Rocky mountain wilderness is breathtaking when seen from a passenger train.

VOCABULARY SECTION EXAM I

26. The team's effort to rally in the final minute of the game "floundered" when a teammate fumbled the ball. Floundered most nearly means
    A. was successful
    B. failed
    C. became interesting
    D. inevitable

27. His home seemed "ordinary" from the outside despite all of the money he spent on remodeling. Ordinary most nearly means
    A. unremarkable
    B. dilapidated
    C. hopeless
    D. plush

28. The assistant manager's thirty minute introduction to the board of directors was only a "prelude" of the lengthy talk yet to come. Prelude most nearly means
    A. documentation
    B. smoke screen
    C. precursor
    D. distraction

29. Some tourists visiting Yellowstone National Park pay little "heed" to the warnings not to feed the bears. Heed most nearly means
    A. gratuity
    B. superstition
    C. attraction
    D. attention

30. Tom really looked "dejected" after being denied a part in the high school play. Dejected most nearly means
    A. defiant
    B. depressed
    C. helpless
    D. gracious

31. The wild blackberry bushes were so thick in the pasture that they created a "labyrinth" for the cattle. Labyrinth most nearly means
    A. maze
    B. museum
    C. haven
    D. den

32. "Maternal" most nearly means
    A. son-like
    B. daughter-like
    C. mother-like
    D. father-like

33. The car "veered" to the right to avoid a head-on collision with the dump truck. Veered most nearly means
    A. skidded
    B. swerved
    C. braked
    D. accelerated

34. John was a "resplendent" example of a hard-working student. Resplendent most nearly means
    A. shameful
    B. disgusting
    C. responsive
    D. shining

35. Many foreign policy experts no longer believe that the NATO "alliance" is as strong as it was 10 years ago. Alliance most nearly means
    A. market
    B. compliance
    C. opposition
    D. accord

36. The patient was "cognizant" during the entire surgical procedure. Cognizant most nearly means
    A. conscious
    B. unconscious
    C. paralyzed
    D. asleep

37. Kids always seem "fidgety" in church. Fidgety most nearly means
    A. quiet
    B. tired
    C. restless
    D. guilty

38. Jovial most nearly means
    A. arrogant
    B. tasteless
    C. merry
    D. dejected

39. Plants in this area have to be "hardy" to survive the long and harsh winter season. Hardy most nearly means
    A. delicate
    B. vigorous
    C. transplanted
    D. frail

40. The left lane of traffic was "obstructed" by construction equipment. Obstructed most nearly means
    A. slowed
    B. turned around
    C. dwarfed
    D. blocked

41. To continue would be "inane". Inane most nearly means
    A. merciful
    B. meaningful
    C. knowledgeable
    D. pointless

42. Despite the pressure exerted by the prosecuting attorney, the detective refused to "divulge" the name of his informant. Divulge most nearly means
    A. reveal
    B. lie
    C. remember
    D. withdraw

43. People living in a rural community setting enjoy their "seclusion". Seclusion most nearly means
    A. fellowship
    B. gregariousness
    C. privacy
    D. companionship

44. Joey was particularly "adept" at wood carving and woodworking. Adept most nearly means
    A. incompetent
    B. inexperienced
    C. troubled
    D. skillful

45. One could only "speculate" what the future would bring. Speculate most nearly means
    A. worry
    B. ponder
    C. discuss
    D. have apprehension

46. A true optimist does not recognize the meaning of "limitations". Limitations most nearly means
    A. restrictions
    B. vocabulary
    C. freedoms
    D. infinities

47. He may not be known for good housekeeping, but his wood pile was "uniformly" stacked. Uniformly most nearly means
    A. evenly
    B. variably
    C. haphazardly
    D. not

48. The further we ventured from the main thoroughfare, the more the road seemed to "taper". Taper most nearly means
    A. deadend
    B. overlap
    C. narrow
    D. disintegrate

49. Grandma's favorite Thanksgiving tablecloth has several "blemishes" on it that testify to years of family use. Blemishes most nearly means
    A. layers of dust
    B. holes
    C. stains
    D. tears

50. It was getting late and this was reflected by his "erratic" driving. Erratic most nearly means
    A. steady
    B. tired
    C. abnormal
    D. cautious

51. This particular fire extinquisher is "dual" purpose; it has the capacity to put out electrical, and chemical fires. Dual most nearly means
    A. single
    B. multi
    C. three-fold
    D. double

52. From the beginning to the end, all of her involvement in the project was "premeditated". Premeditated most nearly means
    A. unscheduled
    B. planned
    C. insignificant
    D. blatant

53. Most of the popular books have interesting "prologues". Prologues most nearly mean
    A. introductions
    B. footnotes
    C. endings
    D. bodies

54. Criminals are "ostracized" from society by being placed in state and federal penal institutions. Ostracized most nearly means
    A. welcomed
    B. excluded
    C. embraced
    D. accepted

55. They need to win this game to "clinch" the divisional title. Clinch most nearly means
    A. secure
    B. lose
    C. continue
    D. give away

56. It was enjoyable to watch the baby bears "frolic" in the stream. Frolic most nearly means
    A. swim
    B. walk
    C. stagger
    D. play

57. The weather was so cold that even with two coats and insulated underwear on, I still "shivered". Shivered most nearly means
    A. could move
    B. felt cold
    C. quivered
    D. sweat

58. Some people believe the "myth" that by breaking a mirror you are certain to suffer seven years of bad luck. Myth most nearly means
    A. truth
    B. legend
    C. unimpeachable fact
    D. treaty

59. The President of the United States is termed a "lame duck" during the last year of his tenure. Lame duck most nearly means
    A. strong
    B. silent
    C. resilient
    D. weak

60. Mark was "exhilarated" just to score a 'C' on his Biochemistry mid-term. Exhilarated most nearly means
    A. elated
    B. banished
    C. dejected
    D. sad

- END OF TEST -

ANSWER SHEET TO READER'S COMPREHENSION/VOCABULARY EXAM I

1. Ⓐ Ⓑ Ⓒ Ⓓ Ⓔ
2. Ⓐ Ⓑ Ⓒ Ⓓ Ⓔ
3. Ⓐ Ⓑ Ⓒ Ⓓ Ⓔ
4. Ⓐ Ⓑ Ⓒ Ⓓ Ⓔ
5. Ⓐ Ⓑ Ⓒ Ⓓ Ⓔ
6. Ⓐ Ⓑ Ⓒ Ⓓ Ⓔ
7. Ⓐ Ⓑ Ⓒ Ⓓ Ⓔ
8. Ⓐ Ⓑ Ⓒ Ⓓ Ⓔ
9. Ⓐ Ⓑ Ⓒ Ⓓ Ⓔ
10. Ⓐ Ⓑ Ⓒ Ⓓ Ⓔ
11. Ⓐ Ⓑ Ⓒ Ⓓ Ⓔ
12. Ⓐ Ⓑ Ⓒ Ⓓ Ⓔ
13. Ⓐ Ⓑ Ⓒ Ⓓ Ⓔ
14. Ⓐ Ⓑ Ⓒ Ⓓ Ⓔ
15. Ⓐ Ⓑ Ⓒ Ⓓ Ⓔ
16. Ⓐ Ⓑ Ⓒ Ⓓ Ⓔ
17. Ⓐ Ⓑ Ⓒ Ⓓ Ⓔ
18. Ⓐ Ⓑ Ⓒ Ⓓ Ⓔ
19. Ⓐ Ⓑ Ⓒ Ⓓ Ⓔ
20. Ⓐ Ⓑ Ⓒ Ⓓ Ⓔ
21. Ⓐ Ⓑ Ⓒ Ⓓ Ⓔ
22. Ⓐ Ⓑ Ⓒ Ⓓ Ⓔ
23. Ⓐ Ⓑ Ⓒ Ⓓ Ⓔ
24. Ⓐ Ⓑ Ⓒ Ⓓ Ⓔ
25. Ⓐ Ⓑ Ⓒ Ⓓ Ⓔ
26. Ⓐ Ⓑ Ⓒ Ⓓ Ⓔ
27. Ⓐ Ⓑ Ⓒ Ⓓ Ⓔ
28. Ⓐ Ⓑ Ⓒ Ⓓ Ⓔ
29. Ⓐ Ⓑ Ⓒ Ⓓ Ⓔ
30. Ⓐ Ⓑ Ⓒ Ⓓ Ⓔ

31. Ⓐ Ⓑ Ⓒ Ⓓ Ⓔ
32. Ⓐ Ⓑ Ⓒ Ⓓ Ⓔ
33. Ⓐ Ⓑ Ⓒ Ⓓ Ⓔ
34. Ⓐ Ⓑ Ⓒ Ⓓ Ⓔ
35. Ⓐ Ⓑ Ⓒ Ⓓ Ⓔ
36. Ⓐ Ⓑ Ⓒ Ⓓ Ⓔ
37. Ⓐ Ⓑ Ⓒ Ⓓ Ⓔ
38. Ⓐ Ⓑ Ⓒ Ⓓ Ⓔ
39. Ⓐ Ⓑ Ⓒ Ⓓ Ⓔ
40. Ⓐ Ⓑ Ⓒ Ⓓ Ⓔ
41. Ⓐ Ⓑ Ⓒ Ⓓ Ⓔ
42. Ⓐ Ⓑ Ⓒ Ⓓ Ⓔ
43. Ⓐ Ⓑ Ⓒ Ⓓ Ⓔ
44. Ⓐ Ⓑ Ⓒ Ⓓ Ⓔ
45. Ⓐ Ⓑ Ⓒ Ⓓ Ⓔ
46. Ⓐ Ⓑ Ⓒ Ⓓ Ⓔ
47. Ⓐ Ⓑ Ⓒ Ⓓ Ⓔ
48. Ⓐ Ⓑ Ⓒ Ⓓ Ⓔ
49. Ⓐ Ⓑ Ⓒ Ⓓ Ⓔ
50. Ⓐ Ⓑ Ⓒ Ⓓ Ⓔ
51. Ⓐ Ⓑ Ⓒ Ⓓ Ⓔ
52. Ⓐ Ⓑ Ⓒ Ⓓ Ⓔ
53. Ⓐ Ⓑ Ⓒ Ⓓ Ⓔ
54. Ⓐ Ⓑ Ⓒ Ⓓ Ⓔ
55. Ⓐ Ⓑ Ⓒ Ⓓ Ⓔ
56. Ⓐ Ⓑ Ⓒ Ⓓ Ⓔ
57. Ⓐ Ⓑ Ⓒ Ⓓ Ⓔ
58. Ⓐ Ⓑ Ⓒ Ⓓ Ⓔ
59. Ⓐ Ⓑ Ⓒ Ⓓ Ⓔ
60. Ⓐ Ⓑ Ⓒ Ⓓ Ⓔ

(This page may be removed to mark answers.)

The Postal Exam Preparation Book

ANSWERS TO MATH EXAM I

1. C	11. D	21. B	31. B
2. B	12. A	22. C	32. A
3. A	13. C	23. D	33. A
4. D	14. D	24. A	34. C
5. C	15. D	25. A	35. B
6. A	16. A	26. C	36. D
7. B	17. C	27. C	37. D
8. A	18. B	28. B	38. D
9. D	19. C	29. A	39. A
10. D	20. D	30. D	40. C

If your score was:

35 or more correct, you have an excellent score
30-34 correct, you have a good score
29 or less correct, you should practice more.

ANSWERS TO READER'S COMPREHENSION AND VOCABULARY EXAM I

1. B	16. B	31. A	46. A
2. A	17. D	32. C	47. A
3. D	18. B	33. B	48. C
4. A	19. D	34. D	49. C
5. C	20. A	35. D	50. C
6. C	21. D	36. A	51. D
7. B	22. D	37. C	52. B
8. D	23. D	38. C	53. A
9. A	24. C	39. B	54. B
10. D	25. A	40. D	55. A
11. B	26. B	41. D	56. D
12. C	27. A	42. A	57. C
13. A	28. C	43. C	58. B
14. A	29. D	44. D	59. D
15. C	30. B	45. B	60. A

If your score was:

53 or more correct, you have an excellent score
45-52 correct, you have a good score
44 or less correct, you should practice more

MATH EXAM II

POSTAGE RATES FOR MAILING PARCELS

Various rates are provided below for determination of the cost of sending parcels weighing 2 to 20 pounds to Areas 1 through 6 and locally.

Wt in exact lbs & not exceeding	Local Area	Areas 1&2	Area 3	Area 4	Area 5	Area 6
2	1.75	2.00	2.05	2.15	2.15	2.65
3	1.95	2.20	2.25	2.35	2.35	2.85
4	1.15	2.40	2.45	2.55	2.55	3.05
5	1.35	2.60	2.65	2.75	2.75	3.25
6	1.55	2.80	2.85	2.95	2.95	3.45
7	1.75	3.00	3.05	3.15	3.15	3.65
8	1.95	3.20	3.25	3.35	3.35	3.85
9	2.15	3.40	3.45	3.55	3.55	4.05
10	2.35	3.60	3.65	3.75	3.75	4.25
11	2.55	3.80	3.85	3.95	3.95	4.45
12	2.75	4.00	4.05	4.15	4.15	4.65
13	2.95	4.20	4.25	4.35	4.35	4.85
14	3.15	4.40	4.45	4.55	4.55	5.05
15	3.35	4.60	4.65	4.75	4.75	5.25
16	3.55	4.80	4.85	4.95	4.95	5.45
17	3.75	5.00	5.05	5.15	5.15	5.65
18	3.95	5.20	5.25	5.35	5.35	5.85
19	4.15	5.40	5.45	5.55	5.55	6.05
20	4.35	5.60	5.65	5.75	5.75	6.25

(Note: These particular postage and wrapping charges are not included unless the customer specifically requests their use. The weights shown below are only applicable up to 2 pounds and not including 2 pounds. Parcels weighing 2 or more pounds are shown above.)

(Hint: Fractional weights over 2 pounds should be rounded to the next hightest figure (i.e., 10-1/4 pounds = 11 pounds on the chart)).

GROUP A

Parcel No.	Price
1 or 2	0.45/oz
3	0.50/oz
4	0.55/oz
5	0.58/oz

PADDED ENVELOPE CHARGE

all sizes=$1.00

GROUP B

All parcels cost 0.32 for the first 2 ounces and 0.07 for each additional ounce.

PACKAGE WRAPPING CHARGES

Pkg size	Cost
1-3	0.75
4-6	1.25
7-10	2.00

TIME: 75 MINUTES
40 QUESTIONS

MATH SECTION EXAM II

1. How much would 12 15-cent stamps and 143 5-cent stamps cost?

    A. $8.95   B. $9.00   C. $8.85   D. none of these

2. What would the expense be to buy 23 22-cent stamps, 400 18-cent stamps and 47 padded envelopes that cost $0.45 each?

    A. $93.21   B. $93.12   C. $98.12   D. $98.21

3. What would it cost to send a 12 pound package to Area 2, a 4 pound package to Area 4, and purchase 139 22-cent stamps?

    A. $36.99   B. $26.18   C. $37.13   D. $38.12

4. What would it cost to send a 19 pound package to Area 6 and a 4 ounce Group B parcel locally?

    A. $7.23   B. $6.27   C. $6.57   D. $6.51

5. If a customer wanted to send a 1-3/4 pound Group A, No. 4 parcel, how much would it cost?

    A. $14.25   B. $15.40   C. $16.50   D. none of these

6. If another customer only had $15.00, how many 8 pound parcels could he send locally for that amount of money?

    A. 5   B. 6   C. 7   D. 8

7. How much would it cost to send a 12 pound, 7 pound, and 15 pound parcel to Areas 5, 3, and 6 respectively?

    A. $12.45   B. $12.50   C. $12.75   D. none of these

8. What would it cost to send a Size 5, wrapped 19 pound package to Area 2?

    A. $12.13   B. 141.25   C. $5.40   D. $6.65

9. What would it cost to send a 9 ounce Group B package stuffed inside a medium-size padded envelope to Santa Fe, New Mexico?

    A. $1.51   B. $1.81   C. $1.49   D. none of these

10. If you only had $7.45, how many 8 ounce Group A, No. 1 parcels could you send for that amount of money?

    A. 3   B. 4   C. 5   D. none of these

11. How much would it cost if you were to send a 7 pound parcel to Area 3 and a 10 pound parcel to Area 6, and have both of them wrapped prior to sending? (Package sizes are 7 and 9, respectively)

    A. $10.03   B. $11.03   C. $11.30   D. $10.30

12. What would it cost if a customer wanted 1250 22-cent stamps, 1600 18-cent stamps, 475 padded envelopes, and to send an 8 pound parcel locally?

    A. $1175.29   B. $1039.95   C. $1000.00   D. $1025.99

13. What would it cost to send a wrapped 20 ounce Group A, No. 5 parcel, considering it is a Size 2 package?

    A. $12.35   B. $13.75   C. $14.80   D. none of these

14. How much would it cost to send fourteen 18 pound parcels to Area 6, thirty-seven 20 pound parcels to Area 1, and sixteen 14 ounce Group B parcels locally?

    A. $483.07   B. $302.93   C. $307.66   D. none of these

15. How many 18-cent stamps could be purchased if a customer had $13.50?

    A. 65   B. 70   C. 75   D. 80

16. What is the cost of sending a 1-1/4 pound Group A, No. 3 parcel in a padded envelope?

    A. $11.00 B. $12.00 C. $13.00 D. $14.00

17. How much would it cost to send a 25 ounce Group A, No. 5, Size 8 wrapped parcel?

    A. $16.00 B. $16.50 C. $15.00 D. none of these

18. If a customer wanted to send forty 2 pound parcels, ten 3 pound parcels, and five 18 pound parcels to Areas 1, 2, and 5 respectively, what would be the total bill?

    A. $137.28 B. $126.00 C. $125.23 D. $128.75

19. What would it cost to send forty 1 pound Group B parcels to Seattle, WA; half of them wrapped as Size 3 packages and the other half as Size 2 packages?

    A. $78.00 B. $80.00 C. $82.00 D. none of these

20. How many 2 Pound Parcels in padded envelopes could be sent to Area 6 if you only had $9.25?

    A. 2 B. 3 C. 4 D. none of these

21. What would it cost to send three Size 3 wrapped 12 pound packages to Area 2, and thirteen 7 ounce Group B parcels in large-size padded envelopes?

    A. $35.96 B. $37.92 C. $33.90 D. none of these

22. How many 15-cent stamps could be purchased if a customer only had $15.00?

    A. 10 B. 100 C. 1000 D. 110

23. What would be the total cost of sending twelve 3 pound packages, sixteen 20 pound packages, eight 12 pound packages, and three 2 pound packages to Areas 2, 3, 6, and 1 respectively?

    A. $2.00 B. $12.00 C. $8.95 D. none of these

24. Look at Question 23 again. This time assume that packages destined to Areas 3 and 6 must be wrapped in Size 7 packaging and the remaining packages being sent need to be wrapped in Size 2 packaging. What would be the total cost of this shipment now?

    A. $147.87 B. $172.63 C. $219.25 D. none of these

25. How much would it cost to send 49 Group A, No. 3, 25-ounce parcels and 50 Group B, 17 ounce parcels?

    A. $625.00 B. $575.00 C. $681.00 D. $620.00

26. How much would it cost to send 157 local 18 pound parcels, 30 Group A, No. 4, 10 ounce parcels, and 16 Group B, 1 pound parcels?

    A. $676.25 B. $795.95 C. $805.95 D. $800.00

27. Look at Question 26 again. Assume you need to have all packages wrapped before shipping and their sizes are 3, 4, and 8 respectively, what would be the new cost?

    A. $993.20 B. $991.20 C. $990.90 D. none of these

28. If you had 135 Group A, No. 1 parcels weighing 1-1/2 pounds each, wrapped in Size 4 packaging, and 75 Group B parcels weighing 18 ounces each, wrapped in Size 7 packaging, what would be the total bill of sending all of these?

    A. $1872.43 B. $1868.57 C. $1848.57 D. $1884.75

29. If one customer had $24.00 and wanted to purchase as many 40-cent stamps as possible and another wanted as many 8-cent stamps as he could buy for $13.04, how many stamps will each customer get for their money?

    A. 60 & 163 B. 90 & 163 C. 60 & 90 D. 120 & 12

30. What would it cost to purchase 1,400 22-cent stamps, 1375 40-cent stamps and 62 large-sized padded envelopes?

    A. $912.00 B. $920.00 C. $930.00 D. $918.00

31. How much would a customer have to spend in order to send thirty-seven 18 pound packages to Area 6, eight 1-1/4 pound Size 5, Group B parcels, and five 3-1/2 pound packages to Area 2?

    A. $262.82 B. $248.73 C. $250.00 D. $251.09

32. How many 40-cent airmail stamps could be purchased for $80.00?

    A. 200 B. 225 C. 20 D. 375

33. If a customer had 20 cassette tapes, each weighing 14 ounces and assuming they are each considered a No. 1, Group A article, how much would it cost to send them individually in small padded envelopes?

    A. $132.70 B. $140.00 C. $146.00 D. none of these

34. What would it cost to send 42 Size 6, wrapped 5 pound packages to Area 2, and 159 Size 7, wrapped 19-3/4 pound packages to Area 3?

    A. $130.00 B. $1358.00 C. $137 D. $1378.05

35. If a bulk mailer wanted to send out a quarter of a million advertisement letters at a discount rate of 7-3/4-cents per piece, how much would it cost the company to mail these ads?

    A. $12,750.00 B. $18,020.00 C. $19,375.00 D. none of these

36. What would a customer have to pay to send two 12 pound packages locally, three Size 7, wrapped 12 pound packages to Area 4, and twenty 4 ounce Group B parcels to Salem, Oregon?

    A. $31.15 B. $34.75 C. $33.00 D. $33.15

37. How many 27 ounce Group B articles stuffed in medium-sized, padded envelopes could be sent for $30.70?

    A. 7 B. 8 C. 9 D. 10

38. How many 13 ounce No. 3, Group A parcels wrapped in Size 2 packaging could be sent for $72.50?

    A. 10 B. 9 C. 8 D. 7

39. What would it cost to send forty-one 17 pound packages, eight 16-1/2 pound packages, and thirty-eight 12-1/4 pound packages to Areas 1, 2, and 3 respectively?

    A. $400.00 B. $406.50 C. $407.00 D. none of these

40. How much would it cost to send a 14-7/8 ounce Group B parcel in a padded envelope to Phoenix, Arizona?

    A. $2.23 B. $2.33 C. $2.43 D. $2.53

- END OF TEST -

ANSWER SHEET TO MATH EXAM II

1. Ⓐ Ⓑ Ⓒ Ⓓ Ⓔ
2. Ⓐ Ⓑ Ⓒ Ⓓ Ⓔ
3. Ⓐ Ⓑ Ⓒ Ⓓ Ⓔ
4. Ⓐ Ⓑ Ⓒ Ⓓ Ⓔ
5. Ⓐ Ⓑ Ⓒ Ⓓ Ⓔ
6. Ⓐ Ⓑ Ⓒ Ⓓ Ⓔ
7. Ⓐ Ⓑ Ⓒ Ⓓ Ⓔ
8. Ⓐ Ⓑ Ⓒ Ⓓ Ⓔ
9. Ⓐ Ⓑ Ⓒ Ⓓ Ⓔ
10. Ⓐ Ⓑ Ⓒ Ⓓ Ⓔ
11. Ⓐ Ⓑ Ⓒ Ⓓ Ⓔ
12. Ⓐ Ⓑ Ⓒ Ⓓ Ⓔ
13. Ⓐ Ⓑ Ⓒ Ⓓ Ⓔ
14. Ⓐ Ⓑ Ⓒ Ⓓ Ⓔ
15. Ⓐ Ⓑ Ⓒ Ⓓ Ⓔ
16. Ⓐ Ⓑ Ⓒ Ⓓ Ⓔ
17. Ⓐ Ⓑ Ⓒ Ⓓ Ⓔ
18. Ⓐ Ⓑ Ⓒ Ⓓ Ⓔ
19. Ⓐ Ⓑ Ⓒ Ⓓ Ⓔ
20. Ⓐ Ⓑ Ⓒ Ⓓ Ⓔ

21. Ⓐ Ⓑ Ⓒ Ⓓ Ⓔ
22. Ⓐ Ⓑ Ⓒ Ⓓ Ⓔ
23. Ⓐ Ⓑ Ⓒ Ⓓ Ⓔ
24. Ⓐ Ⓑ Ⓒ Ⓓ Ⓔ
25. Ⓐ Ⓑ Ⓒ Ⓓ Ⓔ
26. Ⓐ Ⓑ Ⓒ Ⓓ Ⓔ
27. Ⓐ Ⓑ Ⓒ Ⓓ Ⓔ
28. Ⓐ Ⓑ Ⓒ Ⓓ Ⓔ
29. Ⓐ Ⓑ Ⓒ Ⓓ Ⓔ
30. Ⓐ Ⓑ Ⓒ Ⓓ Ⓔ
31. Ⓐ Ⓑ Ⓒ Ⓓ Ⓔ
32. Ⓐ Ⓑ Ⓒ Ⓓ Ⓔ
33. Ⓐ Ⓑ Ⓒ Ⓓ Ⓔ
34. Ⓐ Ⓑ Ⓒ Ⓓ Ⓔ
35. Ⓐ Ⓑ Ⓒ Ⓓ Ⓔ
36. Ⓐ Ⓑ Ⓒ Ⓓ Ⓔ
37. Ⓐ Ⓑ Ⓒ Ⓓ Ⓔ
38. Ⓐ Ⓑ Ⓒ Ⓓ Ⓔ
39. Ⓐ Ⓑ Ⓒ Ⓓ Ⓔ
40. Ⓐ Ⓑ Ⓒ Ⓓ Ⓔ

(This page may be removed to mark answers.)

The Postal Exam Preparation Book

TIME: 90 MINUTES
60 QUESTIONS

READERS' COMPREHENSION SECTION EXAM II

1. For those who have ambitions of painting their own home, car or furniture, particular attention should be given to proper surface preparation. It is futile and costly to attempt to paint a surface that is not adequately prepared. The paint will peel or bubble prematurely. Inevitably, the job must be done again at twice the expense and effort. The surface of the item to be painted needs to be thoroughly cleansed of dust, dirt, and anything foreign. In addition, areas of peeling, cracking or corrosion must be scraped or sanded smooth. A primer coat of paint should be applied to those surfaces that lay bare the material being painted (i.e., wood, steel, aluminum, etc.). Primer coats serve as a bonding agent which effectively hold the second and final coat of paint.

The statement that best supports this paragraph is:
   A. Virtually anyone can do their own painting if they have the spare time and materials to work with.
   B. Proper application of paint to a surface requires a good deal of attention to the preliminary preparation.
   C. A professional painter is the only answer.
   D. Corrosion and dust are two elements that can't be ignored when painting.

2. Insects do have the ability to hear but it differs somewhat from the way humans hear. Insects possess miniscule hairs located on their antennae, or bodies that are particularly well adapted to sensing vibrations. Collectively, these vibrations are processed by the nervous system and interpreted as sound. The method is effective, but it does lack the refined directionality of human hearing.

The statement that best supports this paragraph is:
   A. The mechanics of hearing for an insect are dependent on external vibration-sensitive hairs.
   B. Insects lack sound directionality largely to the simplicity of their nervous system.
   C. An insect devoid of vibration sensitive hairs could be considered essentially deaf.
   D. The greater number of vibration sensitive hairs an insect possesses, the better that insect can hear sound.

3. Glass, as much as it appears to be a solid material, is really liquid. It is not readily apparent, but if you have ever noticed that older windows are rippled and tend to distort your vision, you have witnessed glass liquidity. Gravity causes the rippling effect. In fact, if enough time is allowed, a glass window would eventually turn into an unformed pool of glass. It would be comparable to molten glass poured on a flat surface.

The statement that best supports this paragraph is:
   A. Since glass is as unstable as it is, it really shouldn't be utilized for windows.
   B. Gravity can cause a rippling effect in glass.
   C. Despite appearing solid, glass has liquid properties.
   D. Older windows have the propensity to distort your view.

4. People should be aware that when they purchase expensive gold or silver items such as jewelry, flatware, etc., they are not necessarily getting the purest form of those precious metals. Both gold and silver are considered very soft metals. Without the addition of a stronger element called an alloy, silver or gold would be impractical for everyday use. Typically, copper is the element chosen for alloying. To maintain the integrity of the precious metal, the entire composition is arranged in such a way as to allow no more than ten percent of copper. However, this amount is enough to render acceptable hardness, and can lend a bronze tint to the basic color.

The statement that best supports this paragraph is:
   A. All precious metals require alloying.
   B. Copper is the most common alloy used in gold and silver.
   C. If a bronze tint is apparent in your flatware, it can be attributed to the copper alloy used in its manufacture.
   D. The intrinsic properties of gold and silver are such that copper alloys are used to enhance the metal's endurance.

5. Clearly, one of the most important things to have in a marriage is an open line of communication. Too often couples repress their feelings or desires and this ultimately leads to frustration or depression. It is absolutely necessary that both partners communicate to each other their needs or concerns. Otherwise, it becomes a precarious game of mind-reading or guessing what the other wants or needs. They may think that their assumptions are correct, but nine times out of ten, they

are wrong. No two individuals are alike physically or emotionally. That is why it is so vital to have open discussions within the marriage.

The statement that best supports this paragraph is:

    A. A marriage requires too much work so why bother getting married in the first place.
    B. Open communication between marital partners will always circumvent frustration and depression.
    C. The foundation of a healthy marriage necessitates partners to communicate openly.
    D. There are widely varied physical and emotional differences between marital partners.

6. It is a responsible measure for pet owners to have their pets spay or neutered by their veterinarian. There are distinct advantages to having this procedure done. First and foremost, it prevents unwanted litters. Millions of unwanted cats and dogs are euthanized each year because of overcrowding at local humane societies and the subsequent lack of people willing to adopt these pets. Secondly, once a pet has been sterilized, there is a lesser tendency for aggression and roaming. One other benefit is that your pet has a lower probability of acquiring reproductive tract cancer. Spaying and neutering is a safe procedure that yields a myriad of benefits and warrants consideration on behalf of the pet owner.

The statement that best supports this paragraph is:

    A. It is required for humane reasons to always have your pet sterilized by your veterinarian.
    B. Pets not spay or neutered are more susceptible to reproductive tract cancer.
    C. Anyone that owns a dog or cat and elects not to have their pet spay or neutered can basically be surmised as irresponsible.
    D. The option of having your pet sterilized poses an array of benefits.

7. The human back is really quite remarkable with respect to the amount of abuse inflicted upon it without it breaking down or deteriorating. As we stand or sit, the back always yields support, while at the same time, it lends us the capacity to turn and twist without placing stress on the vertebrae (i.e., the individual bones that are collectively called the spine or backbone). Despite the back's resiliency, it can and does get injured when physical limitations are superceded. When lifting heavy objects, it is critically important to use your legs instead of your back. Flexing your knees while keeping your back straight can circumvent most back injuries.

The statement that best supports this paragraph is:

    A. Backs which are considered to be surprisingly durable, are not exempt from being damaged, so care should be exercised when lifting.
    B. It is suggested to twist your back as you are lifting abnormally heavy loads.
    C. The human back displays tremendous resiliency considering the abuse we put it through.
    D. When presented with a situation that involves lifting something extraordinarily heavy, it is suggested to get the help of friends.

8. If you have the desire to walk, jog or ride a bicycle along the side of a road or public access, it is prudent to wear lightly colored clothing. This is particularly important if you do your activity at dawn or dusk when visibility is reduced. Light colors are more readily seen than darker ones in low light conditions. The best alternative is to wear clothes that are light reflective, although this may be expensive. A less costly, but just as effective approach, is to purchase a small roll of reflective tape and wrap small strips around your pant legs and sleeves. Even in the dead of night, reflective tape is evident in the beam of a headlight. It is tragic that many pedestrians are struck by vehicles, yet with a little precaution most accidents could have been avoided.

The statement that best supports this paragraph is:

    A. It is recommended to curtail most sporting activities when it begins to get dark outside.
    B. It is mandatory to wear light reflective clothing at night to avoid being hit by vehicles.
    C. For your safety, it is judicious to dress in a manner that enhances visibility to motorists.
    D. Sports enthusiasts are more concerned about comfort and style of athletic dress than they are about safety.

9. Cholesterol has been singled out by the medical profession as being one of the leading causes of heart attacks. Research has shown that excessive levels of cholesterol in the blood leads to an eventual build-up of fats on arterial walls. The result is a restriction of blood flow. It is of particular concern when the arteries that supply the heart with blood become occluded. This situation alone sets the stage for a certain heart attack. Fortunately, cholesterol levels can be controlled. Your doctor should determine what your levels are. If you are at high risk, it may be necessary to change or modify your diet. You may not like it initially, but that is far better than facing an inevitable heart attack.

The statement that best supports this paragraph is:

    A. Any amount of cholesterol found in the blood presents a serious problem that should be controlled through diet and exercise.
    B. The detrimental effects of excess cholesterol is good reason to keep levels in check.

C. By becoming more aware of the danger of excessive cholesterol in diets, there has been a noticeable switch to non-cholesterol foods.
D. Moderate levels of cholesterol in our blood is no reason to radically change our eating habits.

10. October is one of the best times of the year to take a vacation. Fewer people tend to travel at that time due to work commitments or children in school. People in the recreational industry term it the off season and it is usually reflected by cheaper lodging and meal prices. This makes the traveler's dollar stretch further. There is also an availability of tour packages, and unlike the on-season, overbookings and cancellations rarely occur. Traveling in October has many advantages that certainly deserve consideration for the next family trip.
The statement that best supports this paragraph is:
A. It is worthwhile to take a trip in October solely due to cheaper rates.
B. Traveling in October hosts several advantages that deem consideration when planning a vacation.
C. The advantages of traveling in the fall are expounded upon.
D. It is difficult for most people to enjoy a Fall vacation because obligations to work and school are priorities.

11. When the topic for discussion is mobile home construction, it is easy to fall prey to a stereotypical frame of mind. Most everyone remembers the "tin lizzie" of yesteryear. They were small, cheaply built fire traps that ended up taking the lives of many people. Over the years, construction codes have been dramatically changed. These days the quality of mobile homes exceeds that of conventional home construction. Better insulation, thicker framing, the use of fire retardant building materials, and a variety of spacious floorplans are just a few of the many salable features.
The statement that best supports this paragraph is:
A. Mobile homes are a thing of the past that most people overlook when considering new housing.
B. Materials that are used in mobile home construction are above standards required by building codes.
C. Utility bills of mobile home residents should be less than those living in comparable conventional housing due to better insulation.
D. The substantial improvements made in mobile home construction warrant consideration when shopping around for new housing.

12. In the 1984 election, the news media was accused of swaying the outcome of the presidential vote. The problem stemmed from coverage of voting results the minute they became available. Since a three hour time difference exists between the East and West coasts, those people going to the polls in the West could actually see the direction of the vote long before they cast their own vote. The news organizations were forecasting a winner even before the polls of some western states were open. Consequently, it made a lot of people in the West feel that their vote was insignificant and thus affected voter turnout. Since then, measures have been taken to prevent a repeat performance in 1988.
The statement that best supports this paragraph is:
A. The news media should be banned from political races.
B. Freedom of the press, as a right guaranteed in the Constitution, prevents any constraints from being placed on the media's coverage of elections.
C. Criticisms directed at the media for influencing the 1984 Presidential election prompted some changes in election coverage to avoid similar problems in the future.
D. Election coverage by the media makes it less desirable to live in a western state.

13. As ridiculous as it may sound, there have been past incidents of people trying to warm the interior of their home with a barbeque grill. Even if there is no apparent smoke, a tremendous danger exists from carbon monoxide emissions, Carbon monoxide is a colorless, odorless gas which even at minimum levels can be lethal. Carbon monoxide has the unique ability to displace oxygen. Without proper ventilation people can fall prey to asphyxiation. The symptoms are subtle. Lethargy is first experienced. Eventually, the victim feels tired enough to fall asleep and death is the inevitable result. This fact, in addition to the obvious fire danger, should be enough to discourage the use of barbeque grills inside homes.
The statement that best supports this paragraph is:
A. The use of a barbeque grill indoors for heating is unsafe and is not recommended.
B. It is fine to have an indoor barbeque as long as a majority of the home's windows are open.
C. Carbon monoxide gas is extremely poisonous.
D. Barbeque grills are a viable means of cheaply heating a home.

14. Organic gardening is a technique used to raise fruits and vegetables without the application of chemicals or pesticides. From a growing concern for health, people have been looking to organically raised foods. Most food items that appear on store shelves have in one respect or another been raised or processed with chemicals and/or pesticides. Markets hosting only organic produce have sprung up all around the country. More farmers, although small scale, are

just beginning to tap this market.

The statement that best supports this statement is:

A. Since pesticides and chemicals are not an integral part of organic farming, organic produce should be cheaper.
B. Organic agriculture is a lucrative market that is largely ignored by most farmers.
C. Commercially raised foods that are not organically raised are unhealthy.
D. The chemical and pesticide-free attributes of organic produce is becoming more popular with health-conscious consumers.

15. It is difficult to understand why the United States has not converted over to the metric system. It is a much easier system to learn because everything is figured in even units. For example, ten centimeters equals one decimeter; ten decimeters equals one meter; ten meters equals one decameter, etc. On the other hand, our current system of measurement require an extensive memorization of odd numbers. For example, twelve inches equals one foot, three feet equals one yard, 5280 feet equal one mile, etc. If we have a need to interchange metric units into our system of measures (i.e., how many meters are in one foot, or how many centimeters are in a yard) it requires the use of conversion tables. For the sake of simplicity and world uniformity, the metric system should be taught in our public schools and implemented in place of our current system.

The statement that best supports this paragraph is:

A. If we continue to use our system of measure long enough most other countries are bound to follow our precedent.
B. For no apparent reason, we continue to embrace an outmoded system of measures in spite of the benefits gained by converting over to metrics.
C. The reason metrics have not been emphasized in our public schools is due to a lack of qualified teachers.
D. Conversion charts would no longer be necessary once metrics become an internationally recognized system of measure.

16. Scuba diving is a sport that is gaining popularity. Through the ages, people have always had a sense of fascination and desire for underwater adventure. That became a possibility with the development and continued design improvement of Self-Contained-Underwater-Breathing-Apparatus (SCUBA) gear. There are a growing number of dive shops that specialize in outfitting and training future divers. Diving isn't a cheap sport to participate in, but the growing availability of scuba equipment has made it more affordable than it was 10 to 15 years ago. The enthusiasm expressed by people that have been diving is unmistakable. There is an entirely different world underwater that awaits discovery.

The statement that best supports this paragraph is:

A. Scuba diving equipment was so expensive 10 to 15 years ago that only a rich elite could enjoy the sport of diving.
B. There are infinite discoveries to be made by new divers.
C. Because scuba diving has become more affordable and accessible, it has captured a larger number of people's interest.
D. As of lately, there have been a proliferation of dive shops that cater to the demands of diving enthusiasts.

17. Most states have adopted stricter laws to curb the incidence of driving while under the influence (DWI) drivers. Tragically, thousands of people are killed on our highways by drunk drivers. It is a fallacy to think that alcohol consumption, regardless of the amount, will not impair driving. Unfortunately, it is the prevalence of this attitude that accounts for a large percentage of auto fatalities nationwide. To curtail this problem, tougher penalties have been enacted to make the potential DWI driver think twice before drinking and then getting behind the wheel of a vehicle.

The statement that best supports this paragraph is:

A. Lawmakers from most areas of the country have taken the stance that tougher punishment is required to diminish the number of DWI related accidents.
B. DWI driving is still tolerated in some states.
C. Drunk driving clearly presents a hazard on public roads.
D. Longer jail sentences imposed on drunk drivers should be an effective deterrent against DWI drivers.

18. Arthroscopic surgery is a medical technique that has proven itself to be invaluable to athletes with ligament or cartilage injuries. Prior to its development, injuries of this nature usually spelled the end of sports competition. The surgery was fairly traumatic and the amount of time required for recuperation and rehabilitation was long. Arthroscopic surgery, on the other hand, is far less traumatic. A minimal amount of skin and muscle tissue is cut to reach the injury directly. The medical instrument used by the surgeon can, in a more precise manner, trim damaged ligaments or cartilage quickly. In general, this does not mean that an athlete's injuries are without risk or pain. But, arthroscopic surgery is an

alternative that affords a better chance of quick recovery and the hope for continued participation in the future sporting activities.

The statement that best supports this paragraph is:

    A. Arthroscopic surgery is the only answer to most athletic injuries.

    B. In the past, injuries sustained to ligaments or cartilage were virtually inoperable.

    C. Today's athletes play with less reservation than their predecessors did because of the new advances made in connective tissue surgery.

    D. Arthroscopic surgery is a technique that can repair injured cartilage and ligament tissue and expediate recovery and the resumption of sports competition.

19. California has very strict building codes for multi-level construction projects due to the prevalence of earthquakes. In the past, buildings were constructed with absolute rigidity. As history has shown those very buildings could not withstand the swaying motions of an earthquake. Either the buildings would collapse altogether or they would sustain extensive superstructure damage that warranted demolition. Fortunately, architectural engineering has developed new designs that allow buildings to give during an earthquake without causing damage.

The statement that best supports this paragraph is:

    A. Earthquakes can be devastating to conventionally constructed buildings.

    B. It is not suggested to build in California.

    C. Architectural engineering has eliminated all the building problems associated with earthquakes.

    D. Earthquakes in California have prompted the development of new construction designs that comply with stricter building codes.

20. When there is ice or frost present on concrete walks and driveways, it is not prudent to use salt. Salt has adverse effects on concrete. It may not be noticeable at first, but if applied over time, salt can literally destroy concrete. Initially, little pockmarks are noticeable and if the use of salt continues, those same pockmarks become deep crevices. Alternatives to salt are sand or gravel. These do not eliminate surface ice, but they give improved traction without destruction of the underlying concrete. Additionally, sand and gravel are cheaper to buy and save on replacement costs of driveways and walkways.

The statement that best supports this paragraph is:

    A. Salt has been a longtime favorite to use in eliminating ice on sidewalks and driveways.

    B. Salt has destructive effects on all building materials.

    C. Because of the inherent disadvantages of using salt on concrete, sand or gravel are recommended as better, cheaper substitutes.

    D. Salt, if used only on a short term basis, will not have adverse effects on concrete walks or drives.

21. Owning a gun may seem like having a security blanket to some people. However, that very form of security can prove tragic if some simple precautions are not followed. Too many times people are shot accidentally because someone didn't realize that the gun they were handling was loaded. Treat every gun as though it is loaded and never point the barrel toward anyone. Most firearms are equipped with a safety switch that inhibits the trigger mechanism, Unfortunately, anything mechanical can and does fail. It is still a safe measure to have the safety on at all times with exception to the moment that a shot is about to be made. Another precaution is the proper storage of a gun and ammunition. If possible, it is best to lock everything in a gun cabinet, chest or closet. If that is not a viable option, then put trigger locks on the guns and store them out of the reach of children. Basically, the use of a little common sense can circumvent accidents involving firearms.

The statement that best supports this paragraph is:

    A. Firearms are unique and therefore pose a constant threat to individuals as well as families.

    B. As long as the safety switch is on, guns can be handled with little regard as to the direction of the barrel.

    C. Several points about gun safety are highlighted.

    D. It is important to keep all firearms and ammunition out of the reach of children.

22. It is foolhardy to think that an individual can control cocaine use. Cocaine is considered by experts worldwide to be one of the most addictive substances known to man. The sadder aspects of the drugs use are the trails of broken marriages, financial losses, disintegration of friendships and deaths that have occurred. The human toll is simply too great to even remotely merit using the drug. There have been significant strides made in cocaine abuse rehabilitation but the simple truth is the best form of rehabilitation is not to start using the drug. This concept needs to be impressed upon our children as well as our friends to circumvent certain tragedy.

The statement that best supports this paragraph is:

    A. The risks that are inherent in cocaine use are far too great to even contemplate its use.

    B. The use of cocaine may be addictive but since there are excellent rehabilitation programs available,

caution can be thrown to the wind.
C. Education is the key to preventing kids from experimenting with cocaine.
D. Cocaine, if used in a very conservative manner, is manageable by most individuals.

23. The bald eagle came very close to extinction a few years ago because of the wide use of the chemical pesticide called DDT. DDT was used extensively by farmers to protect their crops from destructive insects. It was not immediately known that the chemical did not break down naturally as it passed through the food chain. Invariably, sufficient quantities of DDT were ingested by bald eagles feeding on contaminated rodents to cause diminished reproductive capabilities. Thus, DDT was directly responsible for bald eagle eggs having extremely thin shells. As a consequence, few, if any, eggs would hatch. The species would have disappeared entirely if some concerned environmentalists had not stepped forward and forced an end to the use of DDT.

The statement that best supports this paragraph is:
A. Be grateful that we have concerned environmentalists.
B. Farmers were easily convinced that DDT was directly responsible for the bald eagle's demise.
C. Had the application of DDT to crops not been stopped, the bald eagle's extinction would have been a direct result.
D. Bald eagles should have had the discernment of what in their diet was and was not contaminated with DDT; it is their own fault that they almost became extinct.

24. The way a person dresses for a job interview has more bearing on a prospective employer's hiring decision than most people realize. Most interviewers are initially impressed the moment you enter their office. If you are qualified in every regard for a job, yet dress in sloppy attire, you may have destroyed your chances of being hired even before the conventional line of questioning begins. On the other hand, a well-attired job applicant creates the impression of professionalism, a positive attitude and an eager willingness to contribute to the company. First impressions are extremely important when searching for a job.

The statement that best supports this paragraph is:
A. As long as the right answers are given to the questions posed by the interviewer, dress has little significance in employment considerations.
B. It is important to have the right qualifications before seeking any job.
C. How job applicants dress has significant impact on employment hiring decisions.
D. If you only have blue jeans and T-shirts, don't even bother looking for work.

25. Hearing protection is essential for anyone that participates in trap or skeet shooting. If a person's hearing is regularly exposed to the loud extremes of shotgun reports, permanent hearing damage is the end result. The first evidence of hearing loss is a continual ringing in the ears even several days after shooting. If exposure to the noise is prolonged, the capacity to hear is eventually diminished. Hearing is one of the most precious senses that we have. It is nothing short of stupidity to jeopardize losing that sense by simply not wearing proper hearing protection.

The statement that best supports this paragraph is:
A. Hearing protection is not as important to the intermittent shotgunner as it is to the one that regularly practices.
B. The simple precaution of wearing hearing protection while shooting is suggested.
C. Certain degrees of hearing loss can be tolerated by most people.
D. Hearing is the most precious sense that we have.

VOCABULARY SECTION EXAM II

26. Because of poor radio reception, the weather report was "garbled". Garbled most nearly means
    A. misinformed
    B. non-existent
    C. distorted
    D. easy to hear

27. "Zealot" most nearly means
    A. historian
    B. fanatic
    C. economist
    D. politician

28. Of all the different situations that police have to face from day to day, the most unpredictable ones are "domestic" disputes. Domestic most nearly means
    A. drug
    B. home
    C. juvenile
    D. school

29. Bill seemed "arrogant" after winning the local Scrabble meet. Arrogant most nearly means
    A. drug
    B. upset
    C. proud
    D. haughty

30. The new tax revisions are viewed by many with some degree of "trepidation". Trepidation most nearly means
    A. dread
    B. agreement
    C. trivolity
    D. anticipation

31. The dog looked a little "lethargic" after chasing the cat around the house all day long. Lethargic most nearly means
    A. energetic
    B. satisfied
    C. apathetic
    D. nervous

32. The remarks made at the news conference were "innocuous". Innocuous most nearly means
    A. harsh
    B. unfounded
    C. inoffensive
    D. severe

33. This order "supercedes" all other orders previously issued. Supercedes most nearly means
    A. dwarfs
    B. supplants
    C. placates
    D. discards

34. The party was beginning to get "vociferous". Vociferous most nearly means
    A. neighbor's attention
    B. old
    C. packed
    D. loud

35. He had a "lanky" physique despite his appetite for large meals. Lanky most nearly means
    A. lean
    B. chunky
    C. overweight
    D. strange

36. Were it not for the "perseverance" of our forefathers to draft a new constitution, this country would not be what it is now. Perseverance most nearly means
    A. background
    B. tenacity
    C. petulance
    D. education

37. It is an "endeavor" by most college students to at least acquire a bachelor's degree. Endeavor most nearly means
    A. art
    B. guarantee
    C. informal engagement
    D. attempt

The Postal Exam Preparation Book 41

38. Even though the car has been to the garage twice, the engine still "intermittently" runs rough. Intermittently most nearly means
    A. persistently
    B. periodically
    C. internally
    D. regularly

39. Their "intentions" were well meaning. Intentions most nearly means
    A. purposes
    B. strengths
    C. procedures
    D. intensity

40. Shannon had a definite "repugnance" for camping out. Repugnance most nearly means
    A. attraction
    B. observance
    C. dislike
    D. affinity

41. It sounded like a "plausible" way of raising revenues for the school district. Plausible most nearly means
    A. far-reaching
    B. unrealistic
    C. incredible
    D. reasonable

42. He was surprisingly "unabashed" at what he had done. Unabashed most nearly means
    A. sorry
    B. withdrawn
    C. apologetic
    D. shameless

43. The Brown family had "kindred" all over the country. Kindred most nearly means
    A. friends
    B. relatives
    C. business ties
    D. traveled

44. It is against the law to offer "asylum" to escaped convicts. Asylum most nearly means
    A. coffee
    B. transportation
    C. atonement
    D. refuge

45. When the team bowled four strikes in a row, that proved to be the "pivotal" point of the game. Pivotal most nearly means
    A. disturbing
    B. highlight
    C. turning
    D. important

46. Most of the windows in the building were "opaque". Opaque most nearly means
    A. clear
    B. cracked
    C. non-transparent
    D. thick

47. John was "writhing" from the pain in his ankle after his foot slipped off the bicycle pedal. Writhing most nearly means
    A. swallowing hard
    B. panic-stricken
    C. squirming
    D. breathing shallowly

48. She was "reputed" to be the best bridge player in town. Reputed most nearly means
    A. has the distinction
    B. not regarded
    C. without warrant
    D. mistrusted

49. Few people tackle a job with such "fervor" as Tony does. Fervor most nearly means
    A. style
    B. acrimony
    C. bitterness
    D. passion

50. The "ascent" may be difficult but it is worth it once you are at the top. Ascent most nearly means
    A. climb
    B. discent
    C. declination
    D. downfall

51. "Tepid" most nearly means
    A. mild
    B. distressed
    C. tense
    D. magnanimous

52. The "tempo" of the song would be too slow for most teenagers. Tempo most nearly means
    A. notes
    B. singing
    C. rhythm
    D. treble

53. There was a mutual agreement made between both parties, but the actual settlement dates were "tentative". Tentative most nearly means
    A. finalized
    B. provisional
    C. elusive
    D. sketchy

54. A lot of folks thought of him as a "hermit". Hermit most nearly means
    A. popular individual
    B. recluse
    C. good natured
    D. follower

55. Tim is "prone" to catching colds. Prone most nearly means
    A. non-suspectible
    B. immune
    C. superior
    D. predisposed

56. Where the car came from is a "mystery". Mystery most nearly means
    A. an enigma
    B. superstitious
    C. certainty
    D. answered

57. His "self-esteem" was low. Self-esteem most nearly means
    A. health
    B. modesty
    C. pride
    D. well-being

58. When an animal is said to be "omnivorous" that most nearly means
    A. strictly vegetarian
    B. eats only meat
    C. eats only plants
    D. eats everything

59. Considering the fact that it is November, the countryside still looked "verdant". Verdant most nearly means
    A. cold
    B. green
    C. bleak
    D. barren

60. I was in the "vicinity" so I stopped. Vicinity most nearly means
    A. area
    B. city
    C. express lane
    D. open

-END OF TEST-

ANSWER SHEET TO READER'S COMPREHENSION/VOCABULARY EXAM II

1. Ⓐ Ⓑ Ⓒ Ⓓ Ⓔ		31. Ⓐ Ⓑ Ⓒ Ⓓ Ⓔ	
2. Ⓐ Ⓑ Ⓒ Ⓓ Ⓔ		32. Ⓐ Ⓑ Ⓒ Ⓓ Ⓔ	
3. Ⓐ Ⓑ Ⓒ Ⓓ Ⓔ		33. Ⓐ Ⓑ Ⓒ Ⓓ Ⓔ	
4. Ⓐ Ⓑ Ⓒ Ⓓ Ⓔ		34. Ⓐ Ⓑ Ⓒ Ⓓ Ⓔ	
5. Ⓐ Ⓑ Ⓒ Ⓓ Ⓔ		35. Ⓐ Ⓑ Ⓒ Ⓓ Ⓔ	
6. Ⓐ Ⓑ Ⓒ Ⓓ Ⓔ		36. Ⓐ Ⓑ Ⓒ Ⓓ Ⓔ	
7. Ⓐ Ⓑ Ⓒ Ⓓ Ⓔ		37. Ⓐ Ⓑ Ⓒ Ⓓ Ⓔ	
8. Ⓐ Ⓑ Ⓒ Ⓓ Ⓔ		38. Ⓐ Ⓑ Ⓒ Ⓓ Ⓔ	
9. Ⓐ Ⓑ Ⓒ Ⓓ Ⓔ		39. Ⓐ Ⓑ Ⓒ Ⓓ Ⓔ	
10. Ⓐ Ⓑ Ⓒ Ⓓ Ⓔ		40. Ⓐ Ⓑ Ⓒ Ⓓ Ⓔ	
11. Ⓐ Ⓑ Ⓒ Ⓓ Ⓔ		41. Ⓐ Ⓑ Ⓒ Ⓓ Ⓔ	
12. Ⓐ Ⓑ Ⓒ Ⓓ Ⓔ		42. Ⓐ Ⓑ Ⓒ Ⓓ Ⓔ	
13. Ⓐ Ⓑ Ⓒ Ⓓ Ⓔ		43. Ⓐ Ⓑ Ⓒ Ⓓ Ⓔ	
14. Ⓐ Ⓑ Ⓒ Ⓓ Ⓔ		44. Ⓐ Ⓑ Ⓒ Ⓓ Ⓔ	
15. Ⓐ Ⓑ Ⓒ Ⓓ Ⓔ		45. Ⓐ Ⓑ Ⓒ Ⓓ Ⓔ	
16. Ⓐ Ⓑ Ⓒ Ⓓ Ⓔ		46. Ⓐ Ⓑ Ⓒ Ⓓ Ⓔ	
17. Ⓐ Ⓑ Ⓒ Ⓓ Ⓔ		47. Ⓐ Ⓑ Ⓒ Ⓓ Ⓔ	
18. Ⓐ Ⓑ Ⓒ Ⓓ Ⓔ		48. Ⓐ Ⓑ Ⓒ Ⓓ Ⓔ	
19. Ⓐ Ⓑ Ⓒ Ⓓ Ⓔ		49. Ⓐ Ⓑ Ⓒ Ⓓ Ⓔ	
20. Ⓐ Ⓑ Ⓒ Ⓓ Ⓔ		50. Ⓐ Ⓑ Ⓒ Ⓓ Ⓔ	
21. Ⓐ Ⓑ Ⓒ Ⓓ Ⓔ		51. Ⓐ Ⓑ Ⓒ Ⓓ Ⓔ	
22. Ⓐ Ⓑ Ⓒ Ⓓ Ⓔ		52. Ⓐ Ⓑ Ⓒ Ⓓ Ⓔ	
23. Ⓐ Ⓑ Ⓒ Ⓓ Ⓔ		53. Ⓐ Ⓑ Ⓒ Ⓓ Ⓔ	
24. Ⓐ Ⓑ Ⓒ Ⓓ Ⓔ		54. Ⓐ Ⓑ Ⓒ Ⓓ Ⓔ	
25. Ⓐ Ⓑ Ⓒ Ⓓ Ⓔ		55. Ⓐ Ⓑ Ⓒ Ⓓ Ⓔ	
26. Ⓐ Ⓑ Ⓒ Ⓓ Ⓔ		56. Ⓐ Ⓑ Ⓒ Ⓓ Ⓔ	
27. Ⓐ Ⓑ Ⓒ Ⓓ Ⓔ		57. Ⓐ Ⓑ Ⓒ Ⓓ Ⓔ	
28. Ⓐ Ⓑ Ⓒ Ⓓ Ⓔ		58. Ⓐ Ⓑ Ⓒ Ⓓ Ⓔ	
29. Ⓐ Ⓑ Ⓒ Ⓓ Ⓔ		59. Ⓐ Ⓑ Ⓒ Ⓓ Ⓔ	
30. Ⓐ Ⓑ Ⓒ Ⓓ Ⓔ		60. Ⓐ Ⓑ Ⓒ Ⓓ Ⓔ	

(This page may be removed to mark answers.)

ANSWERS TO MATH EXAM II

1. A	11. C	21. A	31. D
2. D	12. B	22. B	32. A
3. C	13. A	23. D	33. C
4. D	14. C	24. C	34. D
5. B	15. C	25. C	35. C
6. C	16. A	26. C	36. D
7. A	17. B	27. A	37. D
8. D	18. D	28. D	38. A
9. B	19. C	29. A	39. B
10. D	20. A	30. B	40. A

If your score was:
    35 or more correct, you have an excellent score
    30-34 correct, you have a good score
    29 or less correct, you should practice more.

ANSWERS TO READER'S COMPREHENSION AND VOCABULARY EXAM II

1. B	16. C	31. C	46. C
2. A	17. A	32. C	47. C
3. C	18. D	33. B	48. A
4. D	19. D	34. D	49. D
5. C	20. C	35. A	50. A
6. D	21. C	36. B	51. A
7. A	22. A	37. D	52. C
8. C	23. C	38. B	53. B
9. B	24. C	39. A	54. B
10. B	25. B	40. C	55. D
11. D	26. C	41. D	56. A
12. C	27. B	42. D	57. C
13. A	28. B	43. B	58. D
14. D	29. D	44. D	59. B
15. B	30. A	45. C	60. A

If your score was:
    53 or more correct, you have an excellent score
    45-52 correct, you have a good score
    44 or less correct, you should practice more

POSTAGE RATES FOR MAILING PARCELS

Various rates are provided below for determination of the cost of sending parcels weighing 2 to 20 pounds to Areas 1 through 6 and locally.

Wt in exact lbs & not exceeding	Local Area	Areas 1&2	Area 3	Area 4	Area 5	Area 6
2	2.52	2.72	2.82	2.97	3.07	3.10
3	2.75	2.95	3.05	3.20	3.30	3.33
4	2.79	2.99	3.09	3.24	3.34	3.37
5	3.04	3.24	3.34	3.49	3.59	3.62
6	3.12	3.32	3.42	3.57	3.67	3.70
7	3.19	3.39	3.49	3.64	3.74	3.77
8	3.26	3.46	3.56	3.71	3.81	3.84
9	3.35	3.55	3.65	3.80	3.90	3.93
10	3.42	3.62	3.72	3.87	3.97	4.00
11	3.57	3.77	3.87	4.02	4.12	4.15
12	3.66	3.86	3.96	4.11	4.21	4.24
13	3.71	3.91	4.01	4.16	4.26	4.29
14	3.79	3.99	4.09	4.24	4.34	4.37
15	3.87	4.07	4.17	4.32	4.42	4.45
16	3.96	4.16	4.26	4.41	4.51	4.54
17	4.05	4.25	4.35	4.50	4.60	4.63
18	4.12	4.32	4.42	4.57	4.67	4.70
19	4.20	4.40	4.50	4.65	4.75	4.78
20	4.26	4.46	4.56	4.71	4.81	4.84

(Note: These particular postage and wrapping charges are not included unless the customer specifically requests their use. The weights shown below are only applicable up to 2 pounds and not including 2 pounds. Parcels weighing 2 or more pounds are shown above.)

(Hint: Fractional weights over 2 pounds should be rounded to the next hightest figure (i.e., 10-1/4 pounds = 11 pounds on the chart).

GROUP A

Parcel No.	Price
1 or 2	0.27/oz
3	0.29/oz
4	0.37/oz
5	0.58/oz

PADDED ENVELOPE CHARGE

all sizes=1.12 each

GROUP B

All parcels cost 0.16 for the first 6 ounces and 0.09 for each additional ounce.

PACKAGE WRAPPING CHARGES

Pkg size	Cost
1-3	0.72
4-6	1.33
7-10	1.67

TIME: 75 MINUTES
40 QUESTIONS

MATH SECTION EXAM III

1. How much would 95 12-cent bulk mail stamps and 80 22-cent stamps cost?

   A. $39.00   B. $29.00   C. $27.00   D. $33.00

2. What would be the cost of 940 22-cent stamps, 137 5-cent stamps, and 960 2-cent stamps?

   A. $352.85   B. $222.58   C. $232.85   D. none of these

3. If you wanted to purchase six rolls (100 count) of 17-cent stamps, 35 and 40-cent stamps, and 19 padded envelopes, how much would all of this cost?

   A. $43.17   B. $92.12   C. $105.08   D. none of these

4. If a customer only had $25.00, how many Size 3, wrapped packages weighing 6 pounds each could be sent to Area 3 (assume that the entire $25.00 is to be spent)?

   A. 6   B. 7   C. 5   D. 8

5. Suppose a customer had $47.00 and seven 5 pound Size 7, wrapped packages to be sent to Area 2. How much money would this customer have left after this transaction?

   A. $15.96   B. $16.12   C. $12.63   D. $14.23

6. Suppose that just before you finished the transaction for the same customer in Question 5, the expense of it all was a little too much. If 4 of the 7 parcels to be sent to Area 2 were made 2 pounds lighter and the remaining 3 packages made 3 pounds lighter, how much money would the customer have let over from the original $47.00?

   A. $15.14   B. $15.35   C. $12.72   D. $16.17

7. How much would it cost to send twenty 1-1/4-pound Group A, No. 4 parcels and three 1-1/4-pound Group B parcels to Miami, Florida?

   A. $153.26   B. $152.26   C. $150.26   D. none of these

8. If fourteen 11 pound packages are to be sent to Area 5 and fifteen 4 pound packages to Area 6, how much will it cost?

   A. $19.1,8   B. $93.07   C. $108.23   D. $127.82

9. A customer wanted to know what the maximum %individual weights could be for 3 identical parcels destined to Area 3 and costing under $13.51 to send.

   A. 19 lbs   B. 18 lbs   C. 17 lbs   D. 16 lbs

10. What would it cost to send four 12 pound, thirty-two 5 pound, and thirteen 19 pound packages to Areas 3, 5 and 6 respectively?

    A. $195.62   B. $183.15   C. $197.18   D. $192.86

11. How many 12 ounce Group A, No. 4 parcels placed in medium-size padded envelopes could be sent to Area 6 for $19.00?

    A. 2   B. 3   C. 4   D. none of these

12. How much would it cost to send a 1-1/4 pound Group B parcel enclosed in a medium-sized padded envelope to Area 4?

    A. $2.54   B. $4.71   C. $1.42   D. none of these

13. Assume a customer has $60.00 and desires to send as many 18 pound, Size 5, wrapped packages locally as possible with enough money left to purchase 9 large padded envelopes. How many packages could be sent under these circumstances?

    A. 6   B. 7   C. 8   D. 9

The Postal Exam Preparation Book 49

14. What would it cost to send 42 Size 8 wrapped parcels each weighing 13 pounds to Area 6 and 27 Group B, 30 ounce articles to Area 2?

    A. $14.92   B. 47.92   C. 32.   D. none of these

15. How many 1-1/2 pound Group B, Size 9 wrapped parcels could be sent locally for $40.00?

    A. 6   B. 5   C. 11   D. 9

16. Suppose a customer only had $43.16 and wished to send as many 9 ounce Group B articles enclosed in large-size padded envelopes as possible to Seattle, Washington. How many articles could be sent?

    A. 25   B. 27   C. 29   D. 31

17. How much would it cost to send twenty 4 pound, Size 2 wrapped packages, seven 19 pound Size 5 wrapped packages, and thirteen 8 pound, Size 9 wrapped packages to Areas 4, 5, and 6 respectively?

    A. $67.53   B. $87.35   C. $47.53   D. none of these

18. How many 1-1/4 pound Group A, No. 4 parcels enclosed in small, padded envelopes could be sent to Area 4 for $35.00?

    A. 4   B. 2   C. 3   D. none of these

19. What would the cost be to send 20 Group A, No. 2, 3/4 pound parcels to Area 6 and 16 Group B, size 6, 10 ounce, wrapped packages to Area 2?

    A. $94.40   B. $89.40   C. $73.40   D. $79.40

20. How much money would be left from $41.00 if four 6 pound packages were sent to Area 3 and fourteen 13 ounce Group B parcels enclosed in small, padded envelopes were sent locally?

    A. $0.68   B. $0.47   C. $0.58   D. none of these

21. If twenty 1/4 pound Group A, No. 5 parcels were sent to New Jersey and thirty-seven 8 pound Size 10, wrapped parcels sent to Area 1, how much would it all cost?

    A. $226.31   B. $236.21   C. $240.00   D. $227.21

22. What would it cost to send four 19 ounce Group A, No. 3 parcels and 352 Size 8, wrapped 15 pound parcels to Area 3?

    A. $2079.20   B. $2702.02   C. $2070.27   D. $2077.72

23. Suppose a customer wanted to purchase 60 padded envelopes, 50 17-cent stamps, and send 40 13-ounce Group B parcels to local destinations. How much would all of this cost?

    A. $107.30   B. $92.53   C. $120.53   D. $122.53

24. If six 5 ounce Group A, No. 3 parcels and twenty-eight 18 ounce Group A, No. 5, Size 4, wrapped parcels were all sent to California, how much would it cost?

    A. $15.07   B. $29.43   C. $18.76   D. none of these

25. How many 20 pound Size 9, wrapped parcels could be sent to Area 6 on a budget of $33.00?

    A. 4   B. 5   C. 6   D. 7

26. What would the cost be to send 15 Size 3, 12- pound wrapped parcels to Area 1, and 37 Size 2, 5 pound wrapped parcels to Area 6?

    A. $212.16   B. $236.52   C. $229.28   D. none of these

27. If a business wanted 140 large size padded envelopes, 1600 22-cent stamps, 150 39-cent stamps and 90 2-cent stamps, how much would the expense be?

    A. $557.81   B. $569.10   C. $579.01   D. $596.01

28. Five packages each weighing 19 pounds, 6 pounds, 10 pounds, 14 pounds and 3 pounds were being sent to Areas 1, 2, 4, 5, and 6 respectively. What would the total bill be for mailing them?

    A. $19.26   B. $18.46   C. $20.16   D. $21.06

29. If two packages each weigh 17-3/4 pounds and were destined to Area 5, what would it cost to mail them?

    A. $9.60   B. $9.20   C. $9.34   D. $9.72

30. What would the expense be to send forty 16-pound parcels locally, ten 8 pound, Size 2 wrapped parcels to Area 1, and fourteen 4 ounce Group B articles to Area 5?

    A. $162.42   B. $173.81   C. $193.59   D. $202.44

31. Suppose a customer had $10.00 and wanted to send as many 5-ounce Group B parcels enclosed in small padded envelopes as possible to a zip code that would classify it as an Area 4 destination. How many parcels could be sent?

    A. 5   B. 6   C. 7   D. none of these

32. Look at Question 31 again. Assume everything remains the same except that the parcels are now classified as Group A, No. 4. How many of these packages could be sent on a budget of $10.00?

    A. 3   B. 4.   C. 2   D. 5

33. What is the cost of sending a 12, 20, 8 and 5-pound packages (all 4 parcels are Size 1 wrapped) to Areas 2, 5, 5, and 6 respectively?

    A. $18.98   B. $19.06   C. $17.06   D. $16.89

34. A customer wanted to purchase 80 22-cent stamps, 15 small padded envelopes, and send thirteen 17-ounce Group A, No, 5 articles to relatives all living in Area 4. How much will it all cost?

    A. $27.55   B. $57.55   C. $81.08   D. none of these

35. If you only had $22.00, how many 15-ounce Group A, No. 2 parcels enclosed in large-size padded envelopes could be sent after having paid postage on five 19 pound packages destined to Area 1?

    A. 3   B. 2   C. 1   D. 0

36. If 42 Size 5, 3-pound wrapped packages, 31 Size 9, 2- pound wrapped packages, and 12 Size 7, 17- pound wrapped packages were sent to Areas 4, 3, and, respectively, what would it cost?

    A. $405.38   B. $400.49   C. $407.08   D. none of these

37. Suppose a customer had to purchase 15 rolls (100 count) of 17-cent stamps and 15 small padded envelopes. If the customer had $300.00, how many 5-pound, size 5 wrapped parcels destined to Area 3 could be mailed with the money left over from the stamps and envelope purchase?

    A. 4   B. 2   C. 8   D. 6

38. What would it cost to send 5 Group B, 5 ounce articles locally, and 15 Group A, No. 4, 18 ounce parcels to New York?

    A. $100.07   B. $107.07   C. $100.70   D. none of these

39. Look at Question 38 again. If a customer had $125.00, how much money would be left from the transaction?

    A. $17.93   B. $24.93   C. $24.31   D. none of these

40. If an equal number of 17-pound parcels were sent to Areas 6, 5, and 3 at a cost of $54.32, how many parcels were sent to each Area destination?

    A. 4   B. 5   C. 3   D. 7

- END OF TEST -

The Postal Exam Preparation Book 51

ANSWER SHEET TO MATH EXAM III

1.	Ⓐ	Ⓑ	Ⓒ	Ⓓ	Ⓔ	21.	Ⓐ	Ⓑ	Ⓒ	Ⓓ	Ⓔ
2.	Ⓐ	Ⓑ	Ⓒ	Ⓓ	Ⓔ	22.	Ⓐ	Ⓑ	Ⓒ	Ⓓ	Ⓔ
3.	Ⓐ	Ⓑ	Ⓒ	Ⓓ	Ⓔ	23.	Ⓐ	Ⓑ	Ⓒ	Ⓓ	Ⓔ
4.	Ⓐ	Ⓑ	Ⓒ	Ⓓ	Ⓔ	24.	Ⓐ	Ⓑ	Ⓒ	Ⓓ	Ⓔ
5.	Ⓐ	Ⓑ	Ⓒ	Ⓓ	Ⓔ	25.	Ⓐ	Ⓑ	Ⓒ	Ⓓ	Ⓔ
6.	Ⓐ	Ⓑ	Ⓒ	Ⓓ	Ⓔ	26.	Ⓐ	Ⓑ	Ⓒ	Ⓓ	Ⓔ
7.	Ⓐ	Ⓑ	Ⓒ	Ⓓ	Ⓔ	27.	Ⓐ	Ⓑ	Ⓒ	Ⓓ	Ⓔ
8.	Ⓐ	Ⓑ	Ⓒ	Ⓓ	Ⓔ	28.	Ⓐ	Ⓑ	Ⓒ	Ⓓ	Ⓔ
9.	Ⓐ	Ⓑ	Ⓒ	Ⓓ	Ⓔ	29.	Ⓐ	Ⓑ	Ⓒ	Ⓓ	Ⓔ
10.	Ⓐ	Ⓑ	Ⓒ	Ⓓ	Ⓔ	30.	Ⓐ	Ⓑ	Ⓒ	Ⓓ	Ⓔ
11.	Ⓐ	Ⓑ	Ⓒ	Ⓓ	Ⓔ	31.	Ⓐ	Ⓑ	Ⓒ	Ⓓ	Ⓔ
12.	Ⓐ	Ⓑ	Ⓒ	Ⓓ	Ⓔ	32.	Ⓐ	Ⓑ	Ⓒ	Ⓓ	Ⓔ
13.	Ⓐ	Ⓑ	Ⓒ	Ⓓ	Ⓔ	33.	Ⓐ	Ⓑ	Ⓒ	Ⓓ	Ⓔ
14.	Ⓐ	Ⓑ	Ⓒ	Ⓓ	Ⓔ	34.	Ⓐ	Ⓑ	Ⓒ	Ⓓ	Ⓔ
15.	Ⓐ	Ⓑ	Ⓒ	Ⓓ	Ⓔ	35.	Ⓐ	Ⓑ	Ⓒ	Ⓓ	Ⓔ
16.	Ⓐ	Ⓑ	Ⓒ	Ⓓ	Ⓔ	36.	Ⓐ	Ⓑ	Ⓒ	Ⓓ	Ⓔ
17.	Ⓐ	Ⓑ	Ⓒ	Ⓓ	Ⓔ	37.	Ⓐ	Ⓑ	Ⓒ	Ⓓ	Ⓔ
18.	Ⓐ	Ⓑ	Ⓒ	Ⓓ	Ⓔ	38.	Ⓐ	Ⓑ	Ⓒ	Ⓓ	Ⓔ
19.	Ⓐ	Ⓑ	Ⓒ	Ⓓ	Ⓔ	39.	Ⓐ	Ⓑ	Ⓒ	Ⓓ	Ⓔ
20.	Ⓐ	Ⓑ	Ⓒ	Ⓓ	Ⓔ	40.	Ⓐ	Ⓑ	Ⓒ	Ⓓ	Ⓔ

(This page may be removed to mark answers.)

TIME: 90 MINUTES
60 QUESTIONS

READER'S COMPREHENSION SECTION EXAM III

1. If speaking before a group of people puts a lump in your throat, you are not alone. However, there are some means of preparation that can make public speaking more comfortable for you. The best speeches are not given on a note of spontaneous inspiration. Preparation time is required to give a good quality speech. It is important to know the subject matter thoroughly to convey confidence. Another facet that requires practice is delivery. Meek or nervous speaking is perceived by an audience as a lack of confidence in yourself or your topic. On the other hand, a strong and dynamic voice indicates self-confidence. Public speaking is by no means a talent that comes naturally to a few select people. Rather, it requires a good degree of work to give a good quality presentation.

   The statement that best supports the above paragraph is:

   A. It is not so much the amount of preparation that goes into developing a speech, but the attention to enunciation of words that makes the difference between giving a good or bad presentation.
   B. Adequate preparation will guarantee a high quality speech.
   C. Nervousness is natural when speaking before a group.
   D. The natural inclination to be nervous about giving a speech can be countered with advance preparation.

2. When the weather turns cold, it is important to dress appropriately to circumvent hypothermia. Since a large percentage of heat loss occurs from the head, it is important to wear a cap or hat and wrap a scarf around the neck and face. Enough clothing should be worn to keep a person warm, yet not promote perspiration. If a person's clothing becomes wet by the elements or perspiration, insulative properties are lost and the prospect of fatal hypothermia becomes real. Wool is the most desirable material used in winter garments because it can insulate even when wet. This is not the case with nylon, acrylic, etc. Regardless of cold winter conditions, there is no need to stay indoors if you dress appropriately.

   The statement that best supports the above paragraph is:

   A. If blizzard conditions exist, it is probably wisest to remain indoors until the weather improves.
   B. Colder weather necessitates us to dress in a warm and dry manner that precludes the possibility of hypothermia.
   C. Wool is a superior material compared to nylon or acrylic because of its insulative properties even when wet.
   D. Since hypothermia in its early stages is very obvious, as long as we recognize it and respect it by seeking shelter, how we dress is not really important.

3. Some people have said that the success of state lotteries has largely occurred because of the people who can least afford it. Studies have shown that primarily middle and lower income people purchase lottery tickets in the faint hope of striking it rich. Taxes that are levied by state and federal governments are designed to progressively get more revenue from an individual that earns more than others. State lotteries, however, have had just the opposite effect. Lotteries are regressive in the sense that poorer people spend more money in lotteries than wealthier people. This sort of dilemma lends credence to the idea that lotteries in the long run, hurt local economies more than help them.

   The statement that best supports the above paragraph is:

   A. State lotteries are nothing more than legalized gambling.
   B. If enough lottery tickets are sold and there are few, if any winners, it can't help but be a boom to a local economy.
   C. There is a large consensus of people that believe state lotteries tax those people who are in a position to least afford it.
   D. A state lottery is considered by some and shown by statistics to be a regressive tax.

4. Most people do not realize that many commercially canned food items are subjected to radiation treatment. As much as it may surprise some people, this has been sanctioned by the FDA for years. There is absolutely no danger posed to the consumer. Canned food is subjected to predefined doses of radiation to eliminate potentially dangerous bacteria. Before radiology was employed in the food industry, it was not uncommon for some people to die from botulism or other bacterially based illnesses. Unfortunately, the mere word radiation conjures anxiety among people. Therefore, it is understandable why a company using radiation in processing does not readily advertise the fact.

   The statement that best supports this paragraph is:

   A. The commercial food industry needs to better educate the public about the uses of radiology in food processing.
   B. Radiation treatment to canned food has its health benefits, but due to the preconceived views held by some people, the practice is not highly publicized.

C. Were it not for radiology in commercial food processing, the incidence of bacterial poisonings would surely increase.

D. Radiation treatment of canned food is well known and well received by most people because of its inherent benefits.

5. Some animals have the remarkable ability to physically change their outer appearance to blend into their environment. This may entail changes in skin color that are either subtle or quite drastic. It may involve various changes of body shape as well. These abilities are the underpinning of survival to some species. If an animal is masterful at the art of camouflage, the chances of being recognized by a predator are greatly reduced. At the same time, it makes it much easier to prey upon unsuspecting insects or other animals. Whether it was by evolutionary design or accident, the species that possesses this innate ability has a much better chance at survival than those without this ability.

The statement that best supports this paragraph is:

A. An animal's ability to change either its color or shape to better blend with an environment is a complex physiological process.

B. If an animal possesses good camouflage skills it ascertains survival.

C. Animals that have the ability to blend into their immediate surroundings stand a much better chance of survival.

D. It has been long established that camouflage characteristics of some species are an evolutionary fluke.

6. It seems like everything changes with time and the Highway Patrol is no exception. Their new method of catching speeders involves the use of a radar-camera unit that is placed on the shoulder of a road facing oncoming traffic. If someone drives by the unit at a speed over what is posted, a snapshot of the vehicle and driver in violation is automatically taken. It is then a simple matter to trace license plate numbers to the owner in question. Traffic citations are then mailed. It is cost effective and very efficient.

The statement that best supports the above paragraph is:

A. If you are a habitual speeder, it would be prudent to avoid driving on primary highways and take the back roads.

B. The manner in which speeders are apprehended by the Highway Patrol has dramatically changed.

C. Radar-camera units are an effective deterrent to speeding.

D. Since the issuance of tickets has become so automated, it is believed that the right to appeal is severely limited.

7. If the opportunity is presented, termites will cause significant structural damage to a home. Wood made soft by continual exposure to moisture is the material preferred by termites. There are a number of factors that are responsible for wood becoming susceptible to termite infestation. Low foundations with poor drainage, lack of or improperly installed flashing around edges, firewood stacked directly against an exterior wall, or constant shade afforded by vegetation too close to the house are only a few examples of how wood can become wet for extended periods of time. When these conditions are present, your home can play host to termites at substantial expense. The best measures taken are preventative, rather than reactive. Anything done that helps to ensure wood from getting and remaining moist is beneficial.

The statement that best supports this paragraph is:

A. It is necessary to prevent wood in a home from becoming constantly wet and soft as that is an open invitation to termites.

B. If wood is subjected to moisture over long periods of time, it has a tendency to soften.

C. A high and dry foundation is a place where termite infestation is not likely to occur.

D. Anyway you look at it, preventing or eradicating an existing termite problem is going to be expensive.

8. The microwave oven has gained increasing popularity as a kitchen appliance. It can cook or defrost food at a far quicker pace than its range top counterparts. Additionally, it is relatively easy to clean and there is little possibility of getting burned. Only the food is heated, not the oven itself. We have become a convenience-minded society and because of that trend, microwave ovens have gained strong favor lately.

The statement that best supports this paragraph is:

A. Microwave ovens are safer for children to operate.

B. Microwaves are advantageous in the respect of cooking meals more quickly than conventional ovens.

C. Microwave ovens have found a niche in our convenience-minded society.

D. Range tops are considerably harder to clean than microwaves.

9. If kids are allowed to use calculators in school, it is feared that they will not learn basic mathematical skills. Virtually anyone can punch numbers into a calculator and come up with a solution to a basic math problem. What happens if, for some reason, a calculator cannot be used? If kids do not properly grasp addition, subtraction, multiplication and division

fundamentals, a problem definitely exists. This illiteracy can become a potential stumbling block in a child's future. Calculators can be invaluable tools to people, but if they are applied improperly in schools, they can hurt kids more than help them.

    The statement that best supports this paragraph is:
        A. Calculators have absolutely no business being used in our public schools.
        B. People that rely on calculators to solve mathematical problems are probably illiterate.
        C. Ironically, calculators can become more of a hindrance to a child's education than a benefit.
        D. If a person has access to a calculator, an understanding of basic mathematical principles is not important.

10. Some consumer groups would like to see farmers stop feeding antibiotics to livestock all together. This practice is believed to spawn various strains of bacteria that are immune to antibiotics. If people ingest meats or other products that have been subjected to antibiotic treatment, any illness they may contract could be more difficult to treat. Bacteria that are unresponsive to conventional antibiotic drugs could pose a danger to people. This concern by consumer groups may be overblown to some extent, but the situation does warrant further study.

    The statement that best supports the above paragraph is:
        A. The practice of feeding livestock antibiotics has been proven to be dangerous to consumers.
        B. Super strains of bacteria are the result of farmers' feeding programs.
        C. More studies on bacterial propagation are needed.
        D. The relationship of antibiotic treatment to livestock feed and bacterial immunities are of prime concern to some consumer groups.

11. If a home has cathedral ceilings, it is well worth it for the homeowner to install a ceiling fan. Heat has the tendency to rise thus leaving floors relatively cool. A ceiling fan however, can eliminate that temperature disparity as it forces heated air to circulate more efficiently. And, better heating efficiency will lower a homeowner's heating bills. Ceiling fans also lend an aesthetic quality to a home. Any way you look at it, the prospect of installing a ceiling fan certainly deserves some consideration.

    The statement that best supports the above paragraph is:
        A. Ceiling fans are only needed in homes with cathedral ceilings.
        B. Cool spots within a home can be alleviated with the installation of ceiling fans.
        C. Considering what ceiling fans have to offer, a homeowner would be well advised to look into their installation.
        D. Heating bills will not reflect a savings worth the cost of installing a ceiling fan.

12. It seems that as the years go by, merchants tend to push the Christmas shopping season on us earlier and earlier. In the past, most businesses would not even hint about Christmas until the day after Thanksgiving. These days it is not uncommon to see Christmas preview sales in October or even late September! Christmas music is now being heard in some stores shortly after Halloween! The more you really think about it, the easier it is to believe that the Christmas season is becoming more and more commercialized. This is a sad commentary if the religious fundamentals of the holiday are overlooked for the sheer sake of sales.

    The statement that best supports the above paragraph is:
        A. All merchants look forward to Christmas because of the expected increase of sales around the holiday.
        B. Christmas advertisements prior to Thanksgiving are considered premature by most people.
        C. The Christmas shopping season should be under full swing by November 1.
        D. Prior to and during the Christmas season, there seems to be more of an emphasis on sales than in the observance of the holiday itself.

13. Fluoride plays a particularly important role in dentistry. It was established through research that fluoride inhibits plaque formation on teeth. Soon after this discovery, fluoride became an integral part of most toothpastes. It is even added to some cities' drinking water. Although fluoride has not completely eliminated the need for regular dental checkups, it has improved the quality of our health by substantially reducing the incidence of tooth dcay.

    The statement that best supports this paragraph is:
        A. Fluoride is indirectly responsible for the large numbers of dentists applying for unemployment.
        B. Since its discovery, fluoride has had a positive impact on the field of dentistry.
        C. Dental problems associated with plaque have been marginally affected by the introduction of fluoride.
        D. Oral hygiene is no longer a problem since fluoride has become an integral part of most toothpastes.

14. While credit cards can be a source of real financial trouble for some they are considered invaluable to the seasoned traveler. Personal checks are almost impossible to cash out-of-town. Ironically, many merchants require at least two forms of identification one of which is a nationally recognized credit card. A traveler can be severely limited if personal

checks are the only means available to pay for goods or services. Credit cards, when used with discretion, afford the traveler several benefits. They are convenient and accepted almost anywhere. Additionally, they are much safer to carry than cash as they can be reissued if lost or stolen. Credit card users are also given a monthly statement of all expenses which can serve as tax records. When credit cards are utilized with good judgment, they are highly recommended for the individual that travels fairly regularly.

The statement that best supports the above paragraph is:

    A. Credit cards are not recommended for people that lack self-control in their spending habits.
    B. Accurate tax records are imperative for the business traveler.
    C. While some people have the propensity to abuse credit cards, they are considered an asset by most travelers because of the conveniences they afford.
    D. Credit cards are substantially safer to carry than cash because if they are lost or stolen, the account can be frozen to prevent theft of funds and the holder can be reissued a new card.

15. Good form is absolutely necessary to a bowler that desires a high average score. The occasional strike or spare bowled by an amateur is all well and good, but the repetition of such bowling is difficult at best without proper and consistent form. The more control you can exert over your ball, the better your chances are of obtaining strikes and spares. Once you have established a routine of controlled ball release, refinements can be made with anticipated results. Eventually, everything will seem very comfortable and bowling scores will vastly improve.

The statement that best supports the above paragraph is:

    A. Professional bowlers are very serious people.
    B. Ball control is what all amateur bowlers lack.
    C. Widely varied bowling scores are a thing of the past once proper ball release is learned.
    D. To perform well in bowling, attention must be given to proper form and consistent ball control.

16. Skunks are not recommended as pets for reasons outside of the obvious odor problems associated with the species. Odor glands can be easily removed by a veterinarian. However, what cannot be ascertained is if the pet skunk is a potential carrier of rabies. Skunks suffer from a particularly high incidence of rabies which it can be passed on directly to offspring by transovarial infection. Rabies can reside within an skunk without manifesting itself until a later time. In other words, your pet skunk may become passively rabid without your knowledge. The disease can be contracted simply by the pet's saliva inadvertently getting into an open cut or wound. Baby skunks are cute, but considering the inherent danger that goes with their ownership, it is an unnecessary risk to take.

The statement that best supports the above paragraph is:

    A. The implication that rabies is inherent in skunks should be reason enough to dissuade people from keeping them as pets.
    B. The primary means of rabies transmission among skunks is through transovarial infection of the offspring.
    C. Rabies does not always manifest itself in its host.
    D. If an individual is determined to own a pet skunk, it is best advised to wear gloves anytime the animal is to be handled.

17. Ethiopia had been in the throes of a severe famine for several years. This was largely ignored by the world until two European journalists video taped some of the extremely graphic consequences of the famine. Emaciated bodies, resembling skeletons were shown to be commonplace. Thousands of children, as well as adults, died from malnutrition or suffered irreversible physical and mental deterioration. The journalists produced video footage that the world could not ignore any longer. World help in terms of food, medical supplies, agricultural technology and money were sent to Ethiopia immediately. Hunger still plagues Ethiopia today, but because of the efforts of two particular journalists, this problem has been substantially abated.

The statement that best supports the above paragraph is:

    A. Ethiopia's famine was caused by an extended drought.
    B. The key to alleviating hunger is through agricultural technical training.
    C. The media played a key role in focusing world attention on Ethiopia's hunger problems.
    D. The famine in Ethiopia was responsible for the deaths of thousands of people.

18. Gambling, whether it be in cards, dice, or the races, can be a great source of entertainment; that is, until it becomes a habit or necessity to one's life. Most people gamble with money they can afford to lose. If luck should have it, and that money is indeed lost, it is prudent to call it quits and choose other things to do for enjoyment. The lack of this discretion can qualify a person as a compulsive gambler. This kind of behavior almost always leads to financial ruin and personal despair. Tragically, this is not uncommon.

The statement that best supports the above paragraph is:

A. The pitfalls of compulsive gambling are an inevitable fate for all gamblers.
B. If you have lost money gambling, get a loan or some other means of credit because your luck is bound to change any minute.
C. Compulsive gambling is a pathological condition.
D. Gambling can be an enjoyable pastime as long as good judgment is exercised toward money management.

19. It's almost inevitable that we will find some form of junk mail in our mailboxes daily. More often than not, it's simply thrown away and the recipient grumbles a little over how he or she was inconvenienced by having to sort through it. Actually, we should be happy to receive it. Were it not for the revenues generated by bulk business mail, the Postal Service would have no choice but to substantially raise the cost of mailing letters and packages. Bulk mail accounts for well over half of the income taken in by the Postal Service, and this, in turn, directly subsidizes the cost of handling other classes of mail. So, the next time you see junk mail in your mail box, you will have the satisfaction of knowing that its presence constitutes a savings to you.
The statement that best supports the above paragraph is:
A. Bulk mail is a major inconvenience for postal customers.
B. Junk mail accounts for a sizable percentage of business handled by the Postal Service.
C. Contrary to people's perception, junk mail is responsible for keeping most other rates lower.
D. The Postal Service could operate without the subsidization of bulk business mail.

20. Tornadoes are particularly destructive storms that have killed many people. If you ever find yourself in a situation where a tornado is imminent, never take it for granted that you are safe just because you are indoors. Regardless of how well a home is built, it can be easily reduced to a pile of rubble by the influences of a tornado. Therefore, it's vitally important to immediately seek shelter in a house's basement. The old line of thinking was that the southwest corner of a basement afforded the best protection as that was a tornado's most common approach. However, it is more important to get under a table or anything that can provide protection from falling debris than it is to be in the southwest corner. If a home does not have a basement, small places such as linen closets or bathrooms are the best places to be. Apparently, the door sills and 2 by 4 construction of smaller spaces are comparatively stronger than larger spaces.
The statement that best supports the above paragraph is:
A. If various safety measures are observed by individuals during a tornado, the prospect of injury or death decreases.
B. Tornadoes are an awesome force of nature that can reduce even the most well constructed home to a pile of rubble.
C. A home that features a basement affords a little more protection to a family during a tornado than a home without one.
D. It's important not to take tornadoes for granted.

21. There have been impressive advancements made in municipal solid waste processing. While standard landfill operations are becoming more and more expensive to operate, the new idea of waste processing involves high technology incineration plants. This concept isn't really that new, but the mechanics employed to attain efficient waste incineration have been improved markedly. Earlier efforts to incinerate waste produced emissions far too toxic for our atmosphere. However, waste can now be burned without detrimental effects to the environment. The energy yielded can be efficiently harnessed as either steam or electricity, both of which are valuable resources.
The statement that best supports the above paragraph is:
A. Incineration plants originally posed an emission control problem.
B. Burning municipal waste is a relatively new procedure.
C. Technological improvements have made waste incineration a viable means of processing waste.
D. Steam and electricity are the end products of incineration.

22. Advertisers of specialty products rely heavily on demographic studies to identify potential customers. Demography is the statistical study of a given population of people; statistics may include marital status, age, household income, or other tangible aspects that can be categorized and profiled. This information can be extremely valuable to companies. If an advertiser is aware of the kind of consumer that has a need for their product, money invested in advertising can be targeted better. Instead of wasting countless advertising dollars on consumers that have little, if any, interest in the product, those same advertising dollars can be channeled toward consumers that have an inclination to buy. The bottom line in business today is efficiency, and demographics offers the information needed to reach that goal.
The statement that best supports the above paragraph is:

A. Demographic studies are absolutely essential for any company desiring to be efficient in marketing.
B. The appropriation of advertising money is better coordinated with the aid of demographic research.
C. If an advertiser is not aware of the kind of customer that may have an interest in his product, money spent on any advertising is frivolous.
D. Consumers are very selective in their tastes.

23. It may come as a surprise to people, but some of the worst driving conditions can be caused by a light rainfall. When pavement remains dry for an extended period of time, oil and other fluids that drip from passing vehicles tend to accumulate. This is particularly true for that area of pavement that lies between the wheel tracks. Light rainfall has the tendency to bring those residues to the surface and create an exceptionally slick driving surface. Most people don't perceive rain as threatening and as a consequence, caution is not exercised in driving. This very perception is the primary reason for many accidents, and in some cases, fatalities.

The statement that best supports the above paragraph is:
A. It is not recommended to drive in the rain.
B. Those who ride motorcycles should be particularly concerned about road conditions after a light rain.
C. Oil residues and precipitation are the culprits responsible for slick road surfaces.
D. A light rain doesn't generally raise concern on the behalf of drivers, but it can render driving dangerous if certain conditions prevail.

24. If you have ever attended a trap or skeet shotgun competition, you may have noticed that practically all the shotguns used have a ventilated rib on top of the barrel. Anytime a firearm is repetitively fired, the barrel gets very warm. The heat expended from the barrel can dramatically affect what the shooter sees as he or she lines the object up with the sight. The heat reflected off the barrel causes a ripple distortion of one's view. The closer a person's line of sight is to the barrel, the worse the distortion. Ventilated ribs, an integral part of a shotgun, serves to reduce heat distortion and increase the accuracy of sight alignment.

The statement that best supports the above paragraph is:
A. On a cold day, heat distortion should not be a problem for a competitive shooter.
B. All shotguns come equipped with ventilated ribs.
C. The closer a person's line of sight is to a source of heat, the worse the view distortion.
D. Ventilated ribs on firearms are designed to reduce view distortion from heat emitted from the barrel.

25. Disciplining children is never an easy task. One of the most common mistakes by parents is inconsistency in punishment. Children are very perceptive. If they realize that a parent feels sorry for them and will relax the penalty for their wrongdoing, the entire point of the punishment is lost. Discipline loses its effectiveness if there'snot a complete follow-through. On the other hand, if a child is told that he is grounded for one week for an infraction, and does, in fact, remain grounded for the entirety, the threat of being grounded for misbehavior has considerably more substance. Hopefully, such a measure of punishment will serve as an effective deterrent to future misbehavior.

The statement that best supports the above paragraph is:
A. If you're unhappy with your child's performance either academically or socially, threaten to ground him for at least one week.
B. Spare the rod and spoil the child.
C. The key to effective discipline for children lies mainly with the consistent administration of punishment.
D. Most children are acutely perceptive to parental emotions.

-CONTINUE ON TO NEXT PAGE-

VOCABULARY EXAM III

26. The acrid smell "permeated" every room in the house. Permeated most nearly means
    A. diminished
    B. barely noticeable
    C. pervaded
    D. dissipated

27. Except for a few "miscellaneous" items, almost everything was sold at the garage sale. Miscellaneous most nearly means
    A. antique
    B. small
    C. mixed
    D. large

28. Fortunately, he was right, but his decision was founded purely on "conjecture". Conjecture most nearly means
    A. fundamentals
    B. strong evidence
    C. group help
    D. a guess

29. The lawn was watered by an "automatic" system. Automatic most nearly means
    A. self-operating
    B. intricate
    C. costly
    D. extensive

30. You can save money on almost any purchase if you "barter" with the retailer. Barter most nearly means
    A. dicker
    B. make installments
    C. associate
    D. negotiate a contract

31. John didn't have an "inkling" as to how to fix the leaky faucet. Inkling most nearly means
    A. clue
    B. schematic
    C. tools
    D. the phone number of a plumber

32. The family's dog was responsible for "rousing" them in time to escape the fire safely. Rousing most nearly means
    A. coaxing
    B. initiating
    C. biting
    D. waken

33. She was "nonchalant" about the news concerning her mother. Nonchalant most nearly means
    A. withdrawn
    B. saddened
    C. indifferent
    D. estatic

34. The donor chose to remain "anonymous". Anonymous most nearly means
    A. known
    B. incognito
    C. present
    D. recognized

35. It was obvious that the idea was "abhorred" by most committee members. Abhorred most nearly means
    A. well received
    B. disliked
    C. accepted
    D. tabled

36. "Abode" most nearly means
    A. without transportation
    B. incline
    C. residence
    D. absurdity

37. The climate in that area of the world is quite "temperate". Temperate most nearly means
    A. violent
    B. sultry
    C. hot
    D. mild

38. "Attire" is considered to be very important when looking for work. Attire most nearly means
    A. attitude
    B. performance
    C. dress
    D. sincerity

39. She kept her home "immaculate". Immaculate most nearly means
    A. cluttered
    B. painted
    C. dirty
    D. spotless

40. His "overtures" to her were not the least bit discreet. Overtures most nearly means
    A. clothing
    B. transgressions
    C. advances
    D. concessions

41. The old oak tree was "rigid" despite the gale force winds. Rigid most nearly means
    A. flexible
    B. swayed
    C. insurmountable
    D. inflexible

42. Some kids like to "instigate" trouble fairly regularly. Instigate most nearly means
    A. incite
    B. prevent
    C. downgrade
    D. discourage

43. "Biennial" most nearly means
    A. one year
    B. two years
    C. two months
    D. two decades

44. Swimming and bicycle riding are considered by most physicians as "salutary" sports. Salutary most nearly means
    A. healthy
    B. detrimental
    C. strenuous
    D. stressful

45. John felt "intimidated" by his friends. Intimidated most nearly means
    A. assured
    B. obliged
    C. threatened
    D. honor

46. The America's Cup is a highly "coveted" trophy among international yachting clubs. Coveted most nearly means
    A. sought after
    B. contested
    C. ranked
    D. obscured

47. The possibility of rescue before nightfall was beginning to seem "remote". Remote most nearly means
    A. plausible
    B. certain
    C. close at hand
    D. unlikely

48. This particular invention was originally thought of as a "ludicrous" idea that had absolutely no practical applications. Ludicrous most nearly means
    A. workable
    B. crazy
    C. expensive
    D. delicate

49. "Truancy" was not a problem for most metropolitan high schools. Truancy most nearly means
    A. drugs
    B. tardiness
    C. absenteeism
    D. bad study habits

50. The politician was beginning to sound "redundant" on some issues. Redundant most nearly means
    A. tiring
    B. repetitive
    C. eloquent
    D. knowledgeable

51. "Longevity" seems to run in their family. Longevity most nearly means
    A. luck
    B. baldness
    C. happiness
    D. long life

52. It is easy to "procrastinate" when it comes to doing household chores we hate. Procrastinate most nearly means
    A. defer
    B. over do it
    C. manage
    D. underestimate the time required

53. Spiders have an innate ability to weave "intricate" webs. Intricate most nearly means
    A. small
    B. complicated
    C. substantial
    D. eloquent

54. The activity was considered to be "clandestine" by most people in the Bureau. Clandestine most nearly means
    A. open to public scrutiny
    B. safe
    C. secretive
    D. large scale

55. "Perpetual" most nearly means
    A. forever
    B. usual
    C. weekly
    D. intermittent

56. Anyone washing a car on a day like this must be pretty "optimistic" that it will not rain. Optimistic most nearly means
   A. nuts
   B. confident
   C. paranoid
   D. likable

57. Our political system is basically "bipartisan". Bipartisan most nearly means
   A. two party
   B. anarchy
   C. patriotic
   D. oligarchy

58. When something is thought of as being "abundant" that most nearly means
   A. short supply
   B. lightweight
   C. rare
   D. plentiful

59. He "liberally" sprinkled pepper on his dinner. Liberally most nearly means
   A. conservatively
   B. ominously
   C. generously
   D. belligerently

60. Tom was careful not to "libel" anyone in his speech to the share holders. Libel most nearly means
   A. compliment
   B. slander
   C. discourage
   D. promote

- END OF TEST -

ANSWER SHEET TO READER'S COMPREHENSION/VOCABULARY EXAM III

1. Ⓐ Ⓑ Ⓒ Ⓓ Ⓔ		31. Ⓐ Ⓑ Ⓒ Ⓓ Ⓔ	
2. Ⓐ Ⓑ Ⓒ Ⓓ Ⓔ		32. Ⓐ Ⓑ Ⓒ Ⓓ Ⓔ	
3. Ⓐ Ⓑ Ⓒ Ⓓ Ⓔ		33. Ⓐ Ⓑ Ⓒ Ⓓ Ⓔ	
4. Ⓐ Ⓑ Ⓒ Ⓓ Ⓔ		34. Ⓐ Ⓑ Ⓒ Ⓓ Ⓔ	
5. Ⓐ Ⓑ Ⓒ Ⓓ Ⓔ		35. Ⓐ Ⓑ Ⓒ Ⓓ Ⓔ	
6. Ⓐ Ⓑ Ⓒ Ⓓ Ⓔ		36. Ⓐ Ⓑ Ⓒ Ⓓ Ⓔ	
7. Ⓐ Ⓑ Ⓒ Ⓓ Ⓔ		37. Ⓐ Ⓑ Ⓒ Ⓓ Ⓔ	
8. Ⓐ Ⓑ Ⓒ Ⓓ Ⓔ		38. Ⓐ Ⓑ Ⓒ Ⓓ Ⓔ	
9. Ⓐ Ⓑ Ⓒ Ⓓ Ⓔ		39. Ⓐ Ⓑ Ⓒ Ⓓ Ⓔ	
10. Ⓐ Ⓑ Ⓒ Ⓓ Ⓔ		40. Ⓐ Ⓑ Ⓒ Ⓓ Ⓔ	
11. Ⓐ Ⓑ Ⓒ Ⓓ Ⓔ		41. Ⓐ Ⓑ Ⓒ Ⓓ Ⓔ	
12. Ⓐ Ⓑ Ⓒ Ⓓ Ⓔ		42. Ⓐ Ⓑ Ⓒ Ⓓ Ⓔ	
13. Ⓐ Ⓑ Ⓒ Ⓓ Ⓔ		43. Ⓐ Ⓑ Ⓒ Ⓓ Ⓔ	
14. Ⓐ Ⓑ Ⓒ Ⓓ Ⓔ		44. Ⓐ Ⓑ Ⓒ Ⓓ Ⓔ	
15. Ⓐ Ⓑ Ⓒ Ⓓ Ⓔ		45. Ⓐ Ⓑ Ⓒ Ⓓ Ⓔ	
16. Ⓐ Ⓑ Ⓒ Ⓓ Ⓔ		46. Ⓐ Ⓑ Ⓒ Ⓓ Ⓔ	
17. Ⓐ Ⓑ Ⓒ Ⓓ Ⓔ		47. Ⓐ Ⓑ Ⓒ Ⓓ Ⓔ	
18. Ⓐ Ⓑ Ⓒ Ⓓ Ⓔ		48. Ⓐ Ⓑ Ⓒ Ⓓ Ⓔ	
19. Ⓐ Ⓑ Ⓒ Ⓓ Ⓔ		49. Ⓐ Ⓑ Ⓒ Ⓓ Ⓔ	
20. Ⓐ Ⓑ Ⓒ Ⓓ Ⓔ		50. Ⓐ Ⓑ Ⓒ Ⓓ Ⓔ	
21. Ⓐ Ⓑ Ⓒ Ⓓ Ⓔ		51. Ⓐ Ⓑ Ⓒ Ⓓ Ⓔ	
22. Ⓐ Ⓑ Ⓒ Ⓓ Ⓔ		52. Ⓐ Ⓑ Ⓒ Ⓓ Ⓔ	
23. Ⓐ Ⓑ Ⓒ Ⓓ Ⓔ		53. Ⓐ Ⓑ Ⓒ Ⓓ Ⓔ	
24. Ⓐ Ⓑ Ⓒ Ⓓ Ⓔ		54. Ⓐ Ⓑ Ⓒ Ⓓ Ⓔ	
25. Ⓐ Ⓑ Ⓒ Ⓓ Ⓔ		55. Ⓐ Ⓑ Ⓒ Ⓓ Ⓔ	
26. Ⓐ Ⓑ Ⓒ Ⓓ Ⓔ		56. Ⓐ Ⓑ Ⓒ Ⓓ Ⓔ	
27. Ⓐ Ⓑ Ⓒ Ⓓ Ⓔ		57. Ⓐ Ⓑ Ⓒ Ⓓ Ⓔ	
28. Ⓐ Ⓑ Ⓒ Ⓓ Ⓔ		58. Ⓐ Ⓑ Ⓒ Ⓓ Ⓔ	
29. Ⓐ Ⓑ Ⓒ Ⓓ Ⓔ		59. Ⓐ Ⓑ Ⓒ Ⓓ Ⓔ	
30. Ⓐ Ⓑ Ⓒ Ⓓ Ⓔ		60. Ⓐ Ⓑ Ⓒ Ⓓ Ⓔ	

(This page may be removed to mark answers.)

ANSWERS TO MATH EXAM III

1. B	11. B	21. B	31. C
2. C	12. A	22. D	32. A
3. D	13. D	23. A	33. A
4. A	14. D	24. D	34. D
5. C	15. C	25. B	35. D
6. B	16. B	26. C	36. B
7. B	17. D	27. B	37. D
8. C	18. A	28. A	38. C
9. A	19. A	29. C	39. D
10. D	20. C	30. D	40. A

If your score was:
- 35 or more correct, you have an excellent score
- 30-34 correct, you have a good score
- 29 or less correct, you should practice more.

ANSWERS TO READER'S COMPREHENSION AND VOCABULARY EXAM III

1. D	16. A	31. A	46. A
2. B	17. C	32. D	47. D
3. D	18. D	33. C	48. B
4. B	19. C	34. B	49. C
5. C	20. A	35. B	50. B
6. B	21. C	36. C	51. D
7. A	22. B	37. D	52. A
8. C	23. D	38. C	53. B
9. C	24. D	39. D	54. C
10. D	25. C	40. C	55. A
11. C	26. C	41. D	56. B
12. D	27. C	42. A	57. A
13. B	28. D	43. B	58. D
14. C	29. A	44. A	59. C
15. D	30. A	45. C	60. B

If your score was:
- 53 or more correct, you have an excellent score
- 45-52 correct, you have a good score
- 44 or less correct, you should practice more

VOCABULARY

Many people consider this section of the exam the most difficult to prepare for. This is very understandable considering there are more than 75,000 words in most dictionaries; it would be a phenomenal task to memorize most of those words. However, there are a few methods that can be used to simplify the Vocabulary section of the exam.

All of the test questions in the Vocabulary section will contain a key word accentuated by quotation marks (" "). Five alternative words are provided from which you will have to select the one word that most nearly means the same as the key word. The benefit of having such a multiple choice exam is that you know only one answer out of the five is correct. So, even if you are unfamiliar with a key word or some of the alternative choices, it becomes largely a matter of narrowing down the possibilities. The more choices you can eliminate, the better your chances are of selecting the correct answer.

Typically, most questions contain two or more alternative choices each having virtually the same meaning. These choices can be eliminated immediately from the selection of answers because you know that only one correct answer is given.

Take a look at the two samples provided and see if you can apply this technique to determine the correct answer.

SAMPLE 1: The restaurant patron was extremely "irritated" when the waiter accidently spilled coffee on his lap. Irritated most nearly means

   A. happy

   B. elated

   C. jubilant

   D. perfunctory

   E. annoyed

You may already know the answer to this question, but did you note the various choices that have basically the same meaning? If you eliminated choices A, B, and C on that premise, you were correct.

Now that you have narrowed your choices, assume for the moment that you are completely unfamiliar with the two remaining choices, D and E. Before you decide which one is the correct choice, note that at this point you have a 50% chance of choosing the correct one. This is a substantially better chance than you had initially. To continue to narrow down the possibilities, exchange the remaining two choices with the key word and examine the content of the resulting statement. The resulting exchanges would read as follows:

   D. The restaurant patron was extremely "perfunctory" when the waiter accidently spilled coffee on his lap.

   E. The restaurant patron was extremely "annoyed" when the waiter accidently spilled coffee on his lap.

Now, listen to how each choice conforms to the sample sentence and its intended meaning. If your choice seems out of place or somehow has little relation to the rest of the sentence, chances are that it is not the correct answer. If you are still unsure which one of the choices to select, it is strongly advised that you choose the word most familiar to you. Sometimes a word that is rarely used and has limited application in general vocabulary will be tossed into a question just to confuse you. As a general rule, select those choices that are most familiar to you. For the record, choice E is the correct answer for SAMPLE 1.

SAMPLE 2: Grandpa always "exaggerated" the size of the fish he caught from the lake. Exaggerated most nearly means

   A. kept secret

   B. stretched the truth

   C. concealed

   D. registered

   E. recorded

Again, the correct answer may be immediately evident to you, but you should have noticed some choices that could be quickly eliminated. If you noticed that choice A and C have the same meaning, you are right. Additionally, choice D and E basically have the same meaning. Thus, you are left with choice B as the correct answer.

Of course, these samples are somewhat oversimplified. However, on the practice exercises contained herein and most importantly, the actual test, it will not always be possible to narrow it down to a correct selection by eliminating synonymous choices.

Another method that can be of some assistance to you in finding the correct word is an understanding of antonyms and their relation in test questions. Antonyms have just the opposite meaning of synonyms and constitute words that have the exact opposite meaning to one another. For example, the words "good and bad", "high and low", "hot and cold", are examples of antonyms.

Thus, if the synonyms are not apparent in a question, then your next approach would be to find any antonyms. Frequently, test questions will have at least one antonym and, as a general rule, the correct answer will be one of the antonyms. This seems to be a common technique among people who design word meaning tests. They seem to think that you can easily eliminate three of the five choices. Therefore, they include the antonym to force you to waiver between the two remaining choices.

SAMPLE 3: Tree leaves become colored and "brittle" when Fall arrives. Brittle most nearly means

A. antique

B. fragile

C. soaked

D. supple

E. wet

Immediately obvious are the synonym choices of C and E. Can you determine what, if any, choices constitute an antonym? If you determined that choices B and D (fragile and supple) represented antonyms, you are correct. Therefore, we should first take a look at choice A as a possible answer. Now put choice A (antique) into the statement. Does it sound appropriate? If you ruled out choice A as a possible correct answer, you are again correct. Return to the antonyms we identified earlier--the only remaining candidates. Some people would waver between the B and D choices. But by inserting each in place of the word that must be defined, you will see that choice B (fragile) is the correct answer for the sample provided.

Granted, it is not always going to be easy for you to methodically eliminate various choices so that the remaining choice is the right answer. Some words that are completely unfamiliar may prevent you from determining antonyms or synonyms in the first place. There is, however, another method that can provide you with additional understanding of unfamiliar terms.

Most words can be broken down into word derivatives such as prefixes, suffixes, and common roots or stems. Word derivatives can lend a partial, if not complete, view into what a term can mean. For example, take a look at the word "injudiciously". The first two letters "in-" represent the prefix and mean 'not' or 'lack of'. The root of the word is "judic" which means 'judgment'. The last portion of the word "-ous/ly" is considered to be the suffix which means 'characterized by'. "Injudiciously" may then be interpreted as a description of someone who lacks judgment.

An etymology table consisting of common word derivatives has been provided for your convenience. Study it, as it will be invaluable in assisting you with not only the practice exercises, but the actual exam as well.

COMMON PREFIXES

Prefix	Meaning	Example
a-	not or without	atypical-not typical
ab-	away from	abnormal-deviating from normal
ac-	to or toward	accredit-to attribute to
ad-	to or toward	adduce-to bring forward as evidence
ag-	to or toward	aggravate-to make more severe
at-	to or toward	attain-to reach to
an-	not or without	anarchy-a society with no government
ante-	before or preceding	antenatal-referencing prior to birth
anti-	against or counter	antisocial-against being social
auto-	self or same	automatic-self acting
bene-	good or well	benevolence-an act of kindness or goodwill
bi-	two or twice	bisect-to divide into two parts
circum	around	circumscribe-draw a line around or encircle
com-, con-	together or with	combine-join conciliate-united or drawn together
contra-	against or opposite	contradict-opposed or against the truth
de-	removal from	decongestant-relieves or removes congestion
dec-	ten	decade - a ten year period
demi	half	demigod-partly divine and partly human
dis-, dys-	apart, negation, or reversal	dishonest-a lack of or negation of honesty
e-, ex-	from or out of	evoke-to draw forth or bring out
extra-	beyond	extraordinary-outside or beyond the usual order
hemi-	half	hemisphere-half of the globe
hyper-	excessive or over	hyperactive-excessively active
hypo-	beneath or under	hypodermic-something introduced under the skin
im-,	not	impersonal-not personal or lacking personality
in-	not	inaccessible-not accessible
ir-	not	irrational-not having reason or understanding
inter-	among or between	interdepartmental-between departments
intra- intro-	inside or within	intracellular-within a cell introspect-to look within
kilo	one thousand	kiloton-one thousand tons
mal-	bad or ill	malcontent-dissatisfied
mis-	wrong	misinterpret-to interpret wrongly
mono-	one or single	monochromatic-only having one color or hue
non-	not	nonresident-person who does not live in a particular place

Prefix	Meaning	Example
ob-	against or opposed	object-declared opposition or disapproval
omni-	all	omnivore-an animal that eats all foods, either plant or flesh
per-	through or thoroughly	perennial-continuing or lasting through the year
poly-	many or much	polychromy-an artistic combination of different colors
post-	after or later	postglacial-after the Glacial period
pre-	before or previous	preexamine-before an examination
pro-	before or supporting	proalliance-supportive of an alliance
re-	again, former state or position	reiterate-to do or say repeatedly
retro-	backward or return	retrogressive-moving backwards
self-	individual or personal	self-defense-act of defending oneself
semi-	half or part	semifinal-half final
sub-	below or under	submarine-reference to something underwater
super-	above or over	superficial-not penetrating the surface
tele-	distant	telegraph-an instrument used for communicating at a distance
trans-	across, over or through	transparent-pervious to light
ultra-	beyond or excessive	ultraconservative-beyond ordinary conservation
un-	not	unaccountable-not accountable or responsible

COMMON SUFFIXES

Suffix	Meaning	Example
-able, -ally, -ible	capacity or capable of being	readable-able to read pastorally-relating to rural life eligible-qualified to be chosen
-ac	like or pertaining to	maniac-mad-like mental condition
-age	function or state of	mileage-length of distance in miles
-ance, -ary,	act or fact of doing or pertaining to	cognizance-knowledge through perception or reason subsidiary-serving to assist or supplement
-ant	person or thing	tyrant-a ruler that is unjustly severe
-ar	of the nature or pertaining to	nuclear-pertaining to nuclear matter or study
-ation	action	excavation-act or process of excavating
-cede, -ceed	to go or come	intercede-to go or come between succeed-to follow
-cide	destroy or kill	homicide-the killing of a person by another
-cy	quality	decency-the state of being decent, proper or becoming

Suffix	Meaning	Example
-dy	condition or character	shoddy-pretentious condition or something poorly made
-ence,	act or fact of	despondence-loss of hope
-ery	doing or pertaining to	confectionery-place of making or selling candies or sweets
-er	of the nature or pertaining to	lawyer-a practitioner of law
-ful	abounding or full of	fretful-tending to fret or be irritable
-ic	like or pertaining to	artistic-having a talent in art
-ify	in a manner	magnify-to enlarge
-ious	full of	laborious-devoted to labor or requiring a lot of work
-ise	to make like	devise-to create from existing ideas
-ish	like	childish-acting like a child
-ism	act or practice of	capitalism-an economic system that revolves around private ownership
-ist	person or thing	idealist-a person who dreams
-ize	to make like	idolize-to make an idol of
-less	without	penniless-without a penny
-logy	the study of	archaeology-the study of historical cultures using artifacts of past activities
-ly	in a manner	shapely-well formed
-ment	the act of	achievement-the act of achieving
-ness	state of or quality	pettiness-being small in nature or insignificant
-or	of the nature or pertaining to	legislator-person responsible for legislative proceeds within government
-ory	place	dormitory-building on or near a campus that provides living quarters for students
-ship	condition or character	censorship-overseeing or excluding items that may be objectionable to those concerned
-tude	state of or result	solitude-state of being alone or apart from society
-ty	condition or character	levity-lack of gravity in character
-y	quality or result	hefty-moderately heavy or weighty
-yze	to make like	analyze-to separate components into their constituent parts for observation

COMMON ROOTS

Root	Meaning	Example
acou	hearing	acoustical-pertaining to sound
acro	furthest or highest point	acrophobia-fear of heights

Root	Meaning	Example
acu	needle	acupuncture-puncturing of body tissue for relief of pain
aero	air or gas	aeronautics-study of the operation of aircraft
alti	high	altitude-a position or a region at an elevated height
ambi	both	ambidextrous-capability of using both hands equally well
anter	in front	anterior-toward the front
anthrop	human being	anthropology-science of mankind
aqueo, aqui	water bearing	aquatic-living in water
audio	hearing	audiology-science of hearing
auto	self	autocratic-ruled by a monarch with absolute rule
avi	bird/flight	aviary-large cage for confining birds
bia, bio	life	biography-written history of a person's life
bona	good	bonafide-with good faith
capit	head	capital-involving the forfeiture of the head or life
carb	carbon	carboniferous-containing or producing carbon or coal
carcin	cancer	carcinogen-substance that initiates cancer
carn	flesh	carnivorous-eating flesh
cent	a hundred	centennial-pertaining to 100 years
centro, centri	center	centrifugal-movement away from the center
cepha	head	hydrocephalus-condition caused by excess fluid in the head
chron	time	synchronize-to happen at the same time
citri	fruit	citric acid—sour tasting juice from fruits
corpori, corp	body	corporate-combined into one body
crypt	covered or hidden	cryptology-art of uncovering a hidden or coded message
culp	fault	culprit-one accused of a crime
cyclo	circular	cyclone-a storm with a low pressure center combined with strong circular winds
demo	people	democracy—government ruled by the people through elections
doc	teach	doctrine-instruction or teaching
dox	opinion	paradox-a self contradictory statement that has plausibility of being truthful
duo	two	duologue-dialogue confined to two persons
dyna	power	dynamometer-device for measuring power
eco	environment	ecosystem-community or organisms interacting with the environment

The Postal Exam Preparation Book 73

Root	Meaning	Example
embry	early	embryonic-pertaining to an embryo or the beginning of life
equi	equal	equilibrium-balance
ethn	race	ethnology-study of human race
exter	outside of	external-on the outside
flori	flower	florist-dealer in flowers
foli	leafy	defoliate-to strip a plant of its leaves
geo	earth	geophysics-the physics of the earth
geri	old age	geriatrics-division of medicine pertaining to old age
graph	write	autograph-a person's own signature
gyro	spiral motion	gyroscope-rotating wheel that can spin on various planes
horti	garden	horticulture-science of cultivating plants
hydro	water	hydroplane-form of boat that glides over the water
hyge	health	hygiene-practice of preservation of health
hygro	wet	hygrometer-instrument used to measure moisture in the atmosphere
hypno	sleep	hypnology—science that treats sleep
ideo	idea	ideology-science of ideas
iso	equal	isotonic-having equal tones or tension
jur	swear	jury-body of persons sworn to tell the truth
lact, lacto	milk	lacteal-resembling milk
lamin	divided	laminate-bond together layers
lingui	tongue	linguistics-study of languages
litho	stone	lithography-art of putting design on stone with a greasy material and producing printed impressions
loco, locus	place	locomotion-act or power of moving from place to place
macro	large	macrocosm-the great world; the universe
man-	hand	manual-made or operated by hand
medi	middle	mediocre-average or middle quality
mega	large	megalopolis-urban area comprising several large adjoining cities
mero, meri	part or fraction of	meroblastic-partial or incomplete cleavage
micro	small or petty	microscopic-so small as to be invisible without the aid of a microscope
mini	small	miniature-an image or representation of something on a smaller scale

Root	Meaning	Example
moto	motion	motive-prompting action
multi	many	multimillionaire-person with several million dollars
navi	naval	navigation-to direct course for a vessel on the sea or in the air
neo	new	neonatal-pertaining to newborn
noct, nocti	night	nocturnal-occurring in the night
oct, octa	eight	octagonal-a shape having eight angles or eight sides
olig, oligo	scant or few	oligarchy-a government which is controlled by a few people
oo	an egg	oology-a branch of ornithology dealing with bird eggs
optic	vision or eye	optometry-profession of testing vision and examining eyes for disease
ortho	straight	orthodontics-dentistry dealing with correcting the teeth
pent, penta	five	pentagon-a shape having five angles or sides
phon	sound	phonograph-instrument for reproducing sound
pod	foot	podiatry-study and treatment of disorders of the foot
pseudo	false	pseudonym-fictitious name
psyche	mental	psychiatry-science of treating mental disorders
pyro	fire	pyrotechnics-art of making or using fireworks
quad	four	quadruped-animal having four feet
quint	five	quintuple-having five parts
sect	part or divide	bisect-divide into two equal parts
spiri	coiled	spirochete-spiral shaped bacteria
stasi	to stand still	hemostatic-serving to stop hemorrhage
techni	skill	technician-skilled person in particular field
terri	to frighten	terrible-to excite terror
tetra	four	tetrahedron-a polyhedron with four faces
therm	heat	thermostat-device that automatically controls desired temperature
toxi	poison	toxicology-science concerning the effects, antidotes and detection of poisonous substances
uni	single	unilateral-involving one person, class or nation
urb	city	suburb-outlying part of a city
uro	urine	urology-science of studying the urinary tract and its diseases
verb	word	proverb-a name, person or thing that has become a byword

Root	Meaning	Example
veri	truthful	verify-to prove truthful
vit	life	vitality-liveliness
vitri	glass or like glass	vitreous-resembling glass
vivi	alive	viviparous-the birth of living young
vol	wish	volunteer-to enter into or offer oneself freely
zo, zoi, zoo	animal	zoology-science of studying animal zoolife

An Easy To Follow Guide

For Taking The

Postal Service
CLERK CARRIER
EXAMINATION

Clerk Carrier Test Content

The Clerk Carrier exam itself consists of two sections; the first part comprises address cross comparison, and the second part entails address memorization. In the first part, two addresses are provided and it must be determined if they are exactly alike. Some examples are shown below.

> 201 Bellingham Ave.   210 Bellingham Ave.
> 1449 Jackson Blvd.   1449 Jacobson Blvd.
> 350 Sunrise Ln. NE   350 Sonrise Ln. NE
> 52 N. Franklin   52 N. Franklin

In the first particular case, the numerical portions of the addresses (201; 210) are different. (In other instances, the spelling may differ.) The answer blank for this section is set up such that there are only two choices that can be selected; either Ⓐ which represents alike or Ⓓ which represents dislike. Since the two Bellingham addresses are not identical answer Ⓓ is appropriately darkened.

Ⓐ ●

This section may seem quite easy, but once again, time is an important consideration. There are 95 addresses to be compared and a matter of six minutes to do as many as possible. To help you save valuable time with this exercise, place your little finger on one column and your index finger (same hand) on the adjacent column and move them in unison down the page. By doing this, it is easier to focus your attention on just the two addresses that are to be compared. There are no other shortcuts to this section as it is principally a matter of speed and accuracy which can be enhanced by practice on the sample tests that are included in this book.

The second part of the exam concerns address memorization. Twenty-five addresses, such as those provided below, are to be memorized within a five minute period.

A	B	C	D	E
1200-1299 Fir	6700-6799 Fir	6900-6999 Fir	2100-2199 Fir	1300-1399 Fir
Hoover Ct.	Highland St.	Beaver Ave.	Lamplight Ct.	Bellvue St.
1400-1499 Blake	2700-2799 Blake	3100-3199 Blake	4200-4299 Blake	0900-0999 Blake
Sycamore St.	Aspen Dr.	Johnson Ave.	Time Square	Harbor View
9200-9299 Terrace	5800-5899 Terrace	1800-1899 Terrace	8700-8799 Terrace	4300-4399 Terrace

If you are like the author and don't happen to have a photographic memory, it would seem that such a test would be next to impossible to pass, let alone score well on. Actually, it has been demonstrated that normally a person can only remember seven things at one time (much less 25 addresses) and beyond that memory begins to falter. By using memory systems employing associative and imagery techniques, any memory task can be simplified. To briefly summarize how this memory system works, it requires an individual to form images in his or her mind relevant to the item to be memorized. Then, link these images by association. For example, street names are items that must be committed to memory for the exam. Take the addresses that are to follow as an example.

> Phillips Ave.
> Washington Dr.
> Times Square
> Salem St.
> Pine Needle Ct.

Different images come to different minds; the important point is that an individual must be able to see the images clearly in the mind's eye. It is easy (and often rather enjoyable) to create and remember images placed in a bizzare context. For instance, picture a mass of Phillips screwdrivers churning in a washing machine; fastened to the outside of the washer is an oversized wristwatch. A witch with a wart on her nose (from Salem, of course) checks the time before flying away on her broomstick, which crashes into a pine tree. Simply by coming up with such a peculiar story, you will be able to remember not only the street names, but the order in which they are placed.

78 The Postal Exam Preparation Book

Now, how about the numbers that must be committed to memory. To look at a mass of numbers it would seem all the much more impossible to remember them, let alone their order! To simplify the matter, numbers can be transposed into letters of the alphabet so words can be formed and associated accordingly. Below is the format for transposition, and it is vital that this be remembered because it will be a key element in working out the memory section of the exam.

0	1	2	3	4	5	6	7	8	9
G or V	B or D	C or K	F or P	M	N	R	S	T	L

(All other letters can be incorporated into words without bearing any significance.)

For instance, let's say you are given the number 10603328157. Memorizing this number and being able to recall it after any length of time would be very difficult. However, by using just such a system, it could interpret the number to spell out a variety of memorable things. (Here is a chance to use your creativity!) After you have had the chance to figure out what words will comprise such a number, one particular problem should become apparent; the more numbers you try to cram into one word, the harder it is to find a compatible word in the English vocabulary. To further simplify matters, there are two alternatives you can choose.

The first way is to take two numbers at a time, form a word, and associate it with the next. Dealing with the same number (10603328157) 10 could spell DOG, 60-RUG, 33-PIPE, 28-CAT, 15-BONE, and 7-S. There are many ways you could imagine and link these words. One possibility would be to mentally picture a dog lying on a rug and smoking a pipe, and a cat prancing by carrying a bone shaped like an S. That is just one way of remembering that long number. There are, of course, other words and stories that would work, too.

You will find that if your images show action, instead of just being strange objects out of place, it is much easier to recall. As an example, the dog smoking the pipe conveyed action; a scene which is hard to forget.

The second alternative, which offers greater flexibility, is using words of any length, but only the first two significant letters are applicable to your story. For example, the word dig/ging could represent 10 in the number 10603328157.

Rav/en - 60		Rug/by - 60		Rev/olver - 60
Pop/ulation - 33	or	Pup/py - 33	or	Pep/per - 33
Cat/erpillar - 28		Cat/tle - 28		Cot/ton - 28
Bin/oculars - 15		Bean/s - 15		Din/ner - 15

By doing this you have a larger number of words at your disposal to put together stories. With a little originality, it can be quite a bit of fun to see what you can dream up for any number placed in front of you.

Now that you have an idea how to remember numbers easier, we will take a typical test sample and break it down as to what kind of order you should follow in memorizing material.

A	B	C	D	E
1200-1299 Fir	6700-6799 Fir	6900-6999 Fir	2100-2199 Fir	1300-1399 Fir
Hoover Ct.	Highland St.	Beaver Ave.	Lamplight Ct.	Bellvue St.
1400-1499 Blake	2700-2799 Blake	3100-3199 Blake	4200-4299 Blake	0900-0999 Blake
Sycamore St.	Aspen Dr.	Johnson Ave.	Time Square	Harbor View
9200-9299 Terrace	5800-5899 Terrace	1800-1899 Terrace	8700-8799 Terrace	4300-4399 Terrace

First, you will notice that there are ten addresses without any numbers, Hoover Ct. and Sycamore St. under Category A, Highland St. and Aspen Dr. under Category B, etc. Since Hoover Ct. and Sycamore St. are under the same cateogry, they can be put together with respective images. For instance, a Sycamore tree hovering upside down above the ground. If you have any difficulty associating the letter A to the images you had just dreamed up, maybe the following key can be used to your advantage.

The Postal Exam Preparation Book 79

Let category A become an apple
" " B " a bee
" " C " the sea
" " D " dumbbells
" " E " an elephant

With a key of this sort in mind, join the image of an <u>apple</u> with the <u>hovering</u> upside down <u>Sycamore</u> tree picture. Now, when you are asked on the exam, what category does Hoover Ct. belong to, the image of an <u>apple</u> being involved will lead you to answer Category A. Let's select another example to further illustrate the point. Lamplight Ct. and Time Square are under Category D. One way to approach this is to picture a street <u>lamp</u>, instead of giving off light like it should, it is showering the vicinity with alarm clocks (<u>time</u> implied). The lamp post incidentally is shaped like a <u>dumbbell</u>. This does make it easier to remember the items. When asked on the exam where either Time Square or Lamplight Ct. belong, answer D. will be apparent.

The rest of what you will have to memorize are numerical portions of three different streets; in this case Fir, Blake, and Terrace. All of them begin with an even number (eg. 1200) and end on 99 (eg. 1299). Take a look at 1200-1299. It would be meaningless to spend any time and effort memorizing the numbers 00-1299 because already it is known that each number goes from 00-99. Instead of trying to memorize all five categories (A through E) as Figure 1 shows, approach it the way Figure 2 illustrates.

(Fig 1)

A	B	C	D	E
1200-1299 Fir	6700-6799 Fir	6900-6999 Fir	2100-2199 Fir	1300-1399 Fir
Hoover Ct.	Highland St.	Beaver Ave.	Lamplight Ct.	Bellvue St.
1400-1499 Blake	2700-2799 Blake	3100-3199 Blake	4200-4299 Blake	0900-0999 Blake
Sycamore St.	Aspen Dr.	Johnson Ave.	Time Square	Harbor View
9200-9299 Terrace	5800-5899 Terrace	1800-1899 Terrace	8700-8799 Terrace	4300-4399 Terrace

(Fig 2)

A	B	C	D	E
12	67	69	21	13
14	27	31	42	09
92	58	18	87	43

You will find that by using such a short cut it will save a lot of test time. As you have already noticed the street names Fir, Blake, and Terrace have been left out, too. The reason is that none of the numbers are repeats and each retains an identity with only one cateogry. If, on the exam, you were asked what category 3100-3199 Blake belongs to you will know that (31) belongs to Category C and only Category C. If the next question asks where 5800- belongs, without looking at the rest of the address, and thinking of 5800 as 58, you will see that it only applies to Category B.

There are two ways an individual can reference this system of memorization. One way is to mentally create an image of the three numbers in a cateogory and associate it to the letter of that category (eg. Category A-12, 14, 92). There is no particular order in which pertinent numbers have to be memorized. Any way you approach it, 12, 14, and 92 will remain under Category A. With that fact in mind, words can be placed in any order to contrive a story. To illustrate the versatility of this system, two different stories are derived from Category A.

For example, you may picture yourself pouring a <u>buc/ket</u> (12) of <u>apples</u> (Category A) on top of a <u>bum/blebee</u> hive (14) and discover, much to your dismay, that the <u>lac/es</u> (92) of your shoes are tied together. A second and more bizzare chain might include a personal friend or relative. You may see Uncle Bob frantically trying to tie his shoe <u>lac/es</u> (92) while <u>bum/blebees</u> (14) hovering overhead are dropping <u>buc/kets</u> of <u>apples</u> (Category A) on his head. Either way, the key words are included in the stories and more than adequately represent Category A on the exam.

The second way of referencing this system of memorization is by memorizing the numbers in a horizontal manner such as illustrated below.

A	B	C	D	E				
12	67	69	21	13;	These	all	represent	Fir
14	27	31	42	09;	"	"	"	Blake
92	58	18	87	43;	"	"	"	Terrace

There will be three stories containing five significant images each. If you choose this method, it is important that the order of numbers remain the same because each belongs to one particular category and cannot be interchanged. If you were to do so, it would result in a large amount of wrong answers. The advantage to you with this system is that you do not have to keep five different stories in mind, just three—it's much easier to reference because the letters A through E do not have to be used with the stories. Instead, if you have a good feel for your stories you can immediately determine what part of your story applies to the question. As an example, let's use the sequence of numbers that represent Fir on the exam.

A	B	C	D	E
12	67	69	21	13

There are virtually hundreds of different words that could be derived from these numbers, but for this particular illustration, the words bucket, roses, rolling, kid, and dip will be used. Imagine, if you will, a buc/ket of ros/es rol/ling down a hillside and abruptly knocks over a kid trying to balance a 30-dip ice cream cone. Undoubtedly, this is a strange story, not to mention a little sticky, but the underlying principle is quite effective. Now suppose you are given the question, to what category does 1300-1399 Fir belong? (Look at it as 13.) Since you changed the number 13 into the word dip it will be immediately apparent that it is the fifth or last image in your story, the answer would be marked E.

Say the next question was, to what category does 6700-6799 belong? Since 67 stands for ros/es and is the second part of the story, answer Ⓑ would be marked. The same procedure applies to the Blake and Terrace serials. You should have 15 numbers changed into key words; all of which belong to three stories; therefore, regardless of what number you are asked as to which category it belongs, its order in one of the stories is evident.

A	B	C	D	E
12	67	69	21	13
14	27	31	42	09
92	58	18	87	43

Buc/ket - Ros/es - Rol/ling - Kid - Dip

Dam/p - Kis/s - Pud/dle - Muc/k - Gl/owing

Loc/k - Net - But/ter - Toes - Mop

You can see why it is necessary to know your stories, and the order of their images. When properly done you can answer questions in seconds, thus finishing the exam, and having time to review your answers. An unprepared individual will only get half way through the exam.

You have the advantage now! You will have exercises for both the address cross-comparison and the memory sections of the exam, but first a few more helpful hints. The practice exercises are all similar to what you will see on the actual exam. Length, time allotment, and difficulty of the material are all taken into consideration. You will need a timer with an alarm, similar to one used in the kitchen for cooking purposes. Set it for the allotted time for the exercise you are working on and begin. Do not watch the clock because you can lose valuable time. If you finish before the period is up, go back over your answers and correct any mistakes. This same advice applies when taking the actual exam.

By working on these exercises, you can figure out what kind of pace will be demanded on the actual exam. If you work the same pace on the real test there should not be any concern about the time remaining to complete that section. If you come across a question you are not sure of, don't hesitate to skip over it. If time permits, go back to the questions you left unanswered. When you choose to skip a question be sure to skip the corresponding blank on the answer sheet.

PART 1.

ADDRESS CROSS COMPARISON

A sample of what is entailed in this section is provided below. If the corresponding addresses are different in any manner, mark answer D for dislike. On the other hand if they're identical, mark answer A for alike.

1.	1201 Britton Circle	1201 Briton Circle	Ⓐ Ⓓ
2.	Seattle, Wash. 98240	Seattle, Wash. 98240	Ⓐ Ⓓ
3.	69871 Stratford Bay Rd.	69817 Stratford Bay Rd.	Ⓐ Ⓓ
4.	Adams, North Dakota	Adams, South Dakota	Ⓐ Ⓓ
5.	Springfield, Ill 48710	Sprinfield, Ill 48710	Ⓐ Ⓓ
6.	Canyon Dr. SW	Canyon Dr. SW	Ⓐ Ⓓ
7.	Halverson Court NE	Halferson Court NE	Ⓐ Ⓓ
8.	109-C Beachside Apts.	190-C Beachside Apts.	Ⓐ Ⓓ
9.	14534 Pinecrest Ave.	14534 Pinecrest Ave.	Ⓐ Ⓓ
10.	Quanochontaug, R.I. 04311	Quonochontaug, R.I. 04311	Ⓐ Ⓓ

Only answers 2, 6, and 9 should be marked alike. If you have missed any go back over the pertinent question(s) and review what was overlooked. On the practice exercises that are to follow you have six minutes to do as many of the 95 questions provided as possible. Do not go beyond the six minute period; otherwise, you will not have an adequate feeling for what will be expected of you on the real exam. It would also be advisable to find a quiet place to do your work; the more simulated to examination room conditions the better. Fewer distractions can allow an individual to concentrate better.

As a final note, don't get discouraged if you don't quite finish the practice tests within the allotted time. It's not expected of you to complete the test in its entirety.

EXERCISE 1.

TIME: 6 MINUTES

1.	1502 Tallagson Ln.	1502 Talagson Ln.
2.	1012 Harrison Dr.	1012 Harrison Ave.
3.	102 9th Ave.	102 9th Ave.
4.	18771 Forrest Pl. NW	18771 Forest Pl. NE
5.	E. Pebble Beach	W. Pebble Beach
6.	Poulsbo, Wash. 98370	Poulsbo, Wash. 98370
7.	4213 NE Lincoln Rd.	4123 NE Lincoln Rd.
8.	16345 Tukwilla Rd.	16435 Tukwilla Rd.
9.	Ames, Ia. 50010	Ames, Ia. 50010
10.	Whiteford Rd. SW	Whiteford Rd. SE
11.	Alturas, Calif. 90081	Alturas, Calf. 90081
12.	Beacon Falls, Conn. 00378	Bacon Falls, Conn. 00378
13.	841 W. Liberty Rd.	814 W. Liberty Rd.
14.	1646 Lassie Ln.	1646 Lassie Lane
15.	29580 Mt. View Dr.	29850 Mt. View Dr.
16.	47751 Orseth Circle	47751 Orseth Circle
17.	Kaumakani, Hawaii	Kaumokani, Hawaii
18.	14189 Frontier Dr.	14198 Frontier Dr.
19.	Keyport, Wash.	Keyport, Wash.
20.	13455 NW Spirit Crt.	13455 NW Sirit Crt.
21.	Cass, Illinois	Cass, Ilinois
22.	Nesika Bay Rd.	Nesika Bay Rd.
23.	20895 Melson Dr.	20095 Melson Dr.
24.	Shelby, New York	Shelby, New York
25.	Cedar Heights, Ark.	Cedar Heights, Ark.
26.	Hernando, Florida 11212	Hernando, Florida 11221
27.	453 Canyon Dr.	435 Canyon Ave.
28.	Yuma, Arizona	Yuma, Arizona
29.	11B Shadow Ct. Apts.	113 Shadow Ct. Apts.
30.	77127 Briar Cliff	77127 Briter Cliff
31.	10101 Blackberry Ln.	10101 Blackberry Ln.
32.	105-C Trevor Pl. SW	105-C Trevor Pl. NE
33.	Billings, Mont	Billings, Mont.

#		
34.	707 Clover Park	707 Clover Park
35.	Trail Ridge, Mo. 58511	Trail Ridge, Ma. 58511
36.	Tombstone, New Mexico	Tombstone, New Mexico
37.	Edgewater Ct. SW	Edgewater Circle SW
38.	11541 Suquamish Dr.	11541 Suqamish Dr.
39.	809 Lemolo Square	908 Lemolo Square
40.	1798 Mulholland SE	1798 Mullholland SE
41.	Quakersville, Penn 10044	Quakersville, Penn 10404
42.	244 Johnston Rd.	2441 Johnston Rd.
43.	185 Division Dr.	185 Division Ave.
44.	10071 Pacific Blvd.	10071 Atlantic Blvd.
45.	Crestview Ct-98	Crestview Ct-98
46.	154 Rindal St.	154 Rindall St.
47.	22252 Woodward Way	22225 Woodward Way
48.	15733 Virginia Pt. Rd.	15733 Virginia Pl. Rd.
49.	903 Knollward Circle	903 Nollward Circle
50.	San Juan Island	San Juan Islands
51.	2350 Sawdust Trail	2350 Sawdust Trail
52.	Bloomingdale, Georgia 30081	Bloomingdale, Georgia 30018
53.	Bridgeview, Del. 05811	Bridgeview Dr. SE
54.	21st Street NE	21st Ave. NE
55.	169340 Peterson Blvd.	169340 Petersun Blvd.
56.	995 Indianola Pl.	985 Indianola Pl.
57.	H.M. Asgard Apt. C	H.M. Atgard Apt. C
58.	Brownsville, Texas 77811	Brownsville, Texas 77811
59.	Apache Jct., Ariz.	Apache Jct., Ariz.
60.	Denver, Colo. 89036	Denver, Colorado
61.	236 Lisir Circle	236 Lisir Circle
62	33810 Melody Lane	33810 Meludy Lane
63.	13102 Dogwood Ave.	13012 Dogwood Ave.
64.	Butte, Mont.	Butte, Mont.
65.	Des Moines, Ia. 50010	Des Moines, Ia. 50011
66.	Down Rapids, Mich.	Down Stream, Mich.
67.	101-D Hoover St. NE	101-D Hoover Dr. NE
68.	48444 Lakeside Shore	48454 Lakeside Shore
69.	2121 8th Ave. N	2121 8th Ave. N

70.	Clay, North Carolina	Clay, South Carolina
71.	Sunnydale, Calif.	Sunnydale, Calif.
72.	Albany, N.Y. 09337	Albany N.M. 09337
73.	Bloomington, Ill.	Blomington, Ill.
74.	East Ely, Nevada	West Ely, Nevada
75.	Bonscillica, Wyo. 77811	Bonscillica, Wyo. 77811
76.	107-C Wingsong Apts.	107-C Windsong Apts.
77.	Brighton, N.H. 08813	Brighton N.M. 08814
78.	Snoqualamine Pass, Wa.	Snoqualamine Pass, Wash.
79.	223411 Wavecrest Ave.	223416 Wavecrest Ave.
80.	Forest Creek Pk.	Forest Ck. Park
81.	59983 Stottlemeyer Rd.	59983 Stottlemeyer Rd.
82.	333 Chesnut Blvd.	888 Chestnut Blvd.
83.	Silverton Bay, Calif.	Silverdale Bay, Calif.
84.	Admirality Pt. Or.	Admirality Point, Oreg.
85.	1656 Sherman Hill Rd.	1656 Sherman Hill Rd.
86.	Vista Center, Okla. 66711	Vista Canter, Okla. 66711
87.	Brockton, square S.	Brockson Square S.
88.	119 Lincolnside Apts.	119 Linconside Apts.
89.	71333 Bayberry Ct.	71333 Bayberry Ct.
90.	35556 Sunde Rd.	35556 Sundae Rd.
91.	431 Arizona Ave.	431 Arizona Ave.
92.	276598 Loveland Dr.	27659 Loveland Dr.
93.	Bridle Pt. NE	Briddle Pt. NE
94.	126 8th Ave. SW	126 8th Ave SW
95.	78441 Oyster Bay Rd.	78414 Oyster Bay Rd.

ANSWER SHEET TO EXERCISE 1

1. Ⓐ Ⓓ		33. Ⓐ Ⓓ		65. Ⓐ Ⓓ	
2. Ⓐ Ⓓ		34. Ⓐ Ⓓ		66. Ⓐ Ⓓ	
3. Ⓐ Ⓓ		35. Ⓐ Ⓓ		67. Ⓐ Ⓓ	
4. Ⓐ Ⓓ		36. Ⓐ Ⓓ		68. Ⓐ Ⓓ	
5. Ⓐ Ⓓ		37. Ⓐ Ⓓ		69. Ⓐ Ⓓ	
6. Ⓐ Ⓓ		38. Ⓐ Ⓓ		70. Ⓐ Ⓓ	
7. Ⓐ Ⓓ		39. Ⓐ Ⓓ		71. Ⓐ Ⓓ	
8. Ⓐ Ⓓ		40. Ⓐ Ⓓ		72. Ⓐ Ⓓ	
9. Ⓐ Ⓓ		41. Ⓐ Ⓓ		73. Ⓐ Ⓓ	
10. Ⓐ Ⓓ		42. Ⓐ Ⓓ		74. Ⓐ Ⓓ	
11. Ⓐ Ⓓ		43. Ⓐ Ⓓ		75. Ⓐ Ⓓ	
12. Ⓐ Ⓓ		44. Ⓐ Ⓓ		76. Ⓐ Ⓓ	
13. Ⓐ Ⓓ		45. Ⓐ Ⓓ		77. Ⓐ Ⓓ	
14. Ⓐ Ⓓ		46. Ⓐ Ⓓ		78. Ⓐ Ⓓ	
15. Ⓐ Ⓓ		47. Ⓐ Ⓓ		79. Ⓐ Ⓓ	
16. Ⓐ Ⓓ		48. Ⓐ Ⓓ		80. Ⓐ Ⓓ	
17. Ⓐ Ⓓ		49. Ⓐ Ⓓ		81. Ⓐ Ⓓ	
18. Ⓐ Ⓓ		50. Ⓐ Ⓓ		82. Ⓐ Ⓓ	
19. Ⓐ Ⓓ		51. Ⓐ Ⓓ		83. Ⓐ Ⓓ	
20. Ⓐ Ⓓ		52. Ⓐ Ⓓ		84. Ⓐ Ⓓ	
21. Ⓐ Ⓓ		53. Ⓐ Ⓓ		85. Ⓐ Ⓓ	
22. Ⓐ Ⓓ		54. Ⓐ Ⓓ		86. Ⓐ Ⓓ	
23. Ⓐ Ⓓ		55. Ⓐ Ⓓ		87. Ⓐ Ⓓ	
24. Ⓐ Ⓓ		56. Ⓐ Ⓓ		88. Ⓐ Ⓓ	
25. Ⓐ Ⓓ		57. Ⓐ Ⓓ		89. Ⓐ Ⓓ	
26. Ⓐ Ⓓ		58. Ⓐ Ⓓ		90. Ⓐ Ⓓ	
27. Ⓐ Ⓓ		59. Ⓐ Ⓓ		91. Ⓐ Ⓓ	
28. Ⓐ Ⓓ		60. Ⓐ Ⓓ		92. Ⓐ Ⓓ	
29. Ⓐ Ⓓ		61. Ⓐ Ⓓ		93. Ⓐ Ⓓ	
30. Ⓐ Ⓓ		62. Ⓐ Ⓓ		94. Ⓐ Ⓓ	
31. Ⓐ Ⓓ		63. Ⓐ Ⓓ		95. Ⓐ Ⓓ	
32. Ⓐ Ⓓ		64. Ⓐ Ⓓ			

(This page may be removed to mark answers.)

The Postal Exam Preparation Book

ANSWERS TO EXERCISE 1.

1.	D	33.	A	65.	D
2.	D	34.	A	66.	D
3.	A	35.	D	67.	D
4.	D	36.	A	68.	D
5.	D	37.	D	69.	A
6.	A	38.	D	70.	D
7.	D	39.	D	71.	A
8.	D	40.	D	72.	D
9.	A	41.	D	73.	D
10.	D	42.	D	74.	D
11.	D	43.	D	75.	A
12.	D	44.	D	76.	D
13.	D	45.	A	77.	D
14.	D	46.	D	78.	D
15.	D	47.	D	79.	D
16.	A	48.	D	80.	D
17.	D	49.	D	81.	A
18.	D	50.	D	82.	D
19.	A	51.	A	83.	D
20.	D	52.	D	84.	D
21.	D	53.	D	85.	A
22.	A	54.	D	86.	D
23.	D	55.	D	87.	D
24.	A	56.	D	88.	D
25.	A	57.	D	89.	A
26.	D	58.	A	90.	D
27.	D	59.	A	91.	A
28.	A	60.	D	92.	D
29.	D	61.	A	93.	D
30.	D	62.	D	94.	A
31.	A	63.	D	95.	D
32.	D	64.	A		

If Your Score Was:
—87 or more correct you have an excellent score
—between 55 and 86 correct you have a good score
—below 54 correct you should practice more

(This page may be removed to mark answers.)

EXERCISE 2.

TIME: 6 MINUTES

1.	Franklin Ave. SW	Franklin Dr. SW
2.	1011 Tripp St.	1011 Trip St.
3.	Chickasaw, Miss. 43506	Chickasaw, Miss. 43506
4.	Bonneville Road S.	Boneville Road S.
5.	Pleasant Dr. SE	Pleasant Dr. SE
6.	111-D Beatrice Apts.	777-D Beatrice Apts.
7.	Aurora, KY 25344	Aurora KY 25844
8.	65783 Baton Rouge Ave.	65783 Baton Rogue Ave.
9.	2095 Serenade Way	2095 Serenade Way
10.	129 Sunset Lane	129 Sunset Lane
11.	Lake Minetonka, MN	Lake Minnetonka, MN
12.	8760 State Hiway 303	8760 State Hiway 303
13.	147 Wycoff S.	147 Wycoff S.
14.	1913 Gregory Blvd.	1913 Gregory Lane
15.	Star Rt. 2, Box 2144	Star Rt. 2, Box 2414
16.	13058 Olalla Valley Dr.	13058 Olalla Valley Dr.
17.	4189 NE Papoose Pt.	4819 NE Papoose Pt.
18.	Portland, Ore. 87483	Portland, Ore. 87783
19.	Oroville, Calif.	Oroville, Calif.
20.	2222 Schley Blvd.	2222 Shley Blvd.
21.	3315 Olympus Ave.	3315 Olympus Ave.
22.	630 N. Towne Pl.	630 N. Town Pl.
23.	1130 Gattling Dr.	1113 Gattling Dr.
24.	Sioux City, Ia. 54050	Sioux City, Ia. 54050
25.	245 4th Ave.	245 4th Ave.
26.	84-D Turnquist Ave.	84-D Turnquist Ave.
27.	808 Brashem Way	880 Brashem Way
28.	Saskatoon, Canada	Sascatoon, Canada
29.	North Platte, Neb.	North Platte, NE
30.	Twin Falls, ID 83091	Twin Falls, ID 83091
31.	Corpus Christi, TX	Corpus Christi, Texas
32.	San Bernadino, CA	San Bernadine, CA
33.	Phoenix, Ariz. 85020	Phoenix, Ariz. 85020

34.	3012 Ridgeview Dr.	3012 Ridgeview Dr.
35.	631 Charlette Rd.	631 Charlotte Rd.
36.	101-E Buckthorn	101-D Buckthorn
37.	324 Constitution Ln.	324 Constetution Ln.
38.	Yreka, CA	Yreka, CA
39.	383 Pinecone Ct.	838 Pinecone Ct.
40.	Powhaton Point, Ohio	Powhaton Point, Ohio
41.	10011 Richmond Rd.	100111 Richmond Rd.
42.	Zanesville, Ohio 53420	Zanesville, Ohio 53420
43.	Madison, WI 49509	Madeson, WI 49509
44.	Eastview Dr. SW	Eastveiw Ave. SW
45.	9955 Fredrickson Ln.	5599 Fredrickson Ln.
46.	Enumclaw, Wash. 98177	Enumclaw, Wash. 48577
47.	1352 Lafayette N.	1352 Lafayette N.
48.	77-B Hemlock Pl.	77-B Hemlock Pl.
49.	29443 Clover Blossom Rd.	29443 Clover Blossum Rd.
50.	5050 Dibb	5050 Dibb
51.	Multnomah, ORE 91507	Multnomah, ORE 91570
52.	Perrysburg, Penn 12744	Perysburg, Penn 12744
53.	Oakwood Dr. NE	Oakwood Dr. NE
54.	S. Bentwer Way	S. Benter Way
55.	111 Caldwell Ct.	111 Caldwell Ct.
56.	Almonesson, New Jersey	Almoneson, New Jersey
57.	6699 Falner Dr.	6699 Falkner Dr.
58.	222 Utica Place	222 Utica Place
59.	Ballantine, Mont. 54533	Ballantine, Mont. 54533
60.	S. Michigan Ave.	N. Michigan Ave.
61.	Bay Springs, Miss.	Bay Springs, Miss.
62.	Cedar Rapids, Ia.	Cedar Rapids, Iowa
63.	122 Cambrian SW	122 Cambrean SW
64.	3217 Perry	3217 Perry
65.	16-A Sunset Beach	16-A Sunset Beach
66.	4288 Russsell Rd.	4288 Russell Rd.
67.	3007 Kennedy St.	3007 Kennedy St.
68.	7774 Altar Vista	7747 Altar Vista
69.	Missionary Pt., NM	Missionary Pt., NM

70.	Aberdeen, MD 04883	Aberden, MD 04883
71.	2814 Sierra Rd.	2814 Sierra Rd.
72.	444 Aegean Blvd.	4444 Aegean Blvd.
73.	7911 Manchester	7911 Manchester
74.	Aleknagnik, Alaska	Aleknagic, Alaska
75.	147 Sereno Cr. Dr.	147 Cereno Cr. Dr.
76.	806 High St.	806 High St.
77.	202 Hoover Pl.	222 Hoover Pl.
78.	Ahwahnee, Calif.	Ahwohnee, Calif.
79.	Payton Ave. NE	Payton Ave. NE
80.	702 Cline	702 Kline
81.	154 Cherrywood Ln.	154 Cherrywood Ln.
82.	1240 8th Ave.	1240 8th St.
83.	Beautford Way E.	Beautford Way E.
84.	444 4th St.	44 44th St.
85.	1699 1/2 Corning Ct.	1699 1/2 Cornning Ct.
86.	1818 Belmont	1818 Belmont
87.	Bennett, Colo. 67011	Benett, Colo. 67011
88.	3060 N. McWilliams	3060 S. McWilliams
89.	11 Goldenrod Cr.	12 Goldenrod Cr.
90.	SW Lakehurst Dr.	SW Lakehurst Dr.
91.	Boncher Way	Boncher Way
92.	910 Sidney	901 Sidney
93.	33481 Jocobsen Blvd.	33481 Jacobson Blvd.
94.	Waimanalo Beach HI	Waimanalo Beach HI
95.	209 Hobb St.	209 Hobb St.

ANSWER SHEET TO EXERCISE 2

1.	Ⓐ Ⓓ	33.	Ⓐ Ⓓ	65.	Ⓐ Ⓓ
2.	Ⓐ Ⓓ	34.	Ⓐ Ⓓ	66.	Ⓐ Ⓓ
3.	Ⓐ Ⓓ	35.	Ⓐ Ⓓ	67.	Ⓐ Ⓓ
4.	Ⓐ Ⓓ	36.	Ⓐ Ⓓ	68.	Ⓐ Ⓓ
5.	Ⓐ Ⓓ	37.	Ⓐ Ⓓ	69.	Ⓐ Ⓓ
6.	Ⓐ Ⓓ	38.	Ⓐ Ⓓ	70.	Ⓐ Ⓓ
7.	Ⓐ Ⓓ	39.	Ⓐ Ⓓ	71.	Ⓐ Ⓓ
8.	Ⓐ Ⓓ	40.	Ⓐ Ⓓ	72.	Ⓐ Ⓓ
9.	Ⓐ Ⓓ	41.	Ⓐ Ⓓ	73.	Ⓐ Ⓓ
10.	Ⓐ Ⓓ	42.	Ⓐ Ⓓ	74.	Ⓐ Ⓓ
11.	Ⓐ Ⓓ	43.	Ⓐ Ⓓ	75.	Ⓐ Ⓓ
12.	Ⓐ Ⓓ	44.	Ⓐ Ⓓ	76.	Ⓐ Ⓓ
13.	Ⓐ Ⓓ	45.	Ⓐ Ⓓ	77.	Ⓐ Ⓓ
14.	Ⓐ Ⓓ	46.	Ⓐ Ⓓ	78.	Ⓐ Ⓓ
15.	Ⓐ Ⓓ	47.	Ⓐ Ⓓ	79.	Ⓐ Ⓓ
16.	Ⓐ Ⓓ	48.	Ⓐ Ⓓ	80.	Ⓐ Ⓓ
17.	Ⓐ Ⓓ	49.	Ⓐ Ⓓ	81.	Ⓐ Ⓓ
18.	Ⓐ Ⓓ	50.	Ⓐ Ⓓ	82.	Ⓐ Ⓓ
19.	Ⓐ Ⓓ	51.	Ⓐ Ⓓ	83.	Ⓐ Ⓓ
20.	Ⓐ Ⓓ	52.	Ⓐ Ⓓ	84.	Ⓐ Ⓓ
21.	Ⓐ Ⓓ	53.	Ⓐ Ⓓ	85.	Ⓐ Ⓓ
22.	Ⓐ Ⓓ	54.	Ⓐ Ⓓ	86.	Ⓐ Ⓓ
23.	Ⓐ Ⓓ	55.	Ⓐ Ⓓ	87.	Ⓐ Ⓓ
24.	Ⓐ Ⓓ	56.	Ⓐ Ⓓ	88.	Ⓐ Ⓓ
25.	Ⓐ Ⓓ	57.	Ⓐ Ⓓ	89.	Ⓐ Ⓓ
26.	Ⓐ Ⓓ	58.	Ⓐ Ⓓ	90.	Ⓐ Ⓓ
27.	Ⓐ Ⓓ	59.	Ⓐ Ⓓ	91.	Ⓐ Ⓓ
28.	Ⓐ Ⓓ	60.	Ⓐ Ⓓ	92.	Ⓐ Ⓓ
29.	Ⓐ Ⓓ	61.	Ⓐ Ⓓ	93.	Ⓐ Ⓓ
30.	Ⓐ Ⓓ	62.	Ⓐ Ⓓ	94.	Ⓐ Ⓓ
31.	Ⓐ Ⓓ	63.	Ⓐ Ⓓ	95.	Ⓐ Ⓓ
32.	Ⓐ Ⓓ	64.	Ⓐ Ⓓ		

(This page may be removed to mark answers.)

ANSWERS TO EXERCISE 2.

1.	D	33.	A	65.	A
2.	D	34.	A	66.	A
3.	A	35.	D	67.	A
4.	D	36.	D	68.	D
5.	A	37.	D	69.	A
6.	D	38.	A	70.	D
7.	D	39.	D	71.	A
8.	D	40.	A	72.	D
9.	A	41.	D	73.	A
10.	A	42.	D	74.	D
11.	D	43.	D	75.	D
12.	A	44.	D	76.	A
13.	A	45.	D	77.	D
14.	D	46.	D	78.	D
15.	D	47.	A	79.	A
16.	A	48.	A	80.	D
17.	D	49.	D	81.	A
18.	D	50.	A	82.	D
19.	A	51.	D	83.	A
20.	D	52.	D	84.	D
21.	A	53.	A	85.	D
22.	D	54.	D	86.	A
23.	D	55.	A	87.	D
24.	A	56.	D	88.	D
25.	A	57.	D	89.	D
26.	A	58.	A	90.	A
27.	D	59.	A	91.	A
28.	D	60.	D	92.	D
29.	D	61.	A	93.	D
30.	A	62.	D	94.	A
31.	D	63.	D	95.	A
32.	D	64.	A		

If Your Score Was:

—87 or more correct you have an excellent score

—between 55 and 86 correct you have a good score

—below 54 correct you should practice more

EXERCISE 3.

TIME: 6 MINUTES

1.	Miami Blvd.	Miami Blvd.
2.	121 Burroughs	112 Burroughs
3.	1489 Van Meter St.	1489 Van Metor St.
4.	789 Holiday Ave.	789 Holliday Ave.
5.	Atlanta, Georgia 35919	Atlanta, Georgia 35919
6.	17666 Shannon Ln.	17666 Shanon Ln.
7.	Kingsley Blvd. SE	Kinsley Blvd. SE
8.	4456 Lamplight Ct.	4654 Lamplight Ct.
9.	8100 Bonteview St.	8010 Bonteview St.
10.	99-B Moonlight Bay	99-B Moonlight Bay
11.	Las Vegas, Nevada 67088	Las Vegas, Nev. 67088
12.	Tucson, Ariz. 85044	Tuscon, Ariz. 85044
13.	Hampton Dr. SW	Hampton Dr. SW
14.	Bonn St. S	Bonn St. N
15.	418 9th Ave.	481 9th Ave.
16.	1000 Terrace St.	10000 Terrace St.
17.	7478 Wellington	7478 Wellington
18.	Plainsville, NE	Planesville, NE
19.	Faunterloy Rd. NW	Faunterloy Rd. NW
20.	1414 Seaview Place	1414 Seaview Point
21.	Little Rock, Ark. 44807	Little Rock, Ark. 44807
22.	158 Johnathon Ln.	158 Jonathon Ln.
23.	Route 6, Box 4342	Route 6, Box 4342
24.	9315 Labador Park	9351 Labador Park
25.	Crysanthanum Place SW	Crysanthinum Place SW
26.	Fullerton, CA	Fullerton, CA
27.	7877 Knotingham Dr.	7877 Knottingham Dr.
28.	323 Warner Ave.	332 Warner Ave.
29.	489 Vermont Pl.	489 Vermont Pl.
30.	Minneapolis, MN 49401	Minneapolis, Minn. 49401
31.	4001 Briginham Rd.	4001 Brigingham Rd.
32.	Constance Bay	Constance Bay

33.	3388 Joplin Blvd.	8833 Joplin Blvd.
34.	684 11th St. NE	684 13th St. NE
35.	210 E Harmont	210 E. Hormont
36.	Tooele, Utah 76900	Tooele, Utah 79600
37.	1717 Carver Dr.	1717 Carver Dr.
38.	546 S. Galveston Ln.	546 W. Galveston Ln.
39.	New York, N.Y. 00723	New Work, N.Y. 00723
40.	3941 Belmont Way	3941 Belmont Way
41.	87-D University Village	87-D Univarsity Village
42.	2815 Monroe Dr.	2815 Monroe Dr.
43.	2211 Northwestern Rd.	2211 Northwestern Pl.
44.	1411 Hawthrone Ct.	1411 Hawthorn Ct.
45.	720 Kellogg	720 Kellogg
46.	2419 S. Douglous	2419 S. Douglous
47.	Holyoke, Mass. 02411	Holyoke, Miss. 02411
48.	707 Pierce Circle	707 Pierce Circle
49.	13251 Harding Dr.	13251 Harding Dr.
50.	2531 Eisenhower	2531 Eisenhower
51.	110 Main St.	110 Main St.
52.	22619 Hayes Point	22619 Heyes Point
53.	435 Wilmoth Ave.	453 Wilmoth Ave.
54.	Bakersville, N.C. 25014	Bakersville, N.C. 25014
55.	334 Lighthouse Pt.	334 Lighthouse Pt.
56.	214 O'neil Dr. S.	214 O'neil Dr. SW
57.	4516 Mulberry Blvd.	4516 Mulberry Blvd.
58.	Greenbriar Circle S.	S. Greenbriar Circle
59.	7000 Marston Ct.	70000 Marston Ct.
60.	3501 Jensen Way	3501 Bensen Way
61.	Murfreesboro, TN	Murfreesboro, Tenn.
62.	Paducah, Kentucky 35114	Paducah, Kentucky 35114
63.	10074 Jackson Dr.	10704 Jackson Dr.
64.	330 42nd Ave.	330 42nd Ave.
65.	1111 Bouldergrant Pl.	1117 Bouldergrant Pl.
66.	SW Symington Way	SW Symington Way
67.	3939 Concord Ave.	9393 Concord Ave.
68.	Dubuque, Ia. 52400	Dubuque, Ia. 52400
69.	41 Blanchard Dr.	41-C Blanchard Dr.

70.	901 K. Stables Blvd.	901 K. Stabbles Blvd.
71.	N. Shoshonee Pl.	N. Shoshownee Pl.
72.	222 Welch Ave.	222 Welch Ave.
73.	1515 1rst Ave.	1515 1rst Ave. S.
74.	103-C King Terrace	103-C King Terrace
75.	4466 Baltic Dr.	4646 Baltic Dr.
76.	Augusta, Maine 00111	Augusta, Maine 01011
77.	New Albany Rd. SW	Old Albany Rd. SW
78.	252 25th Ave. S.	252 22nd Ave. S.
79.	17677 Belfair Square	17677 Belfair Square
80.	111 Washington Blvd.	111 Washinton Blvd.
81.	2029 Isaquah Ln.	2029 Isaquah Ln.
82.	Kansas City, Kansas	Kansas City, Mo.
83.	NW Macnally Dr. 1-B	NW Mcnally Dr. 1-B
84.	3078 S. George St.	3078 Saint George Ave.
85.	40473 Paulson Dr.	40473 Paulson Dr.
86.	Jacksonville, FL 46991	Jacksonville, Fla. 46991
87.	2000 Ebeneezor Place	2000 Ebaneezor Place
88.	1212 Ballen Lake Park	1212 Ballon Lake Park
89.	12 Lester Blvd.	21 Lester Blvd.
90.	4392 Crestwood Circle	4392 Crestwood Circle
91.	78990 Norweigan Trail	78990 Norweigen Trail
92.	327 S. Hazel	327 N. Hazel
93.	Cincinnati, Ohio 48921	Cinncinati, Ohio 48921
94.	RR 5, Box 414-S	RR 5, Box 41-4S
95.	Provo, Utah	Provo, Utah

ANSWER SHEET TO EXERCISE 3

1. Ⓐ Ⓓ	33. Ⓐ Ⓓ	65. Ⓐ Ⓓ
2. Ⓐ Ⓓ	34. Ⓐ Ⓓ	66. Ⓐ Ⓓ
3. Ⓐ Ⓓ	35. Ⓐ Ⓓ	67. Ⓐ Ⓓ
4. Ⓐ Ⓓ	36. Ⓐ Ⓓ	68. Ⓐ Ⓓ
5. Ⓐ Ⓓ	37. Ⓐ Ⓓ	69. Ⓐ Ⓓ
6. Ⓐ Ⓓ	38. Ⓐ Ⓓ	70. Ⓐ Ⓓ
7. Ⓐ Ⓓ	39. Ⓐ Ⓓ	71. Ⓐ Ⓓ
8. Ⓐ Ⓓ	40. Ⓐ Ⓓ	72. Ⓐ Ⓓ
9. Ⓐ Ⓓ	41. Ⓐ Ⓓ	73. Ⓐ Ⓓ
10. Ⓐ Ⓓ	42. Ⓐ Ⓓ	74. Ⓐ Ⓓ
11. Ⓐ Ⓓ	43. Ⓐ Ⓓ	75. Ⓐ Ⓓ
12. Ⓐ Ⓓ	44. Ⓐ Ⓓ	76. Ⓐ Ⓓ
13. Ⓐ Ⓓ	45. Ⓐ Ⓓ	77. Ⓐ Ⓓ
14. Ⓐ Ⓓ	46. Ⓐ Ⓓ	78. Ⓐ Ⓓ
15. Ⓐ Ⓓ	47. Ⓐ Ⓓ	79. Ⓐ Ⓓ
16. Ⓐ Ⓓ	48. Ⓐ Ⓓ	80. Ⓐ Ⓓ
17. Ⓐ Ⓓ	49. Ⓐ Ⓓ	81. Ⓐ Ⓓ
18 Ⓐ Ⓓ	50. Ⓐ Ⓓ	82. Ⓐ Ⓓ
19. Ⓐ Ⓓ	51. Ⓐ Ⓓ	83. Ⓐ Ⓓ
20. Ⓐ Ⓓ	52. Ⓐ Ⓓ	84. Ⓐ Ⓓ
21. Ⓐ Ⓓ	53. Ⓐ Ⓓ	85. Ⓐ Ⓓ
22. Ⓐ Ⓓ	54. Ⓐ Ⓓ	86. Ⓐ Ⓓ
23. Ⓐ Ⓓ	55. Ⓐ Ⓓ	87. Ⓐ Ⓓ
24. Ⓐ Ⓓ	56. Ⓐ Ⓓ	88. Ⓐ Ⓓ
25. Ⓐ Ⓓ	57. Ⓐ Ⓓ	89. Ⓐ Ⓓ
26. Ⓐ Ⓓ	58. Ⓐ Ⓓ	90. Ⓐ Ⓓ
27. Ⓐ Ⓓ	59. Ⓐ Ⓓ	91. Ⓐ Ⓓ
28. Ⓐ Ⓓ	60. Ⓐ Ⓓ	92. Ⓐ Ⓓ
29. Ⓐ Ⓓ	61. Ⓐ Ⓓ	93. Ⓐ Ⓓ
30. Ⓐ Ⓓ	62. Ⓐ Ⓓ	94. Ⓐ Ⓓ
31. Ⓐ Ⓓ	63. Ⓐ Ⓓ	95. Ⓐ Ⓓ
32. Ⓐ Ⓓ	64. Ⓐ Ⓓ	

(This page may be removed to mark answers.)

ANSWERS TO EXERCISE 3.

1.	A	33.	D	65.	D
2.	D	34.	D	66.	A
3.	D	35.	D	67.	D
4.	D	36.	D	68.	A
5.	A	37.	A	69.	D
6.	D	38.	D	70.	D
7.	D	39.	D	71.	D
8.	D	40.	A	72.	A
9.	D	41.	D	73.	D
10.	A	42.	A	74.	A
11.	D	43.	D	75.	D
12.	D	44.	D	76.	D
13.	A	45.	A	77.	D
14.	D	46.	A	78.	D
15.	D	47.	D	79.	A
16.	D	48.	A	80.	D
17.	A	49.	A	81.	A
18.	D	50.	A	82.	D
19.	A	51.	A	83.	D
20.	D	52.	D	84.	D
21.	A	53.	D	85.	A
22.	D	54.	A	86.	D
23.	A	55.	A	87.	D
24.	D	56.	D	88.	D
25.	D	57.	A	89.	D
26.	A	58.	D	90.	A
27.	D	59.	D	91.	D
28.	D	60.	D	92.	D
29.	A	61.	D	93.	D
30.	D	62.	A	94.	D
31.	D	63.	D	95.	A
32.	A	64.	A		

If Your Score Was:
—87 or more correct you have an excellent score
—between 55 and 86 correct you have a good score
—below 54 correct you should practice more

EXERCISE 4.

TIME: 6 MINUTES

1.	421 Briarwood Pl.	421 Briarwood Pl.
2.	2524 Torry Pines Dr.	2524 Torry Pines Dr.
3.	688 John Hoptkins St.	688 John Hopkins St.
4.	Palm Springs, CA 94611	Palm Springs, CA 94611
5.	Bon Vista Industrial Park	Bon Vista Industrial Park
6.	667 66th Ave. SW	667 67th Ave. SW
7.	400431 Monteray Lane	404031 Monteray Lane
8.	15-D Bolstad Blvd.	15-D Bolstad Blvd.
9.	160 South Dakota St.	160 South Dakota St.
10.	150-A Schilleter Village	150-A Schileter Village
11.	Waterbury, Connecticut 22411	Waterbury, Conn. 22411
12.	1419 Wheeler Dr. SE	1419 Wheeler Dr. SE
13.	1711 Meadowlane	1171 Meadowlane
14.	330 Harcomb Ct. N.	330 Harcomb Ct. N.
15.	88 1/2 Walnut Place	88 1/4 Walnut Place
16.	Emerald Bay Apts. 11C	Emerald Bay Apts. 11C
17.	Carson City, Nev. 55811	Carson City, Nev. 55811
18.	126491 Garfield Ave.	126419 Garfield Ave.
19.	240 Quigley Blvd.	240 Quigley Blvd.
20.	Honolulu, Hawaii 99894	Honalulu, Hawaii 99894
21.	50010 Doctrine Place	5010 Doctrine Place
22.	411 Hystead Ave.	411 Histead Ave.
23.	69731 Ferndale Pkwy.	69731 Ferndale Park
24.	N. Palo Alto Dr.	N. Palo Alto Dr.
25.	1451 SW Spannus Dr.	1451 SW Spannus Dr.
26.	Severance Canyon Rd.	Severence Canyon Rd.
27.	4410 Phoenix St.	4410 Phoenix St.
28.	11-B Deer Antler Cr.	11-B Deer Antler Circle
29.	8435 Orchard Grove S.	8435 Orchard Grove S.
30.	Northwest Orient Blvd.	Northwest Orient Blvd.
31.	441 Stanford Ave.	441 Stanford Ave.
32.	67351 Opalamine Circle	67351 Opal Circle
33.	837 Harding Way NE	837 Harding Way

34.	New Orleans, LA 77501	New Orleans, LA 75701
35.	Citronelle, Ala. 67891	Citronelle, Ala. 67891
36.	320 Four Seasons Apts.	302 Four Seasons Apts.
37.	4115 Ontario Dr.	4115 Ontario Dr.
38.	58423 Lincoln Ct.	58423 Lincoln Place
39.	RR 2, Boone, Ia. 50123	RR 2, Boone, ID 50123
40.	Point Defiance, Wash.	Point Defiance, Wash.
41.	221 16th St.	221 16th St.
42.	Norfolk, Neb. 68744	Norfolk, Neb. 68474
43.	108 E. Lime St.	108 W. Lime St.
44.	1707 Amherst Blvd.	1707 Amhurst Blvd.
45.	310 Mathews Dr.	301 Mathews Dr.
46.	Middlebourne, W.V. 05691	Middleborne, W.V. 05691
47.	1461 Madison Ave.	1461 Madison Ave.
48.	Oshkosh, Wisc. 54420	Oshkosh, Wisc. 54420
49.	N. Manitowac Dr.	N. Manatowac Dr.
50.	1599 Bothell Lane SW	1599 Bothell Lane SW
51.	5743 Whitney Park	5734 Whitney Park
52.	711 SW Richardson Pl.	711 SW Richardson Pl.
53.	Port Bolivar, Tex. 67019	Port Bolivar, Tex. 67019
54.	763241 Columbia Ave.	763241 Columbia Ave.
55.	707-C West Minster Park	707-C West Minster Park
56.	Beecher Falls, VT. 08917	Beacher Falls, VT. 08917
57.	4440 Chester Ave.	4440 Chester Ave.
58.	8980 Fauquier Square	8980 Fauquier Square
59.	Duchesne, Utah 79818	Duchesnee, Utah 79818
60.	30045 Montgomery	30045 Montgomery
61.	SE Carroll St.	SE 111 Carroll St.
62.	1477 Newbury Place	1477 Newbury Place
63.	Bryn Mawr, Wash. 78113	Bryn Mawr, Wash. 78113
64.	343 S. Wendover Ave.	343 S. Wendover Ave.
65.	140 W. St. Patrick	140 W. Saint Patrick
66.	1515 Elsinore Dr.	5151 Elsinore Dr.
67.	Centrahoma, Okla. 65077	Centrahoma, Okla. 65077
68.	400-401 Essex Ct.	400-401 Esex Ct.
69.	7581 Box Elder Pkwy	7581 Box Alder Pkwy

70.	7600 Mount Vernon Rd.	7600 Mt. Vernon Road
71.	651 Trinity St.	651 Trinity St.
72.	Chiloquin, ORE 90403	Chiloquin, ORE 90403
73.	3777 Comanche Ct.	3773 Comanche Ct.
74.	404 Hamilton Place	404 Hamilton Place
75.	Philadelphia Dr. SW	Philadelphia Dr. SW
76.	701 Canton Dr.	701 Canton Ave.
77.	11130 Joesephine St.	11130 Joseephine St.
78.	488 Kenwood	488 Kenwood
79.	9080 Lansing Pl.	9080 Lansing Pk.
80.	1501-D Cleveland Hts.	1501-D Cleveland Hts.
81.	2575 Covington Dr.	2575 Covington Dr.
82.	Northumberland, Penn. 09432	Northumberland, Penn. 09432
83.	1616 Drexal	1616 Drexel
84.	705 Tuscarawas Point	705 Tuscarawas Point
85.	54330 Haskins Dr. S.	54338 Haskins Dr. S.
86.	1221 Cortland Way	2112 Cortland Way
87.	100 Preble Beach	100 Preeble Beach
88.	8595 Perry Ave.	8595 Perry Ave.
89.	7734 Clayton Blvd. NW	7734 Clayton Blvd. NW
90.	22441 Lancaster Dr.	22441 Lancaster Dr.
91.	Campbellsburg, Ind. 54013	Campbelsburg, Ind. 54013
92.	Pinckneyville, Ill. 52388	Pinckneyville, Ill. 52388
93.	515 Olmstead Pl.	515 Olmstead Pl.
94.	4016 Thomson	4016 Thomson
95.	Cape Elizabeth, Maine	Cape Elizebeth, Maine

ANSWER SHEET TO EXERCISE 4

1. Ⓐ Ⓓ	33. Ⓐ Ⓓ	65. Ⓐ Ⓓ
2. Ⓐ Ⓓ	34. Ⓐ Ⓓ	66. Ⓐ Ⓓ
3. Ⓐ Ⓓ	35. Ⓐ Ⓓ	67. Ⓐ Ⓓ
4. Ⓐ Ⓓ	36. Ⓐ Ⓓ	68. Ⓐ Ⓓ
5. Ⓐ Ⓓ	37. Ⓐ Ⓓ	69. Ⓐ Ⓓ
6. Ⓐ Ⓓ	38. Ⓐ Ⓓ	70. Ⓐ Ⓓ
7. Ⓐ Ⓓ	39. Ⓐ Ⓓ	71. Ⓐ Ⓓ
8. Ⓐ Ⓓ	40. Ⓐ Ⓓ	72. Ⓐ Ⓓ
9. Ⓐ Ⓓ	41. Ⓐ Ⓓ	73. Ⓐ Ⓓ
10. Ⓐ Ⓓ	42. Ⓐ Ⓓ	74. Ⓐ Ⓓ
11. Ⓐ Ⓓ	43. Ⓐ Ⓓ	75. Ⓐ Ⓓ
12. Ⓐ Ⓓ	44. Ⓐ Ⓓ	76. Ⓐ Ⓓ
13. Ⓐ Ⓓ	45. Ⓐ Ⓓ	77. Ⓐ Ⓓ
14. Ⓐ Ⓓ	46. Ⓐ Ⓓ	78. Ⓐ Ⓓ
15. Ⓐ Ⓓ	47. Ⓐ Ⓓ	79. Ⓐ Ⓓ
16. Ⓐ Ⓓ	48. Ⓐ Ⓓ	80. Ⓐ Ⓓ
17. Ⓐ Ⓓ	49. Ⓐ Ⓓ	81. Ⓐ Ⓓ
18. Ⓐ Ⓓ	50. Ⓐ Ⓓ	82. Ⓐ Ⓓ
19. Ⓐ Ⓓ	51. Ⓐ Ⓓ	83. Ⓐ Ⓓ
20. Ⓐ Ⓓ	52. Ⓐ Ⓓ	84. Ⓐ Ⓓ
21. Ⓐ Ⓓ	53. Ⓐ Ⓓ	85. Ⓐ Ⓓ
22. Ⓐ Ⓓ	54. Ⓐ Ⓓ	86. Ⓐ Ⓓ
23. Ⓐ Ⓓ	55. Ⓐ Ⓓ	87. Ⓐ Ⓓ
24. Ⓐ Ⓓ	56. Ⓐ Ⓓ	88. Ⓐ Ⓓ
25. Ⓐ Ⓓ	57. Ⓐ Ⓓ	89. Ⓐ Ⓓ
26. Ⓐ Ⓓ	58. Ⓐ Ⓓ	90. Ⓐ Ⓓ
27. Ⓐ Ⓓ	59. Ⓐ Ⓓ	91. Ⓐ Ⓓ
28. Ⓐ Ⓓ	60. Ⓐ Ⓓ	92. Ⓐ Ⓓ
29. Ⓐ Ⓓ	61. Ⓐ Ⓓ	93. Ⓐ Ⓓ
30. Ⓐ Ⓓ	62. Ⓐ Ⓓ	94. Ⓐ Ⓓ
31. Ⓐ Ⓓ	63. Ⓐ Ⓓ	95. Ⓐ Ⓓ
32. Ⓐ Ⓓ	64. Ⓐ Ⓓ	

(This page may be removed to mark answers.)

ANSWERS TO EXERCISE 4.

1.	A	33.	D	65.	D
2.	A	34.	D	66.	D
3.	D	35.	A	67.	A
4.	A	36.	D	68.	D
5.	A	37.	A	69.	D
6.	D	38.	D	70.	D
7.	D	39.	D	71.	A
8.	A	40.	A	72.	A
9.	A	41.	A	73.	D
10.	D	42.	D	74.	A
11.	D	43.	D	75.	A
12.	A	44.	D	76.	D
13.	D	45.	D	77.	A
14.	A	46.	D	78.	A
15.	D	47.	A	79.	D
16.	A	48.	A	80.	A
17.	A	49.	D	81.	A
18.	D	50.	A	82.	A
19.	A	51.	D	83.	D
20.	D	52.	A	84.	A
21.	D	53.	A	85.	D
22.	D	54.	A	86.	D
23.	D	55.	A	87.	D
24.	A	56.	D	88.	A
25.	A	57.	A	89.	A
26.	D	58.	A	90.	A
27.	A	59.	D	91.	D
28.	D	60.	A	92.	A
29.	A	61.	D	93.	A
30.	A	62.	A	94.	A
31.	A	63.	A	95.	D
32.	D	64.	A		

If Your Score Was:
—87 or more correct you have an excellent score
—between 55 and 86 correct you have a good score
—below 54 correct you should practice more

EXERCISE 5.

TIME: 6 MINUTES

1.	1717 Wasbash Ave.	1717 Wabash Ave.
2.	2035 Kewanna Dr. SW	2035 Kawanna Dr. SW
3.	404 E. Attica St.	440 E. Attica St.
4.	New Carlisle, Ind. 48113	New Carlile, Ind. 48113
5.	31310 Hartford Ave.	31310 Heartford Ave.
6.	1112 Warsaw Lane NE	1112 Warsaw Lane NE
7.	41141 Maquoketa Blvd.	4114 Maquoketa Blvd.
8.	Hutchinson, Kan. 50897	Hutchinson, Kan. 50897
9.	304 Osborne Dr.	304 Osborn Dr.
10.	1299 Hiawatha Pl.	9912 Hiawatha Pl.
11.	155 NW Bancroft Ave.	155 NW Bancroft Ave.
12.	Cheyenne, Wyo. 79333	Cheyenne, Wyo. 79333
13.	6044 Ullysses Ct.	6044 Ulysses Ct.
14.	Route 4, Box 20053	Route 4, Box 20503
15.	5132 NE Kendall Circle	5132 NE Kendall Circle
16.	106 Murray Dr.	106 Murray Dr.
17.	Council Bluffs, Ia. 53215	Council Bluffs, Ia. 53215
18.	9090 Pocahontas Place	9090 Pocohontas Place
19.	4152 Bondurant Blvd.	4152 Bondurant Blvd.
20.	1119 Versailles Point	1191 Versailles Point
21.	Brandywine, MD 04320	Brandywine, MD 04320
22.	73444 Randolph Trail	74344 Randolph Trail
23.	Battlecreek, Mich 67022	Battlecreek, Mich 67202
24.	4091 Somerset Place	4091 Somerset Place
25.	503 N. Watseka Cr.	503 N. Watsaka Cr.
26.	4017 Ladora Dr.	4017 Ladora Dr.
27.	1514-M Windsor Hts. Apts.	1514-M Windsor Hts. Apts.
28.	3093 NW Ellinwood Ave.	3093 SW Ellinwood Ave.
29.	404 31rst St.	404 33rd St.
30.	Acomita, NM 79443	Acomita, NM 79443
31.	7474 Granite Hill Rd.	7474 Granate Hill Rd.
32.	202 W. Bismark Ave.	202 W. Bismark Ave.
33.	70009 Decator Dr.	70009 Decaitor Dr.

34.	113 Phillips Pt.	113 Phillips Pt.
35.	4531 Rosewood Lane	4531 Rosemary Lane
36.	Barneston, Neb. 67901	Barnesston, Neb. 67901
37.	3031 Springdale Dr.	3130 Springdale Dr.
38.	1418 White Pine Dr.	1418 White Pine Dr.
39.	6060 62nd Ave. SW	606 62nd Ave. SW
40.	322 Chadron Ct.	322 Chadron Ct.
41.	97388 Clinton St. N.	97388 Clinton St.
42.	7070 Ironside Dr.	70707 Ironside Dr.
43.	32-C Chinook Pl.	32-C S. Chinook Pl.
44.	8013 Dodson	8013 Dodson
45.	Contoocook, NH 09433	Contoocook, NH 09433
46.	13133 Hampstead Blvd.	13131 Hampstead Blvd.
47.	7274 Esmeralda Way	7274 Esmerelda Way
48.	702 Beatrice St.	702 Beatrice Street
49.	9093 Moccasin Trail	9093 Moccasin Trail
50.	300 Simms Ave.	300 Simms Ave.
51.	Bayonne, NJ 09444	Bayonne, NJ 09444
52.	4075 Daniels Dr.	4075 Daniels Dr. SW
53.	1091 Osage Beach	1091 Osage Beach
54.	31372 Henrietta Blvd.	31372 Henrietta Blvd.
55.	1696 Bucklin Hill Rd.	1669 Bucklin Hill Rd.
56.	73051 Dekalb Ave.	73051 Dekelb Ave.
57.	47910 Magnolia Dr.	47910 Magnolia Dr.
58.	Batesville, Miss 49330	Batsville, Miss 49330
59.	707 Maple Grove	7070 Maple Grove
60.	126 Lucerne Ln.	126 Lucerne Ln.
61.	Bellefontaine, MO 54355	Bellefontaine, MO 54355
62.	40002 Laddonia Dr.	40003 Laddonia Dr.
63.	1313 Wilkinson Blvd.	1313 Wilkenson Blvd.
64.	988 Raymond Way S.	988 S. Raymond Way
65.	5577 Beaumont St.	7755 Beaumont St.
66.	1111 Concordia Jct.	1111 Concordia Jct.
67.	Golconda, NEV 84328	Golkonda, NEV 84328
68.	48932 Marshall Terrace	48932 Marshall Terrace
69.	3197 Dolomite Ridge	3197 Dolomitic Ridge

The Postal Exam Preparation Book

70.	811 Robins	811 Robins
71.	80706 Jasper Jct. SW	80706 Jasper Jct. SW
72.	Mount Edgecumbe, AK	Mt. Edgecumbe, AK
73.	9810 Oak Knolls S.	9810 Oak Knolls S.
74.	7351 Hollister Ave.	7315 Hollister Ave.
75.	1507 Yellow Pine	1507 Green Pine Dr.
76.	Ehrenberg, Ariz. 85123	Ehrenburg, Ariz. 85123
77.	1413 3rd St. SW	1413 6th Ave. SW
78.	41378 Tallapoosa Circle	41378 Tallapoosa Circle
79.	105 NW Addison Dr.	105 NW Addison Dr.
80.	4899 Winston Hill	48999 Winston Hill
81.	2043 Fremont Way	2043 Fremont Way
82.	77-D Grandview Apts.	77-D Grandview Apts.
83.	1414 Frazier Park	1414 Frazier Park
84.	4149 Capistrano Beach	4149 Capistreno Beach
85.	83140 Holliwood Blvd.	83410 Holliwood Blvd.
86.	Attawaugan, Conn. 48590	Atawaugan, Conn. 48590
87.	5020 Bristol St.	5020 Bristol St.
88.	10956 Cromwell Dr.	10956 Cromwell Ct.
89.	198 Kent	198 Kent
90.	401 Willow Branch	401 Willow Branch
91.	Cheswold, DEL 03211	Cheswald, DEL 03211
92.	3400 Bowers	3400 Bowens
93.	2020 N. Laporte Ave.	2020 N. Laport Ave.
94.	120 Santa Cruz Circle	120 Santa Cruz Circle
95.	9011 Sedgwick Dr. SW	9011 Segwick Dr. SW

ANSWER SHEET TO EXERCISE 5

1.	Ⓐ	Ⓓ	33.	Ⓐ	Ⓓ	65.	Ⓐ	Ⓓ
2.	Ⓐ	Ⓓ	34.	Ⓐ	Ⓓ	66.	Ⓐ	Ⓓ
3.	Ⓐ	Ⓓ	35.	Ⓐ	Ⓓ	67.	Ⓐ	Ⓓ
4.	Ⓐ	Ⓓ	36.	Ⓐ	Ⓓ	68.	Ⓐ	Ⓓ
5.	Ⓐ	Ⓓ	37.	Ⓐ	Ⓓ	69.	Ⓐ	Ⓓ
6.	Ⓐ	Ⓓ	38.	Ⓐ	Ⓓ	70.	Ⓐ	Ⓓ
7.	Ⓐ	Ⓓ	39.	Ⓐ	Ⓓ	71.	Ⓐ	Ⓓ
8.	Ⓐ	Ⓓ	40.	Ⓐ	Ⓓ	72.	Ⓐ	Ⓓ
9.	Ⓐ	Ⓓ	41.	Ⓐ	Ⓓ	73.	Ⓐ	Ⓓ
10.	Ⓐ	Ⓓ	42.	Ⓐ	Ⓓ	74.	Ⓐ	Ⓓ
11.	Ⓐ	Ⓓ	43.	Ⓐ	Ⓓ	75.	Ⓐ	Ⓓ
12.	Ⓐ	Ⓓ	44.	Ⓐ	Ⓓ	76.	Ⓐ	Ⓓ
13.	Ⓐ	Ⓓ	45.	Ⓐ	Ⓓ	77.	Ⓐ	Ⓓ
14.	Ⓐ	Ⓓ	46.	Ⓐ	Ⓓ	78.	Ⓐ	Ⓓ
15.	Ⓐ	Ⓓ	47.	Ⓐ	Ⓓ	79.	Ⓐ	Ⓓ
16.	Ⓐ	Ⓓ	48.	Ⓐ	Ⓓ	80.	Ⓐ	Ⓓ
17.	Ⓐ	Ⓓ	49.	Ⓐ	Ⓓ	81.	Ⓐ	Ⓓ
18	Ⓐ	Ⓓ	50.	Ⓐ	Ⓓ	82.	Ⓐ	Ⓓ
19.	Ⓐ	Ⓓ	51.	Ⓐ	Ⓓ	83.	Ⓐ	Ⓓ
20.	Ⓐ	Ⓓ	52.	Ⓐ	Ⓓ	84.	Ⓐ	Ⓓ
21.	Ⓐ	Ⓓ	53.	Ⓐ	Ⓓ	85.	Ⓐ	Ⓓ
22.	Ⓐ	Ⓓ	54.	Ⓐ	Ⓓ	86.	Ⓐ	Ⓓ
23.	Ⓐ	Ⓓ	55.	Ⓐ	Ⓓ	87.	Ⓐ	Ⓓ
24.	Ⓐ	Ⓓ	56.	Ⓐ	Ⓓ	88.	Ⓐ	Ⓓ
25.	Ⓐ	Ⓓ	57.	Ⓐ	Ⓓ	89.	Ⓐ	Ⓓ
26.	Ⓐ	Ⓓ	58.	Ⓐ	Ⓓ	90.	Ⓐ	Ⓓ
27.	Ⓐ	Ⓓ	59.	Ⓐ	Ⓓ	91.	Ⓐ	Ⓓ
28.	Ⓐ	Ⓓ	60.	Ⓐ	Ⓓ	92.	Ⓐ	Ⓓ
29.	Ⓐ	Ⓓ	61.	Ⓐ	Ⓓ	93.	Ⓐ	Ⓓ
30.	Ⓐ	Ⓓ	62.	Ⓐ	Ⓓ	94.	Ⓐ	Ⓓ
31.	Ⓐ	Ⓓ	63.	Ⓐ	Ⓓ	95.	Ⓐ	Ⓓ
32.	Ⓐ	Ⓓ	64.	Ⓐ	Ⓓ			

(This page may be removed to mark answers.)

ANSWERS TO EXERCISE 5

1.	D	33.	D	65.	D
2.	D	34.	A	66.	A
3.	D	35.	D	67.	D
4.	D	36.	D	68.	A
5.	D	37.	D	69.	D
6.	A	38.	A	70.	A
7.	D	39.	D	71.	A
8.	A	40.	A	72.	D
9.	D	41.	D	73.	A
10.	D	42.	D	74.	D
11.	A	43.	D	75.	D
12.	A	44.	A	76.	D
13.	D	45.	A	77.	D
14.	D	46.	D	78.	A
15.	A	47.	D	79.	A
16.	A	48.	D	80.	D
17.	A	49.	A	81.	A
18.	D	50.	A	82.	A
19.	A	51.	A	83.	A
20.	D	52.	D	84.	D
21.	A	53.	A	85.	D
22.	D	54.	A	86.	D
23.	D	55.	D	87.	A
24.	A	56.	D	88.	D
25.	D	57.	A	89.	A
26.	A	58.	D	90.	A
27.	A	59.	D	91.	D
28.	D	60.	A	92.	D
29.	D	61.	A	93.	D
30.	A	62.	D	94.	A
31.	D	63.	D	95.	D
32.	A	64.	D		

If Your Score Was:
—87 or more correct you have an excellent score
—between 55 and 86 correct you have a good score
—below 54 correct you should practice more

EXERCISE 6.

TIME: 6 MINUTES

1.	75011 Pearl Bay	75011 Pearl Bay
2.	Denver, Colo. 83007	Denver, Colo. 83007
3.	179-C Bauxite Gardens	179-C Bauxite Gardens
4.	8819 Lawrence Blvd.	8819 Lawrance Blvd.
5.	427 Imperial Way	427 Imperial Way
6.	Mineral Springs, Ark. 44041	Mineral Springs, Ark. 44041
7.	830 Ariton Dr. SW	803 Ariton Dr. SW
8.	7081 Grand Canyon Rd.	7081 Grand Canyon Rd.
9.	2453 St. Johns Rd.	2453 Saint Johns Rd.
10.	40744 Monteray Ln.	40474 Monteray Ln.
11.	4933 Cutler Ave.	4933 Cuttler Ave.
12.	3201 Ventura Blvd.	3021 Ventura Blvd.
13.	Kalaupapa, Hawaii 99831	Kalaupapa, Hawaii 99831
14.	4027 NW McNeil	4027 NE McNeil
15.	5151 Norwood Dr.	5151 Norwood Dr.
16.	6262 Bradley Ave.	6262 Bradly Ave.
17.	1520 Appleton Way	1520 Appleton Way
18.	2501 Sandy Ridge	2501 Sandy Ridge
19.	Guadalupe, Ariz. 84077	Guadalupe, Ariz. 84707
20.	91911 Alberta Dr.	91911 Alburta Dr.
21.	7921 22nd St. SW	7921 42nd St. SW
22.	8080 Maverick Ave.	8080 Maverick Ct.
23.	1293 Van Buran	1293 Van Burien
24.	601 Slyvan Way	601 Slyvan Way
25.	4358 Wauconda Dr.	4358 Wauconda Dr.
26.	1844 New Providence	1844 New Providence
27.	1308 Cherokee Lane	1380 Cherokee Lane
28.	991 Newton Blvd.	991 Newton Blvd.
29.	1345 Tripoli St. S.	1345 Tripoli St. N.
30.	494 Wheatcroft Dr.	494 Wheatcraft Dr.
31.	5535 Roxbury Ln.	5355 Roxbury Lane
32.	412 Plymoth Rock Pt.	412 Plymouth Rock Pt.
33.	67617 Knoxberry Ave.	67617 Knowberry Ave.

#	Address 1	Address 2
34.	741 Cottonwood St.	741 Cottonwood St.
35.	Bargersville, Ind. 49132	Bargersville, Ind. 41932
36.	Anacoco, LA 39542	Anacoca, LA 39542
37.	3052 Elkhorn Ln.	3052 Elkhorne Ln.
38.	Benton Harbour, Mich.	Benton Harbour, Mich.
39.	1588 Atchinson Place	1588 Atchinson Place
40.	70935 Biddeford Way	70935 Bideford Way
41.	311 Bellefonte	311 Bellefonte
42.	20716 Bloomfield Dr.	20761 Bloomfield Dr.
43.	1212 Panama Park	1212 Panama Place
44.	3838 Scott Ln.	3883 Scott Ln.
45.	91701 Woodridge Pl.	91701 Woodridge Pl.
46.	10013 Spencer Dr.	10013 Spencer Dr.
47.	181-E Oak Ridge Apts.	181-E Oak Ridge Apts.
48.	Bethleham, KY 54566	Bethlehem, KY 54566
49.	11190 Florence Dr.	11190 Florance Dr.
50.	4040 Hanover Blvd.	4040 Hanover Blvd.
51.	54990 Swanson Dr.	54990 Swanson Dr.
52.	165 W. Barthell St.	165 E. Barthell St.
53.	7833 Northbrook	7833 Northbrook
54.	1544 Greendale	1544 Greendale
55.	17178 Morgan View	17178 Morgan View Dr.
56.	505 Vermillian Blvd.	505 Vermillion Blvd.
57.	7039 Sheridan Rd.	7039 Sherman Rd.
58.	470 Shellfield Dr.	470 Shellfield Dr.
59.	Valantine, Neb. 67902	Valentine, Neb. 67902
60.	1410 Taft	1410 Taft
61.	540 Campbell Dr.	540 Campbell Dr.
62.	1111 Boston St.	1111 Boston St.
63.	Apt. F, Bayview Apts.	Apt. F, Bayview Apts.
64.	6060 Highland Ave.	60606 Highland Ave.
65.	711 Pleasant St.	711 Plesant
66.	4073 Hampson Way	4073 Hampson Way
67.	11 Bon Dileroy Rd.	11 Bon Dilleroy Rd.
68.	7018 Clifton Ave.	7018 Clifton Ave.
69.	90681 Paramount Blvd	90861 Paramount Blvd.

70.	1616 Madrona St.	1616 Madrona St.
71.	Gainsville, FLA 08911	Gainsville, FLA 09811
72.	1733 Copper Dr.	1733 Copper Dr.
73.	Memphis, Tenn. 24101	Memphis, TN 24101
74.	4027 Sinclair Pl.	4027 Sinclair Place
75.	30391 Peppermint Ave.	30391 Peppermint Ave.
76.	108-B Briarcliff	108-B Briarcliff
77.	9041 Balkner Pl.	9041 Balkner Pl.
78.	8011 Sutherland Ct.	8011 Sutherland Pkwy
79.	Fredericksburg, Ind. 80541	Fredericksburg, Ind. 80541
80.	2793 Armstrong St.	2379 Armstrong St.
81.	Toledo, Ohio 89400	Toledo, Ohio 89400
82.	6869 Stronghurst Dr.	6869 Stronghurst Ave.
83.	2425 Huntington Pt.	2425 Huntington Pl.
84.	181 Pennington Dr.	181 Penington Dr.
85.	59540 Parker Blvd.	59540 Parker Blvd.
86.	4012 Sullivan Pl.	4012 Sulliven Pl.
87.	3384 Ballard Dr. SW	3384 Ballard Dr. NW
88.	301 N. Victor Lane	103 N. Victor Lane
89.	Brownville Jct., Maine	Brownsville Jct., Maine
90.	2340 Zackery Ct.	2340 Zackery Ct.
91.	Alexandria, LA 54911	Alexandria, LA 54191
92.	415 Jennings Ave.	415 Jennings Ave.
93.	2010 Livingston Ln.	2010 Livingston Ln.
94.	NW Evangeline Way	429 NW Evangeline Way
95.	121 Newcastle Dr	211 New Castle Dr.

ANSWER SHEET TO EXERCISE 6

1. Ⓐ Ⓓ	33. Ⓐ Ⓓ	65. Ⓐ Ⓓ
2. Ⓐ Ⓓ	34. Ⓐ Ⓓ	66. Ⓐ Ⓓ
3. Ⓐ Ⓓ	35. Ⓐ Ⓓ	67. Ⓐ Ⓓ
4. Ⓐ Ⓓ	36. Ⓐ Ⓓ	68. Ⓐ Ⓓ
5. Ⓐ Ⓓ	37. Ⓐ Ⓓ	69. Ⓐ Ⓓ
6. Ⓐ Ⓓ	38. Ⓐ Ⓓ	70. Ⓐ Ⓓ
7. Ⓐ Ⓓ	39. Ⓐ Ⓓ	71. Ⓐ Ⓓ
8. Ⓐ Ⓓ	40. Ⓐ Ⓓ	72. Ⓐ Ⓓ
9. Ⓐ Ⓓ	41. Ⓐ Ⓓ	73. Ⓐ Ⓓ
10. Ⓐ Ⓓ	42. Ⓐ Ⓓ	74. Ⓐ Ⓓ
11. Ⓐ Ⓓ	43. Ⓐ Ⓓ	75. Ⓐ Ⓓ
12. Ⓐ Ⓓ	44. Ⓐ Ⓓ	76. Ⓐ Ⓓ
13. Ⓐ Ⓓ	45. Ⓐ Ⓓ	77. Ⓐ Ⓓ
14. Ⓐ Ⓓ	46. Ⓐ Ⓓ	78. Ⓐ Ⓓ
15. Ⓐ Ⓓ	47. Ⓐ Ⓓ	79. Ⓐ Ⓓ
16. Ⓐ Ⓓ	48. Ⓐ Ⓓ	80. Ⓐ Ⓓ
17. Ⓐ Ⓓ	49. Ⓐ Ⓓ	81. Ⓐ Ⓓ
18 Ⓐ Ⓓ	50. Ⓐ Ⓓ	82. Ⓐ Ⓓ
19. Ⓐ Ⓓ	51. Ⓐ Ⓓ	83. Ⓐ Ⓓ
20. Ⓐ Ⓓ	52. Ⓐ Ⓓ	84. Ⓐ Ⓓ
21. Ⓐ Ⓓ	53. Ⓐ Ⓓ	85. Ⓐ Ⓓ
22. Ⓐ Ⓓ	54. Ⓐ Ⓓ	86. Ⓐ Ⓓ
23. Ⓐ Ⓓ	55. Ⓐ Ⓓ	87. Ⓐ Ⓓ
24. Ⓐ Ⓓ	56. Ⓐ Ⓓ	88. Ⓐ Ⓓ
25. Ⓐ Ⓓ	57. Ⓐ Ⓓ	89. Ⓐ Ⓓ
26. Ⓐ Ⓓ	58. Ⓐ Ⓓ	90. Ⓐ Ⓓ
27. Ⓐ Ⓓ	59. Ⓐ Ⓓ	91. Ⓐ Ⓓ
28. Ⓐ Ⓓ	60. Ⓐ Ⓓ	92. Ⓐ Ⓓ
29. Ⓐ Ⓓ	61. Ⓐ Ⓓ	93. Ⓐ Ⓓ
30. Ⓐ Ⓓ	62. Ⓐ Ⓓ	94. Ⓐ Ⓓ
31. Ⓐ Ⓓ	63. Ⓐ Ⓓ	95. Ⓐ Ⓓ
32. Ⓐ Ⓓ	64. Ⓐ Ⓓ	

(This page may be removed to mark answers.)

ANSWERS TO EXERCISE 6

1.	A	33.	D	65.	D
2.	A	34.	A	66.	A
3.	A	35.	D	67.	D
4.	D	36.	D	68.	A
5.	A	37.	D	69.	D
6.	A	38.	A	70.	A
7.	D	39.	A	71.	D
8.	A	40.	D	72.	A
9.	D	41.	A	73.	D
10.	D	42.	D	74.	D
11.	D	43.	D	75.	A
12.	D	44.	D	76.	A
13.	A	45.	A	77.	A
14.	D	46.	A	78.	D
15.	A	47.	A	79.	A
16.	D	48.	D	80.	D
17.	A	49.	D	81.	A
18.	A	50.	A	82.	D
19.	D	51.	A	83.	D
20.	D	52.	D	84.	D
21.	D	53.	A	85.	A
22.	D	54.	A	86.	D
23.	D	55.	D	87.	D
24.	A	56.	D	88.	D
25.	A	57.	D	89.	D
26.	A	58.	A	90.	A
27.	D	59.	D	91.	D
28.	A	60.	A	92.	A
29.	D	61.	A	93.	A
30.	D	62.	A	94.	D
31.	D	63.	A	95.	D
32.	D	64.	D		

If Your Score Was:
—87 or more correct you have an excellent score
—between 55 and 86 correct you have a good score
—below 54 correct you should practice more

EXERCISE 7.

TIME: 6 MINUTES

1.	484 Berkeley Ct.	484 Berceley Ct.
2.	Buckingham, VA 84311	Buckingham, VA 84311
3.	3312 Applegate Pl.	3312 Applegate Place
4.	4040 Bishop Ave.	4040 Bishop Ave.
5.	5541 North Ogden Dr.	5541 North Ogden Dr.
6.	2461 Bennington	2641 Bennington
7.	42-C N. Victoria Rd.	42-C S. Victoria Rd.
8.	770 Richland Hills	770 Richland Hills
9.	Bomoseen, VT 47831	Bomoseen, VT 48731
10.	412 Walnut Springs	214 Walnut Springs
11.	Annabella, Utah 87940	Anabella, Utah 87940
12.	24359 Rio Grande Dr.	24359 Rio Grand Dr.
13.	7781 Weatherford	7781 Weatherford
14.	4940 Swanton Ave.	4904 Swanton Ave.
15.	Darrington, Wash. 97480	Darrington, Idaho
16.	1213 Garfield Rd.	1213 Garfield Rd.
17.	43571 Pilot Point S.	43571 Pilot Point S.
18.	232 Pleasanton NW	232 Pleasanton NW
19.	Jacksonburg, WV 04311	Jacksonberg, WV 04311
20.	4358 Dunbar Lane	4358 Dunnbar Lane
21.	13507 Marion Ave.	13507 Marion Ave.
22.	Antigonish, Nova Scotia	Antigonish, Nova Scotia
23.	389 Saxton Blvd.	398 Saxton Blvd.
24.	94119 Rogers St.	94119 Rodgers St.
25.	1000 Windsor Place	10000 Windsor Place
26.	909 Federal Way	909 Federal Way
27.	401 Gasglow Ridge	401 Gasglow Terrace
28.	Trentwood, WA 94972	Trentwood, WA 94792
29.	9734 Fremont Ln.	9734 Fremont Ln.
30.	4646 Montpilier Dr.	6464 Montpilier Dr.
31.	2015 Drayton	2015 Draxton
32.	7777 Beaver Ave.	1111 Beaver Ave.
33.	6014 Pleasant View	6014 Pleasant View

34.	4318 Whitesboro Ct.	4318 Whitesboro Ct.
35.	5266 Rockdale Dr.	5266 Rockdale Dr.
36.	1092 Lansing Ave. NW	1092 Lansing Ave. NW
37.	Canonchet, RI 03451	Cannonchet, RI 03451
38.	2077 Donalds	2077 Donalds
39.	77th Ave. SW	77th Ave. NW
40.	5802 Tillman Dr.	5802 Tillmon Dr.
41.	1006 Anchor Pt.	1060 Anchor Pt.
42.	3703 Gifford Blvd.	3703 Gifford Blvd.
43.	Salem, ORE 96710	Salem, OR 96710
44.	2166 Tanner Dr.	2166 Tanner Dr.
45.	44556 Lebaron Way	45456 Lebaron Way
46.	Northville, South Dakota	Southville, North Dakota
47.	4510 Columbus Lane	4510 Columbus Lane
48.	20031 Auburn Dr.	20031 S. Auburn Dr.
49.	Spokane, WA 94033	Spokane, WA 94033
50.	Brunswick, Tenn. 30911	Brunswick, TN 30911
51.	4040 Harriott Ln.	4040 Harriot Ln.
52.	3700 Wallace Dr.	3700 Wallace Blvd.
53.	Aumsville, Oreg. 89701	Aumville, Oreg. 89701
54.	60993 Buckeye Hill	60993 Buckeye Hill
55.	8142 Bonanza Pl.	8142 Bonanza Place
56.	Cameron, Penn. 39411	Cameron, Penn. 39411
57.	7839 Minerva Park	7839 Minarva Park
58.	7460 Layton Blvd.	7460 Layton Blvd.
59.	311 Trenton South	311 Trenton North
60.	Austwell, Texas 53189	Austwell TX 53189
61.	1450 Sherwood Point	1540 Sherwood Point
62.	78-C Seneca Falls	78-C Seneca Falls
63.	807 Sprague Square	870 Sprague Square
64.	Billings, Okla. 74388	Billings, Okla. 74388
65.	93083 Coalgate Pl.	93083 Coalgate Pl.
66.	770 Willowick Way	707 Willowick Way
67.	11-B Darlington	11-B Darlington
68.	483 Sardinas	483 Sardinnas
69.	20079 Corsica Cr.	20079 Corsica Cr.

The Postal Exam Preparation Book 121

70.	Campobello, SC 34791	Campobello, SC 34971
71.	Arnold Mills, RI 04931	Arnold Mills, RI 04931
72.	2314 Rickman Dr.	2314 Rickman Dr.
73.	7304-E Edgemont	7314-E Edgemont
74.	30607 Dole Ave.	30706 Dole Ave.
75.	1405 Canistota Rd.	1504 Canistota Rd.
76.	Burlington, Ohio 65033	Burlington, Ohio 65033
77.	8735 Victory Lane	8735 Victory Lane
78.	303 Darwin Ave.	303 N. Darwin Ave.
79.	4011 Champlin St.	4011 Champlin St.
80.	Johnston, Ill 54361	Johnson, Ill 54361
81.	1313 Bellvue Dr.	1313 Bellington Dr.
82.	307 Sandy Park	307 Sandy Park
83.	Broken Bow, Okla. 48935	Broken Bow, Okla. 48935
84.	5011 Santa Clara St.	5011 Santa Clara St.
85.	27811 Ashland Dr.	27881 Ashland Dr.
86.	113 NW Chartoff	113 NW Chartove
87.	2394 Barton Pl.	2934 Barton Pl.
88.	Center Pt., Ia. 53510	Center Pkwy., Ia. 53510
89.	919 Ralston Ave.	919 Ralston Ave.
90.	7515 Sugar Creek Ln.	7515 Sugar Creek Lane
91.	8081 Cardington Dr.	8081 Cardington
92.	135 9th St.	135 9th St.
93.	3315 Pandora Dr.	3315 Pandora Dr. NW
94.	4573 Crescent Bay	4573 Crescent Bay
95.	113 Rosevelt Pl.	113 Rosevelt Pl.

ANSWER SHEET TO EXERCISE 7

1. Ⓐ Ⓓ	33. Ⓐ Ⓓ	65. Ⓐ Ⓓ
2. Ⓐ Ⓓ	34. Ⓐ Ⓓ	66. Ⓐ Ⓓ
3. Ⓐ Ⓓ	35. Ⓐ Ⓓ	67. Ⓐ Ⓓ
4. Ⓐ Ⓓ	36. Ⓐ Ⓓ	68. Ⓐ Ⓓ
5. Ⓐ Ⓓ	37. Ⓐ Ⓓ	69. Ⓐ Ⓓ
6. Ⓐ Ⓓ	38. Ⓐ Ⓓ	70. Ⓐ Ⓓ
7. Ⓐ Ⓓ	39. Ⓐ Ⓓ	71. Ⓐ Ⓓ
8. Ⓐ Ⓓ	40. Ⓐ Ⓓ	72. Ⓐ Ⓓ
9. Ⓐ Ⓓ	41. Ⓐ Ⓓ	73. Ⓐ Ⓓ
10. Ⓐ Ⓓ	42. Ⓐ Ⓓ	74. Ⓐ Ⓓ
11. Ⓐ Ⓓ	43. Ⓐ Ⓓ	75. Ⓐ Ⓓ
12. Ⓐ Ⓓ	44. Ⓐ Ⓓ	76. Ⓐ Ⓓ
13. Ⓐ Ⓓ	45. Ⓐ Ⓓ	77. Ⓐ Ⓓ
14. Ⓐ Ⓓ	46. Ⓐ Ⓓ	78. Ⓐ Ⓓ
15. Ⓐ Ⓓ	47. Ⓐ Ⓓ	79. Ⓐ Ⓓ
16. Ⓐ Ⓓ	48. Ⓐ Ⓓ	80. Ⓐ Ⓓ
17. Ⓐ Ⓓ	49. Ⓐ Ⓓ	81. Ⓐ Ⓓ
18. Ⓐ Ⓓ	50. Ⓐ Ⓓ	82. Ⓐ Ⓓ
19. Ⓐ Ⓓ	51. Ⓐ Ⓓ	83. Ⓐ Ⓓ
20. Ⓐ Ⓓ	52. Ⓐ Ⓓ	84. Ⓐ Ⓓ
21. Ⓐ Ⓓ	53. Ⓐ Ⓓ	85. Ⓐ Ⓓ
22. Ⓐ Ⓓ	54. Ⓐ Ⓓ	86. Ⓐ Ⓓ
23. Ⓐ Ⓓ	55. Ⓐ Ⓓ	87. Ⓐ Ⓓ
24. Ⓐ Ⓓ	56. Ⓐ Ⓓ	88. Ⓐ Ⓓ
25. Ⓐ Ⓓ	57. Ⓐ Ⓓ	89. Ⓐ Ⓓ
26. Ⓐ Ⓓ	58. Ⓐ Ⓓ	90. Ⓐ Ⓓ
27. Ⓐ Ⓓ	59. Ⓐ Ⓓ	91. Ⓐ Ⓓ
28. Ⓐ Ⓓ	60. Ⓐ Ⓓ	92. Ⓐ Ⓓ
29. Ⓐ Ⓓ	61. Ⓐ Ⓓ	93. Ⓐ Ⓓ
30. Ⓐ Ⓓ	62. Ⓐ Ⓓ	94. Ⓐ Ⓓ
31. Ⓐ Ⓓ	63. Ⓐ Ⓓ	95. Ⓐ Ⓓ
32. Ⓐ Ⓓ	64. Ⓐ Ⓓ	

(This page may be removed to mark answers.)

The Postal Exam Preparation Book

ANSWERS TO EXERCISE 7

1.	D	33.	A	65.	A
2.	A	34.	A	66.	D
3.	D	35.	A	67.	A
4.	A	36.	A	68.	D
5.	A	37.	D	69.	A
6.	D	38.	A	70.	D
7.	D	39.	D	71.	A
8.	A	40.	D	72.	A
9.	D	41.	D	73.	D
10.	D	42.	A	74.	D
11.	D	43.	D	75.	D
12.	D	44.	A	76.	A
13.	A	45.	D	77.	A
14.	D	46.	D	78.	D
15.	D	47.	A	79.	A
16.	A	48.	D	80.	D
17.	A	49.	A	81.	D
18.	A	50.	D	82.	A
19.	D	51.	D	83.	A
20.	D	52.	D	84.	A
21.	A	53.	D	85.	D
22.	A	54.	A	86.	D
23.	D	55.	D	87.	D
24.	D	56.	A	88.	D
25.	D	57.	D	89.	A
26.	A	58.	A	90.	D
27.	D	59.	D	91.	D
28.	D	60.	D	92.	A
29.	A	61.	D	93.	D
30.	D	62.	A	94.	A
31.	D	63.	D	95.	A
32.	D	64.	A		

If Your Score Was:
—87 or more correct you have an excellent score
—between 55 and 86 correct you have a good score
—below 54 correct you should practice more

EXCERCISE 8.

TIME: 6 MINUTES

1.	Brice Canyon Dr.	Brice Canyon Rd.
2.	701 Callister Blvd.	710 Callister Blvd.
3.	Albuquerque, NM 79443	Albuquerque, NM 79443
4.	1912 St Vincent Pl.	1912 St Vinsent Pl.
5.	Island Lake, Wash.	Island Lake, Minn
6.	Anchorage, AK 99493	Anchorage, AK 99493
7.	30201 W. Fargo St.	30201 W. Fargo St.
8.	119 Foremann Dr.	119 Foreman Dr.
9.	7874 S. Buena Vista	7874 S. Buena Vista
10.	4237 Waverly Ave.	4237 Waverly Ave.
11.	Boulder, Colo 67351	Boulder, Colo 67351
12.	7400 Holbrook	7400 Holbrook
13.	13-B SW Kingman St.	13-B SW Kinsman St.
14.	32489 College Square	32498 College Square
15.	1516 Topp Ave.	1516 Top Ave.
16.	3040 Pumpkin Ln.	3040 Pumpkin Ln.
17.	80731 Dennis Dr.S.	80731 Dennis Dr. E.
18.	Grand Forks, ND 66761	Grand Forks ND 66671
19.	Miles City, MT 86940	Miles City, Mont. 86940
20.	3817 Winnipeg Terrace	3817 Winnepeg Terrace
21.	4220 Norway Apt 302	4220 Norway Apt 302
22.	69696 Regina Blvd.	69669 Regina Blvd.
23.	805 NW Yorkton Dr.	805 NW York Dr.
24.	3333 Olympia Ave.	3333 Olympia Ave.
25.	Fort Dodge, IA 53066	Fort Dodge, IA 53066
26.	67011 Watson Way	67011 Watson Way
27.	2027 Beaufort Bay	2027 Beauford Bay
28.	790 Valleyview	790 Valleyview
29.	Duluth, MN 49700	Duluth, NM 49700
30.	70140 Syracuse Dr.	70140 Syarcuse Dr.
31.	Watertown, NY 03515	Watertown, Del. 03515
32.	404 Marathon Blvd.	404 Marathon Blvd.
33.	1513 6th St SE	1513 6th St SE

#		
34.	75032 Geraldine Ave.	75023 Geraldine Ave.
35.	8894 Falcon Dr.	8894 Falcon Dr.
36.	Detroit, Mich 50533	Detroyt, Mich 50533
37.	3780 Medford Ave.	3780 Medford Ave.
38.	Sasktoon, Canada	Saskatoon, Canada
39.	2221 Yukon Place	2212 Yukon Place
40.	32104 Valdez Cr.	32104 Vadlez Cr.
41.	410 Ross	410 Rose
42.	Scranton, Penn. 05817	Scranton, Penn 05817
43.	9132 Montreal Dr.	91232 Montreal Dr.
44.	10844 Edmenton SW	10844 Edmanton SW
45.	891 Calgary St.	891 Calgary St.
46.	Rawlins, Wyo. 80832	Rawlins, Wyo. 80832
47.	3120 Glacierbay Dr.	3120 Glacier Bay Rd.
48.	7741 Vancouver Dr.	7714 Vancouver Dr.
49.	10902 Cranberry Ln.	10902 Cranberry Ln.
50.	505 Independance Way	505 Independance Way
51.	Boise, Idaho 86703	Boise, Idahoe 86703
52.	1309 Fulmer Blvd.	1309 Fulmer Blvd.
53.	16167 National Ave.	16167 S. National Ave.
54.	11370 Cambridge Ln.	11370 Cambridge Dr.
55.	2010 Brooks Dr.	2010 Brooks Dr.
56.	1341 NE Estevan Way	1341 NE Estavan Way
57.	Alexandria, LA 20344	Alexandria, LA 20344
58.	North Platte, Neb. 67019	North Platte, Neb. 67019
59.	Mt. Carmel Jct., Utah	Mt. Camel Jct., Utah
60.	51550 San Angelo Dr.	55150 San Angelo Dr.
61.	7070 Trinidad	7070 SW Trinidad
62.	1208 Cortez Circle	1208 Cortez Circle
63.	San Antonio, Texas 49711	San Antonio, Texas 49711
64.	2458 Ozark Lane	2458 Ozark Lane
65.	98712 Pierce Dr. NW	98712 Peirce Dr. NW
66.	1310 Barkley Ave.	1310 Barkley St.
67.	Lexington, KY 35087	Lexington, KY 35087
68.	1414 Englehart Pl.	1414 Engleheart Pl.
69.	8073 Evans St.	8073 Evans St.

70.	93222 S. La Crosse Rd.	93222 S. La Cross Rd.
71.	40399 Sleepy Hollow	40939 Sleepy Hollow
72.	Tallahassee, FLA 32140	Tallahasse, FLA 32140
73.	2049 Audubon Blvd.	2049 Audubon Ridge
74.	Pittsburgh, Penn 04321	Pittsburg, Penn 04321
75.	371 Dayton Dr.	371 Dayton Dr.
76.	Scottsbluff, Neb 69088	Scottsbluff, Neb. 69088
77.	33447 Redfield Dr.	33447 Redfeld Dr.
78.	16321 Laramie Ln.	16321 Laramie Lane
79.	1515 Salty Bay Rd.	1515 Salty Bay Rd.
80.	4000 Durham Dr. NE	4000 Durhamn Dr. NE
81.	Waterloo, IA 53440	Waterloo, IA 53440
82.	2080 Luverne Cr.	2080 Luvern Cr.
83.	13490 Winchester Way	13409 Winchester Way
84.	Strasburg, COLO 79810	Strasburg, COLO 79810
85.	Coconino, Ariz. 85611	Cocoanino, Ariz. 85611
86.	101 45th St. NE	101 45th Ave. NE
87.	So. Burle Ives Dr.	No. Burle Ives Dr.
88.	Glendale, Nev. 89033	Glendall, Nev. 89033
89.	40731 Los Padres Ln.	40731 Las Padres Ln.
90.	3201 Kimberly Dr.	3201 Kimberly Dr.
91.	Charleston, S.C. 11479	Charleston, S.C. 11470
92.	1084 Hermosillo Dr.	1084 Hermosillo Dr.
93.	74031 Caribou St.	743031 Caribou St.
94.	Santa Fe, NM 80449	Sante Fe, NY 80449
95.	4079 Carson	4079 Carsen

ANSWER SHEET TO EXERCISE 8

1. Ⓐ Ⓓ		33. Ⓐ Ⓓ		65. Ⓐ Ⓓ	
2. Ⓐ Ⓓ		34. Ⓐ Ⓓ		66. Ⓐ Ⓓ	
3. Ⓐ Ⓓ		35. Ⓐ Ⓓ		67. Ⓐ Ⓓ	
4. Ⓐ Ⓓ		36. Ⓐ Ⓓ		68. Ⓐ Ⓓ	
5. Ⓐ Ⓓ		37. Ⓐ Ⓓ		69. Ⓐ Ⓓ	
6. Ⓐ Ⓓ		38. Ⓐ Ⓓ		70. Ⓐ Ⓓ	
7. Ⓐ Ⓓ		39. Ⓐ Ⓓ		71. Ⓐ Ⓓ	
8. Ⓐ Ⓓ		40. Ⓐ Ⓓ		72. Ⓐ Ⓓ	
9. Ⓐ Ⓓ		41. Ⓐ Ⓓ		73. Ⓐ Ⓓ	
10. Ⓐ Ⓓ		42. Ⓐ Ⓓ		74. Ⓐ Ⓓ	
11. Ⓐ Ⓓ		43. Ⓐ Ⓓ		75. Ⓐ Ⓓ	
12. Ⓐ Ⓓ		44. Ⓐ Ⓓ		76. Ⓐ Ⓓ	
13. Ⓐ Ⓓ		45. Ⓐ Ⓓ		77. Ⓐ Ⓓ	
14. Ⓐ Ⓓ		46. Ⓐ Ⓓ		78. Ⓐ Ⓓ	
15. Ⓐ Ⓓ		47. Ⓐ Ⓓ		79. Ⓐ Ⓓ	
16. Ⓐ Ⓓ		48. Ⓐ Ⓓ		80. Ⓐ Ⓓ	
17. Ⓐ Ⓓ		49. Ⓐ Ⓓ		81. Ⓐ Ⓓ	
18. Ⓐ Ⓓ		50. Ⓐ Ⓓ		82. Ⓐ Ⓓ	
19. Ⓐ Ⓓ		51. Ⓐ Ⓓ		83. Ⓐ Ⓓ	
20. Ⓐ Ⓓ		52. Ⓐ Ⓓ		84. Ⓐ Ⓓ	
21. Ⓐ Ⓓ		53. Ⓐ Ⓓ		85. Ⓐ Ⓓ	
22. Ⓐ Ⓓ		54. Ⓐ Ⓓ		86. Ⓐ Ⓓ	
23. Ⓐ Ⓓ		55. Ⓐ Ⓓ		87. Ⓐ Ⓓ	
24. Ⓐ Ⓓ		56. Ⓐ Ⓓ		88. Ⓐ Ⓓ	
25. Ⓐ Ⓓ		57. Ⓐ Ⓓ		89. Ⓐ Ⓓ	
26. Ⓐ Ⓓ		58. Ⓐ Ⓓ		90. Ⓐ Ⓓ	
27. Ⓐ Ⓓ		59. Ⓐ Ⓓ		91. Ⓐ Ⓓ	
28. Ⓐ Ⓓ		60. Ⓐ Ⓓ		92. Ⓐ Ⓓ	
29. Ⓐ Ⓓ		61. Ⓐ Ⓓ		93. Ⓐ Ⓓ	
30. Ⓐ Ⓓ		62. Ⓐ Ⓓ		94. Ⓐ Ⓓ	
31. Ⓐ Ⓓ		63. Ⓐ Ⓓ		95. Ⓐ Ⓓ	
32. Ⓐ Ⓓ		64. Ⓐ Ⓓ			

(This page may be removed to mark answers.)

The Postal Exam Preparation Book

ANSWERS TO EXERCISE 8.

1.	D	33.	A	65.	D
2.	D	34.	D	66.	D
3.	A	35.	A	67.	A
4.	D	36.	D	68.	D
5.	D	37.	A	69.	A
6.	A	38.	D	70.	D
7.	A	39.	D	71.	D
8.	D	40.	D	72.	D
9.	A	41.	D	73.	D
10.	A	42.	A	74.	D
11.	A	43.	D	75.	A
12.	A	44.	D	76.	A
13.	D	45.	A	77.	D
14.	D	46.	A	78.	D
15.	D	47.	D	79.	A
16.	A	48.	D	80.	D
17.	D	49.	A	81.	A
18.	D	50.	A	82.	D
19.	D	51.	D	83.	D
20.	D	52.	A	84.	A
21.	A	53.	D	85.	D
22.	D	54.	D	86.	D
23.	D	55.	A	87.	D
24.	A	56.	D	88.	D
25.	A	57.	A	89.	D
26.	A	58.	A	90.	A
27.	D	59.	D	91.	D
28.	A	60.	D	92.	A
29.	D	61.	D	93.	D
30.	D	62.	A	94.	D
31.	D	63.	A	95.	D
32.	A	64.	A		

If Your Score Was:
—87 or more correct you have an excellent score
—between 55 and 86 correct you have a good score
—below 54 correct you should practice more

PART 2.

ADDRESS MEMORIZATION

A sample of what is entailed in this section is provided below. Study the 25 addresses for five minutes, and disregard the other part of this test for the moment. Try to implement what had been discussed earlier to make memorizing this exercise an easier task. When your allotted time is up, cover the key with a piece of paper, and do your best to match the given addresses to the appropriate category (ie. A, B, C, D, or E).

A	B	C	D	E
1500-1599 Trip	1700-1799 Trip	0700-0799 Trip	1300-1399 Trip	1800-1899 Trip
Bearclaw Ct.	Lantern Dr.	Harding Ave.	Bay View Dr.	Lynx Ct.
6600-6699 Brooks	5800-5899 Brooks	6000-6099 Brooks	7200-7299 Brooks	7400-7499 Brooks
Cherokee Blvd.	Post Cr.	Hampton Dr.	Mountainside Ln.	Willow St.
4300-4399 Carlson	4000-4099 Carlson	4900-4999 Carlson	3200-3299 Carlson	3600-3699 Carlson

1. 1500-1599 Trip
2. Post Cr.
3. 4900-4999 Carlson
4. 6000-6099 Brooks
5. Lynx Ct.
6. Cherokee Blvd.
7. 1300-1399 Trip
8. 7400-7499 Brooks
9. 4000-4099 Carlson
10. Hampton Dr.
11. 7200-7299 Brooks
12. Mountainside Ln.
13. Bearclaw Ct.
14. 0700-0799 Trip
15. Willow St.
16. 6600-6699 Brooks
17. 1500-1599 Trip
18. 4300-4399 Carlson
19. 7400-7499 Brooks
20. Bayview Dr.

1. Ⓐ Ⓑ Ⓒ Ⓓ Ⓔ
2. Ⓐ Ⓑ Ⓒ Ⓓ Ⓔ
3. Ⓐ Ⓑ Ⓒ Ⓓ Ⓔ
4. Ⓐ Ⓑ Ⓒ Ⓓ Ⓔ
5. Ⓐ Ⓑ Ⓒ Ⓓ Ⓔ
6. Ⓐ Ⓑ Ⓒ Ⓓ Ⓔ
7. Ⓐ Ⓑ Ⓒ Ⓓ Ⓔ
8. Ⓐ Ⓑ Ⓒ Ⓓ Ⓔ
9. Ⓐ Ⓑ Ⓒ Ⓓ Ⓔ
10. Ⓐ Ⓑ Ⓒ Ⓓ Ⓔ
11. Ⓐ Ⓑ Ⓒ Ⓓ Ⓔ
12. Ⓐ Ⓑ Ⓒ Ⓓ Ⓔ
13. Ⓐ Ⓑ Ⓒ Ⓓ Ⓔ
14. Ⓐ Ⓑ Ⓒ Ⓓ Ⓔ
15. Ⓐ Ⓑ Ⓒ Ⓓ Ⓔ
16. Ⓐ Ⓑ Ⓒ Ⓓ Ⓔ
17. Ⓐ Ⓑ Ⓒ Ⓓ Ⓔ
18. Ⓐ Ⓑ Ⓒ Ⓓ Ⓔ
19. Ⓐ Ⓑ Ⓒ Ⓓ Ⓔ
20. Ⓐ Ⓑ Ⓒ Ⓓ Ⓔ

Uncover the address key to see how well you did. If you scored 10 correct or better at this point you are doing terrific! If you didn't quite get that many correct, don't get discouraged. This kind of memory system is probably new to you and it will take a little practice to get an adequate feeling as to how to turn it to your advantage. Hopefully, at the end of this section, you will not only be able to work through the exercises in their entirety before the allotted time is up, but also acquire accuracy with speed.

These exercises are principally set up the same way in which you will see them on the actual exam. The first page of the exercise will provide you with an address similar to the former example you have just worked with, and you will be given three minutes (not five) to initially study it. After the allotted three minutes are up then proceed to the practice section of the exercise on the next couple of pages. This section is specifically designed to allow you to become more familiar in recalling answers and subsequently marking the appropriate categories. You will see that the address key is provided too; use it ONLY as a periodic reference in the cases of where you are unsure of an answer. Do not become too dependent on it as it will not be present as an aid while working on the actual test section. When you have run out of time working on the practice section, turn back to the first page of the exercise and study the address key for another five minutes. After the allotted time for final review is over turn to the back of the exercise and proceed with the actual test. You will have five minutes to complete as many of the 88 questions as possible. Again, do not become discouraged if you don't quite finish the exercise; it is not intended for you to do so, BUT do not be surprised if by the seventh or eighth exercise you can work completely through them and have a little extra time to spare!

EXERCISE 1.

TIME: 3 MINUTES

A	B	C	D	E
3300-3399 Burns	3900-3999 Burns	4500-4599 Burns	3600-3699 Burns	4000-4099 Burns
Harrison Dr.	Beaver Ave.	Liberty Rd.	Gregory Blvd.	Sunset Ln.
0800-0899 Pine	1100-1199 Pine	1000-1099 Pine	1500-1599 Pine	0700-0799 Pine
Olympic Ave.	Beatrice St.	Charlette Ct.	Salem	Monteray Pl.
9500-9599 Dibb	7300-7399 Dibb	8400-8499 Dibb	7600-7699 Dibb	8500-8599 Dibb

Study the address key above for three minutes. Then turn to page 134 and begin working on the practice exercise for three minutes, writing the appropriate letter next to the address. (There is no answer sheet for this practice section.) When you are through practicing, turn back to this page and study the address key for another five minutes. Once you have given the key a final review within the allotted time, immediately proceed to the test section of the exercise on page 135. You will have five minutes to do as many of the 88 questions as possible. The answers to the test are provided on page 139.

The same format will apply to the rest of the address memory exercises.

TIME: 3 MINUTES

A	B	C	D	E
3300-3399 Burns	3900-3999 Burns	4500-4599 Burns	3600-3699 Burns	4000-4099 Burns
Harrison Dr.	Beaver Ave.	Liberty Rd.	Gregory Blvd.	Sunset Ln.
0800-0899 Pine	1100-1199 Pine	1000-1099 Pine	1500-1599 Pine	0700-0799 Pine
Olympic Ave.	Beatrice St.	Charlette Ct.	Salem	Monteray Pl.
9500-9599 Dibb	7300-7399 Dibb	8400-8499 Dibb	7600-7699 Dibb	8500-8599 Dibb

1. Beatrice St.
2. 3300-3399 Burns
3. 3900-3999 Burns
4. Salem
5. Olympic Ave.
6. 0800-0899 Pine
7. 8400-8499 Dibb
8. Harrison Dr.
9. 4000-4099 Burns
10. 1000-1099 Pine
11. 7600-7699 Dibb
12. Harrison Dr.
13. Liberty Rd.
14. Beaver Ave.
15. 1500-1599 Pine
16. Monteray Pl.
17. 4500-4599 Burns
18. 9500-9599 Dibb
19. 8500-8599 Dibb
20. Gregory Blvd.
21. 1100-1199 Pine
22. Sunset Ln.
23. Charlette Ct.
24. 4500-4599 Burns
25. 3300-3399 Burns
26. Beatrice St.
27. Sunset Ln.
28. 1000-1099 Pine
29. 7300-7399 Dibb
30. Olympic Ave.
31. 3900-3999 Burns
32. Liberty Rd.
33. 8500-8599 Dibb
34. 1500-1599 Pine
35. Salem
36. Gregory Blvd.
37. 4000-4099 Burns
38. 8500-8599 Dibb
39. 1500-1599 Pine
40. Monteray Pl.
41. Gregory Blvd.
42. Charlette Ct.
43. 8500-8599 Dibb
44. 3600-3699 Burns
45. 0800-0899 Pine
46. 7300-7399 Dibb
47. Salem
48. Harrison Dr.
49. 3300-3399 Burns
50. 1100-1199 Pine
51. Beatrice St.
52. Beaver Ave.
53. 3600-3699 Burns
54. Monteray Pl.
55. 0700-0799 Pine
56. 9500-9599 Dibb
57. Olympic Ave.
58. 8400-8499 Dibb
59. 1100-1199 Pine
60. 4000-4099 Burns
61. Charlette Ct.
62. 1000-1099 Pine
63. 9500-9599 Dibb
64. 4500-4599 Burns
65. Beatrice St.
66. Harrison Dr.
67. 7300-7399 Dibb
68. 1500-1599 Pine
69. Monteray Pl.
70. 7600-7699 Dibb
71. 4500-4599 Burns
72. Sunset Ln.
73. Liberty Rd.
74. 8400-8499 Dibb
75. Beaver Ave.
76. 0700-0799 Pine
77. 7600-7699 Dibb
78. Salem
79. Gregory Blvd.
80. 0700-0799 Pine
81. 0800-0899 Pine
82. Olympic Ave.
83. Charlette Ct.
84. 3600-3699 Burns
85. Liberty Rd.
86. 1100-1199 Pine
87. 3900-3999 Burns
88. Salem

1. 9500-9599 Dibb
2. 0800-0899 Pine
3. Harrison Dr.
4. Beaver Ave.
5. 8400-8499 Dibb
6. 3900-3999 Burns
7. Gregory Blvd.
8. 7300-7399 Dibb
9. 1100-1199 Pine
10. Beatrice St.
11. 3300-3399 Burns
12. 0700-0799 Pine
13. Liberty Rd.
14. 7600-7699 Dibb
15. 4000-4099 Burns
16. Sunset Ln.
17. Salem
18. 1000-1099 Pine
19. 3600-3699 Burns
20. 0700-0799 Pine
21. Charlette Ct.
22. 8400-8499 Dibb
23. 3300-3399 Burns
24. Monteray Pl.
25. Gregory Blvd.
26. Olympic Ave.
27. 8500-8599 Dibb
28. 3900-3999 Burns
29. Charlette Ct.
30. 1100-1199 Pine
31. Beatrice St.
32. Harrison Dr.
33. 8400-8499 Dibb
34. Salem
35. 7300-7399 Dibb
36. Liberty Rd.
37. 0800-0899 Pine
38. 3900-3999 Burns
39. 9500-9599 Dibb
40. Beaver Ave.
41. Sunset Ln.
42. 1000-1099 Pine
43. 3300-3399 Burns
44. Beatrice St.
45. 1100-1199 Pine
46. 3600-3699 Burns
47. Olympic Ave.
48. Monteray Pl.
49. 9500-9599 Dibb
50. 4500-4599 Burns
51. Gregory Blvd.
52. 8500-8599 Dibb
53. Charlette Ct.
54. 1000-1099 Pine
55. 4000-4099 Burns
56. Liberty Rd.
57. 7600-7699 Dibb
58. Sunset Ln.
59. Olympic Ave.
60. Salem
61. 0700-0799 Pine
62. 3900-3999 Burns
63. Harrison Dr.
64. Monteray Pl.
65. 9500-9599 Dibb
66. 4000-4099 Burns
67. Beaver Ave.
68. Gregory Blvd.
69. 7300-7399 Dibb
70. 1100-1199 Pine
71. 3600-3699 Burns
72. Beatrice St.
73. 0800-0899 Pine
74. 4500-4599 Burns
75. 8400-8499 Dibb
76. Charlette Ct.
77. Monteray Pl.
78. 7600-7699 Dibb
79. Beaver Ave.
80. 4500-4599 Burns
81. Olympic Ave.
82. Sunset Ln.
83. 8500-8599 Dibb
84. Salem
85. 0800-0899 Pine
86. 3300-3399 Burns
87. Liberty Rd.
88. Harrison Dr.

The Postal Exam Preparation Book 135

ANSWER SHEET TO EXERCISE 1

1. Ⓐ Ⓑ Ⓒ Ⓓ Ⓔ   31. Ⓐ Ⓑ Ⓒ Ⓓ Ⓔ   61. Ⓐ Ⓑ Ⓒ Ⓓ Ⓔ
2. Ⓐ Ⓑ Ⓒ Ⓓ Ⓔ   32. Ⓐ Ⓑ Ⓒ Ⓓ Ⓔ   62. Ⓐ Ⓑ Ⓒ Ⓓ Ⓔ
3. Ⓐ Ⓑ Ⓒ Ⓓ Ⓔ   33. Ⓐ Ⓑ Ⓒ Ⓓ Ⓔ   63. Ⓐ Ⓑ Ⓒ Ⓓ Ⓔ
4. Ⓐ Ⓑ Ⓒ Ⓓ Ⓔ   34. Ⓐ Ⓑ Ⓒ Ⓓ Ⓔ   64. Ⓐ Ⓑ Ⓒ Ⓓ Ⓔ
5. Ⓐ Ⓑ Ⓒ Ⓓ Ⓔ   35. Ⓐ Ⓑ Ⓒ Ⓓ Ⓔ   65. Ⓐ Ⓑ Ⓒ Ⓓ Ⓔ
6. Ⓐ Ⓑ Ⓒ Ⓓ Ⓔ   36. Ⓐ Ⓑ Ⓒ Ⓓ Ⓔ   66. Ⓐ Ⓑ Ⓒ Ⓓ Ⓔ
7. Ⓐ Ⓑ Ⓒ Ⓓ Ⓔ   37. Ⓐ Ⓑ Ⓒ Ⓓ Ⓔ   67. Ⓐ Ⓑ Ⓒ Ⓓ Ⓔ
8. Ⓐ Ⓑ Ⓒ Ⓓ Ⓔ   38. Ⓐ Ⓑ Ⓒ Ⓓ Ⓔ   68. Ⓐ Ⓑ Ⓒ Ⓓ Ⓔ
9. Ⓐ Ⓑ Ⓒ Ⓓ Ⓔ   39. Ⓐ Ⓑ Ⓒ Ⓓ Ⓔ   69. Ⓐ Ⓑ Ⓒ Ⓓ Ⓔ
10. Ⓐ Ⓑ Ⓒ Ⓓ Ⓔ   40. Ⓐ Ⓑ Ⓒ Ⓓ Ⓔ   70. Ⓐ Ⓑ Ⓒ Ⓓ Ⓔ
11. Ⓐ Ⓑ Ⓒ Ⓓ Ⓔ   41. Ⓐ Ⓑ Ⓒ Ⓓ Ⓔ   71. Ⓐ Ⓑ Ⓒ Ⓓ Ⓔ
12. Ⓐ Ⓑ Ⓒ Ⓓ Ⓔ   42. Ⓐ Ⓑ Ⓒ Ⓓ Ⓔ   72. Ⓐ Ⓑ Ⓒ Ⓓ Ⓔ
13. Ⓐ Ⓑ Ⓒ Ⓓ Ⓔ   43. Ⓐ Ⓑ Ⓒ Ⓓ Ⓔ   73. Ⓐ Ⓑ Ⓒ Ⓓ Ⓔ
14. Ⓐ Ⓑ Ⓒ Ⓓ Ⓔ   44. Ⓐ Ⓑ Ⓒ Ⓓ Ⓔ   74. Ⓐ Ⓑ Ⓒ Ⓓ Ⓔ
15. Ⓐ Ⓑ Ⓒ Ⓓ Ⓔ   45. Ⓐ Ⓑ Ⓒ Ⓓ Ⓔ   75. Ⓐ Ⓑ Ⓒ Ⓓ Ⓔ
16. Ⓐ Ⓑ Ⓒ Ⓓ Ⓔ   46. Ⓐ Ⓑ Ⓒ Ⓓ Ⓔ   76. Ⓐ Ⓑ Ⓒ Ⓓ Ⓔ
17. Ⓐ Ⓑ Ⓒ Ⓓ Ⓔ   47. Ⓐ Ⓑ Ⓒ Ⓓ Ⓔ   77. Ⓐ Ⓑ Ⓒ Ⓓ Ⓔ
18. Ⓐ Ⓑ Ⓒ Ⓓ Ⓔ   48. Ⓐ Ⓑ Ⓒ Ⓓ Ⓔ   78. Ⓐ Ⓑ Ⓒ Ⓓ Ⓔ
19. Ⓐ Ⓑ Ⓒ Ⓓ Ⓔ   49. Ⓐ Ⓑ Ⓒ Ⓓ Ⓔ   79. Ⓐ Ⓑ Ⓒ Ⓓ Ⓔ
20. Ⓐ Ⓑ Ⓒ Ⓓ Ⓔ   50. Ⓐ Ⓑ Ⓒ Ⓓ Ⓔ   80. Ⓐ Ⓑ Ⓒ Ⓓ Ⓔ
21. Ⓐ Ⓑ Ⓒ Ⓓ Ⓔ   51. Ⓐ Ⓑ Ⓒ Ⓓ Ⓔ   81. Ⓐ Ⓑ Ⓒ Ⓓ Ⓔ
22. Ⓐ Ⓑ Ⓒ Ⓓ Ⓔ   52. Ⓐ Ⓑ Ⓒ Ⓓ Ⓔ   82. Ⓐ Ⓑ Ⓒ Ⓓ Ⓔ
23. Ⓐ Ⓑ Ⓒ Ⓓ Ⓔ   53. Ⓐ Ⓑ Ⓒ Ⓓ Ⓔ   83. Ⓐ Ⓑ Ⓒ Ⓓ Ⓔ
24. Ⓐ Ⓑ Ⓒ Ⓓ Ⓔ   54. Ⓐ Ⓑ Ⓒ Ⓓ Ⓔ   84. Ⓐ Ⓑ Ⓒ Ⓓ Ⓔ
25. Ⓐ Ⓑ Ⓒ Ⓓ Ⓔ   55. Ⓐ Ⓑ Ⓒ Ⓓ Ⓔ   85. Ⓐ Ⓑ Ⓒ Ⓓ Ⓔ
26. Ⓐ Ⓑ Ⓒ Ⓓ Ⓔ   56. Ⓐ Ⓑ Ⓒ Ⓓ Ⓔ   86. Ⓐ Ⓑ Ⓒ Ⓓ Ⓔ
27. Ⓐ Ⓑ Ⓒ Ⓓ Ⓔ   57. Ⓐ Ⓑ Ⓒ Ⓓ Ⓔ   87. Ⓐ Ⓑ Ⓒ Ⓓ Ⓔ
28. Ⓐ Ⓑ Ⓒ Ⓓ Ⓔ   58. Ⓐ Ⓑ Ⓒ Ⓓ Ⓔ   88. Ⓐ Ⓑ Ⓒ Ⓓ Ⓔ
29. Ⓐ Ⓑ Ⓒ Ⓓ Ⓔ   59. Ⓐ Ⓑ Ⓒ Ⓓ Ⓔ
30. Ⓐ Ⓑ Ⓒ Ⓓ Ⓔ   60. Ⓐ Ⓑ Ⓒ Ⓓ Ⓔ

(This page may be removed to mark answers.)

ANSWERS TO EXERCISE 1.

1.	A	31.	B	61.	E
2.	A	32.	A	62.	B
3.	A	33.	C	63.	A
4.	B	34.	D	64.	E
5.	C	35.	B	65.	A
6.	B	36.	C	66.	E
7.	D	37.	A	67.	B
8.	B	38.	B	68.	D
9.	B	39.	A	69.	B
10.	B	40.	B	70.	B
11.	A	41.	E	71.	D
12.	E	42.	C	72.	B
13.	C	43.	A	73.	A
14.	D	44.	B	74.	C
15.	E	45.	B	75.	C
16.	E	46.	D	76.	C
17.	D	47.	A	77.	E
18.	C	48.	E	78.	D
19.	D	49.	A	79.	B
20.	E	50.	C	80.	C
21.	C	51.	D	81.	A
22.	C	52.	E	82.	E
23.	A	53.	C	83.	E
24.	E	54.	C	84.	D
25.	D	55.	E	85.	A
26.	A	56.	C	86.	A
27.	E	57.	D	87.	C
28.	B	58.	E	88.	A
29.	C	59.	A		
30.	B	60.	D		

If Your Score Was:
—70 or more correct you have an excellent score
—between 45 and 69 correct you have a good score
—44 or below correct you should practice more

EXERCISE 2.

TIME: 3 MINUTES

A	B	C	D	E
7700-7799 Rose	6200-6299 Rose	7100-7199 Rose	5400-5499 Rose	6600-6699 Rose
Cactus Ln.	Maleroy Rd.	Phillips Dr.	Falcon Ridge	Franklin
6100-6199 Clem	4900-4999 Clem	8500-8599 Clem	6000-6099 Clem	5900-5999 Clem
Beechnut Dr.	Carver Blvd.	Washington Ave.	Scotts Bluff	Keyport St.
2300-2399 King	2700-2799 King	1900-1999 King	3000-3099 King	2000-2099 King

TIME: 3 MINUTES

A	B	C	D	E
7700-7799 Rose	6200-6299 Rose	7100-7199 Rose	5400-5499 Rose	6600-6699 Rose
Cactus Ln.	Maleroy Rd.	Phillips Dr.	Falcon Ridge	Franklin
6100-6199 Clem	4900-4999 Clem	8500-8599 Clem	6000-6099 Clem	5900-5999 Clem
Beechnut Dr.	Carver Blvd.	Washington Ave.	Scotts Bluff	Keyport St.
2300-2399 King	2700-2799 King	1900-1999 King	3000-3099 King	2000-2099 King

1. Maleroy Rd.
2. Phillips Dr.
3. 7700-7799 Rose
4. 4900-4999 Clem
5. Falcon Ridge
6. 1900-1999 King
7. Cactus Ln.
8. 6200-6299 Rose
9. Washington Ave.
10. 2300-2399 King
11. Beechnut Dr.
12. 8500-8599 Clem
13. 5400-5499 Rose
14. Franklin
15. 2000-2099 King
16. 6000-6099 Clem
17. Carver Blvd.
18. Keyport St.
19. 6600-6699 Rose
20. Scotts Bluff
21. 5400-5499 Rose
22. 6100-6199 Clem
23. Cactus Ln.
24. Washington Ave.
25. Franklin
26. 7700-7799 Rose
27. Maleroy Rd.
28. 5900-5999 Clem
29. Falcon Ridge
30. 1900-1999 King
31. Beechnut Dr.
32. 6000-6099 Clem
33. 2000-2099 King
34. 7100-7199 Rose
35. Phillips Dr.
36. 7700-7799 Rose
37. Scotts Bluff
38. 8500-8599 Clem
39. 2000-2099 King
40. Carver Blvd.
41. Falcon Ridge
42. Keyport St.
43. 1900-1999 King
44. Beechnut Dr.
45. 6000-6099 Clem
46. 2000-2099 King
47. Franklin
48. 6100-6199 Clem
49. 2700-2799 King
50. Cactus Ln.
51. Maleroy Rd.
52. 7100-7199 Rose
53. 3000-3099 King
54. Carver Blvd.
55. 6200-6299 Rose
56. 5900-5999 Clem
57. Scotts Bluff
58. 2300-2399 King
59. 6600-6699 Rose
60. Washington Ave.
61. 4900-4999 Clem
62. Keyport St.
63. 3000-3099 King
64. 7700-7799 Rose
65. Cactus Ln.
66. Phillips Dr.
67. 2700-2799 King
68. 6100-6199 Clem
69. 7100-7199 Rose
70. 6000-6099 Clem
71. Maleroy Rd.
72. 3000-3099 King
73. 8500-8599 Clem
74. Scotts Bluff
75. 5400-5499 Rose
76. 5900-5999 Clem
77. Keyport St.
78. Franklin
79. 6600-6699 Rose
80. Scotts Bluff
81. Phillips Dr.
82. 2300-2399 King
83. Falcon Ridge
84. 4900-4999 Clem
85. 6200-6299 Rose
86. Beechnut Dr.
87. Washington Ave.
88. Carver Blvd.

1. Franklin
2. Carver Blvd.
3. 1900-1999 King
4. 6000-6099 Clem
5. 2700-2799 King
6. Cactus Ln.
7. 6200-6299 Rose
8. 8500-8599 Clem
9. 2000-2099 King
10. Beechnut Dr.
11. Maleroy Rd.
12. 6100-6199 Clem
13. 5400-5499 Rose
14. Falcon Ridge
15. Scotts Bluff
16. 2300-2399 King
17. 7700-7799 Rose
18. Phillips Dr.
19. Keyport St.
20. 6200-6299 Rose
21. 4900-4999 Clem
22. 1900-1999 King
23. 3000-3099 King
24. 6600-6699 Rose
25. Washington Ave.
26. Franklin
27. 5400-5499 Rose
28. 8500-8599 Clem
29. Beechnut Dr.
30. 7100-7199 Rose
31. Carver Blvd.
32. 2300-2399 King
33. 6200-6299 Rose
34. 5900-5999 Clem
35. Cactus Ln.
36. Maleroy Rd.
37. 8500-8599 Clem
38. 2700-2799 King
39. 6600-6699 Rose
40. Phillips Dr.
41. Keyport St.
42. Washington Ave.
43. Falcon Ridge
44. Franklin
45. 6100-6199 Clem
46. Scotts Bluff
47. 7700-7799 Rose
48. 4900-4999 Clem
49. 3000-3099 King
50. Beechnut Dr.
51. 8500-8599 Clem
52. 6600-6699 Rose
53. Cactus Ln.
54. Scotts Bluff
55. 3000-3099 King
56. 5900-5999 Clem
57. Carver Blvd.
58. Phillips Dr.
59. 5400-5499 Rose
60. 4900-4999 Clem
61. 3000-3099 King
62. Falcon Ridge
63. 6000-6099 Clem
64. 7100-7199 Rose
65. Maleroy Rd.
66. Keyport St.
67. 2000-2099 King
68. Beechnut Dr.
69. 6200-6299 Rose
70. Washington Ave.
71. 2700-2799 King
72. 7100-7199 Rose
73. 6000-6099 Clem
74. Keyport St.
75. Franklin
76. Washington Ave.
77. 5900-5999 Clem
78. Scotts Bluff
79. Maleroy Rd.
80. 2000-2099 King
81. 7700-7799 Rose
82. 6100-6199 Clem
83. Phillips Dr.
84. Falcon Ridge
85. 1900-1999 King
86. 2300-2399 King
87. Carver Blvd.
88. Cactus Ln.

ANSWER SHEET TO EXERCISE 2

1. Ⓐ Ⓑ Ⓒ Ⓓ Ⓔ	31. Ⓐ Ⓑ Ⓒ Ⓓ Ⓔ	61. Ⓐ Ⓑ Ⓒ Ⓓ Ⓔ	
2. Ⓐ Ⓑ Ⓒ Ⓓ Ⓔ	32. Ⓐ Ⓑ Ⓒ Ⓓ Ⓔ	62. Ⓐ Ⓑ Ⓒ Ⓓ Ⓔ	
3. Ⓐ Ⓑ Ⓒ Ⓓ Ⓔ	33. Ⓐ Ⓑ Ⓒ Ⓓ Ⓔ	63. Ⓐ Ⓑ Ⓒ Ⓓ Ⓔ	
4. Ⓐ Ⓑ Ⓒ Ⓓ Ⓔ	34. Ⓐ Ⓑ Ⓒ Ⓓ Ⓔ	64. Ⓐ Ⓑ Ⓒ Ⓓ Ⓔ	
5. Ⓐ Ⓑ Ⓒ Ⓓ Ⓔ	35. Ⓐ Ⓑ Ⓒ Ⓓ Ⓔ	65. Ⓐ Ⓑ Ⓒ Ⓓ Ⓔ	
6. Ⓐ Ⓑ Ⓒ Ⓓ Ⓔ	36. Ⓐ Ⓑ Ⓒ Ⓓ Ⓔ	66. Ⓐ Ⓑ Ⓒ Ⓓ Ⓔ	
7. Ⓐ Ⓑ Ⓒ Ⓓ Ⓔ	37. Ⓐ Ⓑ Ⓒ Ⓓ Ⓔ	67. Ⓐ Ⓑ Ⓒ Ⓓ Ⓔ	
8. Ⓐ Ⓑ Ⓒ Ⓓ Ⓔ	38. Ⓐ Ⓑ Ⓒ Ⓓ Ⓔ	68. Ⓐ Ⓑ Ⓒ Ⓓ Ⓔ	
9. Ⓐ Ⓑ Ⓒ Ⓓ Ⓔ	39. Ⓐ Ⓑ Ⓒ Ⓓ Ⓔ	69. Ⓐ Ⓑ Ⓒ Ⓓ Ⓔ	
10. Ⓐ Ⓑ Ⓒ Ⓓ Ⓔ	40. Ⓐ Ⓑ Ⓒ Ⓓ Ⓔ	70. Ⓐ Ⓑ Ⓒ Ⓓ Ⓔ	
11. Ⓐ Ⓑ Ⓒ Ⓓ Ⓔ	41. Ⓐ Ⓑ Ⓒ Ⓓ Ⓔ	71. Ⓐ Ⓑ Ⓒ Ⓓ Ⓔ	
12. Ⓐ Ⓑ Ⓒ Ⓓ Ⓔ	42. Ⓐ Ⓑ Ⓒ Ⓓ Ⓔ	72. Ⓐ Ⓑ Ⓒ Ⓓ Ⓔ	
13. Ⓐ Ⓑ Ⓒ Ⓓ Ⓔ	43. Ⓐ Ⓑ Ⓒ Ⓓ Ⓔ	73. Ⓐ Ⓑ Ⓒ Ⓓ Ⓔ	
14. Ⓐ Ⓑ Ⓒ Ⓓ Ⓔ	44. Ⓐ Ⓑ Ⓒ Ⓓ Ⓔ	74. Ⓐ Ⓑ Ⓒ Ⓓ Ⓔ	
15. Ⓐ Ⓑ Ⓒ Ⓓ Ⓔ	45. Ⓐ Ⓑ Ⓒ Ⓓ Ⓔ	75. Ⓐ Ⓑ Ⓒ Ⓓ Ⓔ	
16. Ⓐ Ⓑ Ⓒ Ⓓ Ⓔ	46. Ⓐ Ⓑ Ⓒ Ⓓ Ⓔ	76. Ⓐ Ⓑ Ⓒ Ⓓ Ⓔ	
17. Ⓐ Ⓑ Ⓒ Ⓓ Ⓔ	47. Ⓐ Ⓑ Ⓒ Ⓓ Ⓔ	77. Ⓐ Ⓑ Ⓒ Ⓓ Ⓔ	
18. Ⓐ Ⓑ Ⓒ Ⓓ Ⓔ	48. Ⓐ Ⓑ Ⓒ Ⓓ Ⓔ	78. Ⓐ Ⓑ Ⓒ Ⓓ Ⓔ	
19. Ⓐ Ⓑ Ⓒ Ⓓ Ⓔ	49. Ⓐ Ⓑ Ⓒ Ⓓ Ⓔ	79. Ⓐ Ⓑ Ⓒ Ⓓ Ⓔ	
20. Ⓐ Ⓑ Ⓒ Ⓓ Ⓔ	50. Ⓐ Ⓑ Ⓒ Ⓓ Ⓔ	80. Ⓐ Ⓑ Ⓒ Ⓓ Ⓔ	
21. Ⓐ Ⓑ Ⓒ Ⓓ Ⓔ	51. Ⓐ Ⓑ Ⓒ Ⓓ Ⓔ	81. Ⓐ Ⓑ Ⓒ Ⓓ Ⓔ	
22. Ⓐ Ⓑ Ⓒ Ⓓ Ⓔ	52. Ⓐ Ⓑ Ⓒ Ⓓ Ⓔ	82. Ⓐ Ⓑ Ⓒ Ⓓ Ⓔ	
23. Ⓐ Ⓑ Ⓒ Ⓓ Ⓔ	53. Ⓐ Ⓑ Ⓒ Ⓓ Ⓔ	83. Ⓐ Ⓑ Ⓒ Ⓓ Ⓔ	
24. Ⓐ Ⓑ Ⓒ Ⓓ Ⓔ	54. Ⓐ Ⓑ Ⓒ Ⓓ Ⓔ	84. Ⓐ Ⓑ Ⓒ Ⓓ Ⓔ	
25. Ⓐ Ⓑ Ⓒ Ⓓ Ⓔ	55. Ⓐ Ⓑ Ⓒ Ⓓ Ⓔ	85. Ⓐ Ⓑ Ⓒ Ⓓ Ⓔ	
26. Ⓐ Ⓑ Ⓒ Ⓓ Ⓔ	56. Ⓐ Ⓑ Ⓒ Ⓓ Ⓔ	86. Ⓐ Ⓑ Ⓒ Ⓓ Ⓔ	
27. Ⓐ Ⓑ Ⓒ Ⓓ Ⓔ	57. Ⓐ Ⓑ Ⓒ Ⓓ Ⓔ	87. Ⓐ Ⓑ Ⓒ Ⓓ Ⓔ	
28. Ⓐ Ⓑ Ⓒ Ⓓ Ⓔ	58. Ⓐ Ⓑ Ⓒ Ⓓ Ⓔ	88. Ⓐ Ⓑ Ⓒ Ⓓ Ⓔ	
29. Ⓐ Ⓑ Ⓒ Ⓓ Ⓔ	59. Ⓐ Ⓑ Ⓒ Ⓓ Ⓔ		
30. Ⓐ Ⓑ Ⓒ Ⓓ Ⓔ	60. Ⓐ Ⓑ Ⓒ Ⓓ Ⓔ		

(This page may be removed to mark answers.)

ANSWERS TO EXERCISE 2.

1.	E	31.	B	61.	D
2.	B	32.	A	62.	D
3.	C	33.	B	63.	D
4.	D	34.	E	64.	C
5.	B	35.	A	65.	B
6.	A	36.	B	66.	E
7.	B	37.	C	67.	E
8.	C	38.	B	68.	A
9.	E	39.	E	69.	B
10.	A	40.	C	70.	C
11.	B	41.	E	71.	B
12.	A	42.	C	72.	C
13.	D	43.	D	73.	D
14.	D	44.	E	74.	E
15.	D	45.	A	75.	E
16.	A	46.	D	76.	C
17.	A	47.	A	77.	E
18.	C	48.	B	78.	D
19.	E	49.	D	79.	B
20.	B	50.	A	80.	E
21.	B	51.	C	81.	A
22.	C	52.	E	82.	A
23.	D	53.	A	83.	C
24.	E	54.	D	84.	D
25.	C	55.	D	85.	C
26.	E	56.	E	86.	A
27.	D	57.	B	87.	B
28.	C	58.	C	88.	A
29.	A	59.	D		
		60.	B		

If Your Score Was:
—70 or more correct you have an excellent score
—between 45 and 69 correct you have a good score
—44 or below correct you should practice more

EXERCISE 3.

TIME: 3 MINUTES

A	B	C	D	E
3700-3799 Boston	4300-4399 Boston	3500-3599 Boston	4000-4099 Boston	5000-5099 Boston
Eagle Ct.	Michigan Ave.	Alderwood	Falkner Dr.	Stevens Ln.
8200-8299 Sievers	8700-8799 Sievers	9400-9499 Sievers	9000-9099 Sievers	8000-8099 Sievers
Apache Jct.	Mt. Springs	Caldwell	Swanson Ave.	Benchard Dr.
0400-0499 St. John	1000-1099 St. John	2500-2599 St. John	0900-0999 St. John	2200-2299 St. John

TIME: 3 MINUTES

A	B	C	D	E
3700-3799 Boston	4300-4399 Boston	3500-3599 Boston	4000-4099 Boston	5000-5099 Boston
Eagle Ct.	Michigan Ave.	Alderwood	Falkner Dr.	Stevens Ln.
8200-8299 Sievers	8700-8799 Sievers	9400-9499 Sievers	9000-9099 Sievers	8000-8099 Sievers
Apache Jct.	Mt. Springs	Caldwell	Swanson Ave.	Benchard Dr.
0400-0499 St. John	1000-1099 St. John	2500-2599 St. John	0900-0999 St. John	2200-2299 St. John

1. 8700-8799 Sievers
2. 4300-4399 Boston
3. Michigan Ave.
4. 0400-0499 St. John
5. Eagle Ct.
6. Mt. Springs
7. 9000-9099 Sievers
8. 2200-2299 St. John
9. 5000-5099 Boston
10. Stevens Ln.
11. Alderwood
12. 1000-1099 St. John
13. 9400-9499 Sievers
14. Apache Jct.
15. Swanson Ave.
16. 3500-3599 Boston
17. Benchard Dr.
18. 8000-8099 Sievers
19. 2500-2599 St. John
20. Caldwell
21. Mt. Springs
22. 8000-8099 Sievers
23. 3700-3799 Boston
24. Falkner Dr.
25. 0900-0999 St. John
26. 8700-8799 Sievers
27. Eagle Ct.
28. 4000-4099 Boston
29. Michigan Ave.
30. Stevens Ln.
31. 4300-4399 Boston
32. 8200-8299 Sievers
33. 2500-2599 St. John
34. Alderwood
35. Apache Jct.
36. Michigan Ave.
37. Benchard Dr.
38. 9000-9099 Sievers
39. 2200-2299 St. John
40. Falkner Dr.
41. 5000-5099 Boston
42. Caldwell
43. Swanson Ave.
44. 1000-1099 St. John
45. 4300-4399 Boston
46. Apache Jct.
47. Mt. Springs
48. Stevens Ln.
49. 0400-0499 St. John
50. 8200-8299 Sievers
51. Caldwell
52. Eagle Ct.
53. 1000-1099 St. John
54. 4000-4099 Boston
55. 8700-8799 Sievers
56. Falkner Dr.
57. 3500-3599 Boston
58. 3700-3799 Boston
59. Swanson Ave.
60. Alderwood
61. 2200-2299 St. John
62. 3500-3599 Boston
63. 8200-8299 Sievers
64. Eagle Ct.
65. Benchard Dr.
66. 3700-3799 Boston
67. 8000-8099 Sievers
68. 2500-2599 St. John
69. Caldwell
70. 5000-5099 Boston
71. 9400-9499 Sievers
72. 0900-0999 St. John
73. Mt. Springs
74. 4000-4099 Boston
75. Swanson Ave.
76. Stevens Ln.
77. Benchard Dr.
78. 3700-3799 Boston
79. 9000-9099 Sievers
80. Caldwell
81. 9400-9499 Sievers
82. Michigan Ave.
83. 0400-0499 St. John
84. Alderwood
85. 0900-0999 St. John
86. 1000-1099 St. John
87. Falkner Dr.
88. Apache Jct.

The Postal Exam Preparation Book 147

1. 2500-2599 St. John
2. Benchard Dr.
3. Alderwood
4. 8700-8799 Sievers
5. Mt. Springs
6. Eagle Ct.
7. 0400-0499 St. John
8. 9000-9099 Sievers
9. 5000-5099 Boston
10. Michigan Ave.
11. 0900-0999 St. John
12. 8200-8299 Sievers
13. Apache Jct.
14. Stevens Ln.
15. 2200-2299 St. John
16. 1000-1099 St. John
17. Swanson Ave.
18. 9400-9499 Sievers
19. 3700-3799 Boston
20. Falkner Dr.
21. 4000-4099 Boston
22. 3500-3599 Boston
23. 8000-8099 Sievers
24. Alderwood
25. Caldwell
26. Michigan Ave.
27. 8000-8099 Sievers
28. 5000-5099 Boston
29. Apache Jct.
30. 2500-2599 St. John
31. 8700-8799 Sievers
32. Benchard Dr.
33. 4000-4099 Boston
34. Mt. Springs
35. 4300-4399 Boston
36. 8000-8099 Sievers
37. Falkner Dr.
38. 0400-0499 St. John
39. Swanson Ave.
40. Caldwell
41. Eagle Ct.
42. Stevens Ln.
43. 8700-8799 Sievers
44. Alderwood
45. 1000-1099 St. John
46. 3500-3599 Boston
47. Mt. Springs
48. 9400-9499 Sievers
49. Benchard Dr.
50. Falkner Dr.
51. Caldwell
52. Stevens Ln.
53. 2200-2299 St. John
54. 9000-9099 Sievers
55. 4300-4399 Boston
56. Michigan Ave.
57. Benchard Dr.
58. 4000-4099 Boston
59. 0900-0999 St. John
60. Alderwood
61. 8200-8299 Sievers
62. 5000-5099 Boston
63. Apache Jct.
64. Alderwood
65. 2500-2599 St. John
66. Eagle Ct.
67. 8700-8799 Sievers
68. Michigan Ave.
69. Stevens Ln.
70. 3700-3799 Boston
71. 3500-3599 Boston
72. 9400-9499 Sievers
73. Benchard Dr.
74. 2200-2299 St. John
75. Swanson Ave.
76. Eagle Ct.
77. Falkner Dr.
78. 0900-0999 St. John
79. 4300-4399 Boston
80. Apache Jct.
81. 1000-1099 St. John
82. Mt. Springs
83. Caldwell
84. 3700-3799 Boston
85. 9000-9099 Sievers
86. Swanson Ave.
87. 8200-8299 Sievers
88. 0400-0499 St. John

ANSWER SHEET TO EXERCISE 3.

1. Ⓐ Ⓑ Ⓒ Ⓓ Ⓔ 31. Ⓐ Ⓑ Ⓒ Ⓓ Ⓔ 61. Ⓐ Ⓑ Ⓒ Ⓓ Ⓔ
2. Ⓐ Ⓑ Ⓒ Ⓓ Ⓔ 32. Ⓐ Ⓑ Ⓒ Ⓓ Ⓔ 62. Ⓐ Ⓑ Ⓒ Ⓓ Ⓔ
3. Ⓐ Ⓑ Ⓒ Ⓓ Ⓔ 33. Ⓐ Ⓑ Ⓒ Ⓓ Ⓔ 63. Ⓐ Ⓑ Ⓒ Ⓓ Ⓔ
4. Ⓐ Ⓑ Ⓒ Ⓓ Ⓔ 34. Ⓐ Ⓑ Ⓒ Ⓓ Ⓔ 64. Ⓐ Ⓑ Ⓒ Ⓓ Ⓔ
5. Ⓐ Ⓑ Ⓒ Ⓓ Ⓔ 35. Ⓐ Ⓑ Ⓒ Ⓓ Ⓔ 65. Ⓐ Ⓑ Ⓒ Ⓓ Ⓔ
6. Ⓐ Ⓑ Ⓒ Ⓓ Ⓔ 36. Ⓐ Ⓑ Ⓒ Ⓓ Ⓔ 66. Ⓐ Ⓑ Ⓒ Ⓓ Ⓔ
7. Ⓐ Ⓑ Ⓒ Ⓓ Ⓔ 37. Ⓐ Ⓑ Ⓒ Ⓓ Ⓔ 67. Ⓐ Ⓑ Ⓒ Ⓓ Ⓔ
8. Ⓐ Ⓑ Ⓒ Ⓓ Ⓔ 38. Ⓐ Ⓑ Ⓒ Ⓓ Ⓔ 68. Ⓐ Ⓑ Ⓒ Ⓓ Ⓔ
9. Ⓐ Ⓑ Ⓒ Ⓓ Ⓔ 39. Ⓐ Ⓑ Ⓒ Ⓓ Ⓔ 69. Ⓐ Ⓑ Ⓒ Ⓓ Ⓔ
10. Ⓐ Ⓑ Ⓒ Ⓓ Ⓔ 40. Ⓐ Ⓑ Ⓒ Ⓓ Ⓔ 70. Ⓐ Ⓑ Ⓒ Ⓓ Ⓔ
11. Ⓐ Ⓑ Ⓒ Ⓓ Ⓔ 41. Ⓐ Ⓑ Ⓒ Ⓓ Ⓔ 71. Ⓐ Ⓑ Ⓒ Ⓓ Ⓔ
12. Ⓐ Ⓑ Ⓒ Ⓓ Ⓔ 42. Ⓐ Ⓑ Ⓒ Ⓓ Ⓔ 72. Ⓐ Ⓑ Ⓒ Ⓓ Ⓔ
13. Ⓐ Ⓑ Ⓒ Ⓓ Ⓔ 43. Ⓐ Ⓑ Ⓒ Ⓓ Ⓔ 73. Ⓐ Ⓑ Ⓒ Ⓓ Ⓔ
14. Ⓐ Ⓑ Ⓒ Ⓓ Ⓔ 44. Ⓐ Ⓑ Ⓒ Ⓓ Ⓔ 74. Ⓐ Ⓑ Ⓒ Ⓓ Ⓔ
15. Ⓐ Ⓑ Ⓒ Ⓓ Ⓔ 45. Ⓐ Ⓑ Ⓒ Ⓓ Ⓔ 75. Ⓐ Ⓑ Ⓒ Ⓓ Ⓔ
16. Ⓐ Ⓑ Ⓒ Ⓓ Ⓔ 46. Ⓐ Ⓑ Ⓒ Ⓓ Ⓔ 76. Ⓐ Ⓑ Ⓒ Ⓓ Ⓔ
17. Ⓐ Ⓑ Ⓒ Ⓓ Ⓔ 47. Ⓐ Ⓑ Ⓒ Ⓓ Ⓔ 77. Ⓐ Ⓑ Ⓒ Ⓓ Ⓔ
18. Ⓐ Ⓑ Ⓒ Ⓓ Ⓔ 48. Ⓐ Ⓑ Ⓒ Ⓓ Ⓔ 78. Ⓐ Ⓑ Ⓒ Ⓓ Ⓔ
19. Ⓐ Ⓑ Ⓒ Ⓓ Ⓔ 49. Ⓐ Ⓑ Ⓒ Ⓓ Ⓔ 79. Ⓐ Ⓑ Ⓒ Ⓓ Ⓔ
20. Ⓐ Ⓑ Ⓒ Ⓓ Ⓔ 50. Ⓐ Ⓑ Ⓒ Ⓓ Ⓔ 80. Ⓐ Ⓑ Ⓒ Ⓓ Ⓔ
21. Ⓐ Ⓑ Ⓒ Ⓓ Ⓔ 51. Ⓐ Ⓑ Ⓒ Ⓓ Ⓔ 81. Ⓐ Ⓑ Ⓒ Ⓓ Ⓔ
22. Ⓐ Ⓑ Ⓒ Ⓓ Ⓔ 52. Ⓐ Ⓑ Ⓒ Ⓓ Ⓔ 82. Ⓐ Ⓑ Ⓒ Ⓓ Ⓔ
23. Ⓐ Ⓑ Ⓒ Ⓓ Ⓔ 53. Ⓐ Ⓑ Ⓒ Ⓓ Ⓔ 83. Ⓐ Ⓑ Ⓒ Ⓓ Ⓔ
24. Ⓐ Ⓑ Ⓒ Ⓓ Ⓔ 54. Ⓐ Ⓑ Ⓒ Ⓓ Ⓔ 84. Ⓐ Ⓑ Ⓒ Ⓓ Ⓔ
25. Ⓐ Ⓑ Ⓒ Ⓓ Ⓔ 55. Ⓐ Ⓑ Ⓒ Ⓓ Ⓔ 85. Ⓐ Ⓑ Ⓒ Ⓓ Ⓔ
26. Ⓐ Ⓑ Ⓒ Ⓓ Ⓔ 56. Ⓐ Ⓑ Ⓒ Ⓓ Ⓔ 86. Ⓐ Ⓑ Ⓒ Ⓓ Ⓔ
27. Ⓐ Ⓑ Ⓒ Ⓓ Ⓔ 57. Ⓐ Ⓑ Ⓒ Ⓓ Ⓔ 87. Ⓐ Ⓑ Ⓒ Ⓓ Ⓔ
28. Ⓐ Ⓑ Ⓒ Ⓓ Ⓔ 58. Ⓐ Ⓑ Ⓒ Ⓓ Ⓔ 88. Ⓐ Ⓑ Ⓒ Ⓓ Ⓔ
29. Ⓐ Ⓑ Ⓒ Ⓓ Ⓔ 59. Ⓐ Ⓑ Ⓒ Ⓓ Ⓔ
30. Ⓐ Ⓑ Ⓒ Ⓓ Ⓔ 60. Ⓐ Ⓑ Ⓒ Ⓓ Ⓔ

(This page may be removed to mark answers.)

The Postal Exam Preparation Book

ANSWERS TO EXERCISE 3.

1.	C	31.	B	61.	A
2.	E	32.	E	62.	E
3.	C	33.	D	63.	A
4.	B	34.	B	64.	C
5.	B	35.	B	65.	C
6.	A	36.	E	66.	A
7.	A	37.	D	67.	B
8.	D	38.	A	68.	B
9.	E	39.	D	69.	E
10.	B	40.	C	70.	A
11.	D	41.	A	71.	C
12.	A	42.	E	72.	C
13.	A	43.	B	73.	E
14.	E	44.	C	74.	E
15.	E	45.	B	75.	D
16.	B	46.	C	76.	A
17.	D	47.	B	77.	D
18.	C	48.	C	78.	D
19.	A	49.	E	79.	B
20.	D	50.	D	80.	A
21.	D	51.	C	81.	B
22.	C	52.	E	82.	B
23.	E	53.	E	83.	C
24.	C	54.	D	84.	A
25.	C	55.	B	85.	D
26.	B	56.	B	86.	D
27.	E	57.	E	87.	A
28.	E	58.	D	88.	A
29.	A	59.	D		
30.	C	60.	C		

If Your Score Was:
—70 or more correct you have an excellent score
—between 45 and 69 correct you have a good score
—44 or below correct you should practice more

EXERCISE 4.

TIME: 3 MINUTES

A	B	C	D	E
1100-1199 Bryan	1700-1799 Bryan	0500-0599 Bryan	0700-0799 Bryan	1400-1499 Bryan
Burnett Dr.	Agatha Pass	Cranapple Dr.	Chestnut Rd.	Halverson Blvd.
420-4299 Bonn	360-3699 Bonn	3100-3199 Bonn	3200-3299 Bonn	4000-4099 Bonn
Clayburn	Wicker Way	Grey Ave.	Brownville St.	Tener Dr.
9900-9999 Dixon	9000-9099 Dixon	7400-7499 Dixon	8300-8399 Dixon	8900-8999 Dixon

TIME: 3 MINUTES

	A	B	C	D	E
	1100-1199 Bryan	1700-1799 Bryan	0500-0599 Bryan	0700-0799 Bryan	1400-1499 Bryan
	Burnett Dr.	Agatha Pass	Cranapple Dr.	Chestnut Rd.	Halverson Blvd.
	420-4299 Bonn	360-3699 Bonn	3100-3199 Bonn	3200-3299 Bonn	4000-4099 Bonn
	Clayburn	Wicker Way	Grey Ave.	Brownville St.	Tener Dr.
	9900-9999 Dixon	9000-9099 Dixon	7400-7499 Dixon	8300-8399 Dixon	8900-8999 Dixon

1. Tener Dr.
2. Wicker Way
3. Clayburn
4. 9900-9999 Dixon
5. 3600-3699 Bonn
6. 1100-1199 Bryan
7. Agatha Pass
8. 4000-4099 Bonn
9. Grey Ave.
10. 8300-8399 Dixon
11. Chestnut Rd.
12. 0500-0599 Bryan
13. Brownville St.
14. Burnett Dr.
15. 8900-8999 Dixon
16. 3100-3199 Bonn
17. 1700-1799 Bryan
18. Wicker Way
19. 7400-7499 Dixon
20. Cranapple Dr.
21. Burnett Dr.
22. 9000-9099 Dixon
23. 4000-4099 Bonn
24. Grey Ave.
25. Halverson Blvd.
26. 0500-0599 Bryan
27. 3600-3699 Bonn
28. 7400-7499 Dixon
29. Clayburn
30. Agatha Pass
31. Tener Dr.
32. 4200-4299 Bonn
33. 1400-1499 Bryan
34. Chestnut Rd.
35. 8300-8399 Dixon
36. Brownville St.
37. Cranapple Dr.
38. 0700-0799 Bryan
39. 3100-3199 Bonn
40. 8900-8999 Dixon
41. Clayburn
42. Grey Ave.
43. 1100-1199 Bryan
44. 7400-7499 Dixon
45. Halverson Blvd.
46. 0500-0599 Bryan
47. Wicker Way
48. 9900-9999 Dixon
49. 3200-3299 Bonn
50. Burnett Dr.
51. 1400-1499 Bryan
52. 9000-9099 Dixon
53. 3200-3299 Bonn
54. 0700-0799 Bryan
55. Tener Dr.
56. Cranapple Dr.
57. 1700-1799 Bryan
58. 3100-3199 Bonn
59. Halverson Blvd.
60. Agatha Pass
61. 1400-1499 Bryan
62. Cranapple Dr.
63. 9900-9999 Dixon
64. 4200-4299 Bonn
65. Clayburn
66. Brownville St.
67. 0700-0799 Bryan
68. Tener Dr.
69. 3600-3699 Bonn
70. Chestnut Rd.
71. 1700-1799 Bryan
72. Clayburn
73. Agatha Pass
74. 8300-8399 Dixon
75. 3200-3299 Bonn
76. 1100-1199 Bryan
77. Chestnut Rd.
78. 9000-9099 Dixon
79. 4000-4099 Bonn
80. Grey Ave.
81. Halverson Blvd.
82. Brownville St.
83. 8900-8999 Dixon
84. 4200-4299 Bonn
85. Cranapple Dr.
86. Wicker Way
87. Burnett Dr.
88. 7400-7499 Dixon

The Postal Exam Preparation Book 153

1. Grey Ave.
2. Brownville St.
3. 1100-1199 Bryan
4. 3600-3699 Bonn
5. Wicker Way
6. 0500-0599 Bryan
7. Clayburn
8. 7400-7499 Dixon
9. 3100-3199 Bonn
10. 1400-1499 Bryan
11. Cranapple Dr.
12. Tener Dr.
13. 9990-9999 Dixon
14. 3200-3299 Bonn
15. Burnett Dr.
16. Agatha Pass
17. 1700-1799 Bryan
18. 8300-8399 Dixon
19. Tener Dr.
20. 3100-3199 Bonn
21. 8900-8999 Dixon
22. Wicker Way
23. Grey Ave.
24. 4000-4099 Bonn
25. Burnett Dr.
26. Chestnut Rd.
27. 3600-3699 Bonn
28. Agatha Pass
29. 9900-9999 Dixon
30. 8300-8399 Dixon
31. 1100-1199 Bryan
32/ Grey Ave.
33. 1700-1799 Bryan
34. Burnett Dr.
35. Halverson Blvd.
36. 4200-4299 Bonn
37. 9000-9099 Dixon
38. Clayburn
39. Tener Dr.
40. 0700-0799 Bryan
41. 3100-3199 Bonn
42. Cranapple Dr.
43. 1400-1499 Bryan
44. Wicker Way
45. Halverson Blvd.
46. 0700-0799 Bryan
47. 4000-4099 Bonn
48. Chestnut Rd.
49. 7400-7499 Dixon
50. Brownville St.
51. Tener Dr.
52. Burnett Dr.
53. 3200-3299 Bonn
54. Halverson Blvd.
55. Clayburn
56. 3600-3699 Bonn
57. 1400-1499 Bryan
58. 9900-9999 Dixon
59. Grey Ave.
60. Agatha Pass
61. 8900-8999 Dixon
62. 0500-0599 Bryan
63. 4200-4299 Bonn
64. 8300-8399 Dixon
65. Brownville St.
66. Cranapple Dr.
67. 8900-8999 Dixon
68. Chestnut Rd.
69. 9000-9099 Dixon
70. 1700-1799 Bryan
71. 4000-4099 Bonn
72. 7400-7499 Dixon
73. 0700-0799 Bryan
74. Chestnut Rd.
75. Wicker Way
76. Agatha Pass
77. Cranapple Dr.
78. 4200-4299 Bonn
79. 1100-1199 Bryan
80. Clayburn
81. Brownville St.
82. 9000-9099 Dixon
83. 3200-3299 Bonn
84. Halverson Blvd.
85. 1400-1499 Bryan
86. Grey Ave.
87. 0500-0599 Bryan
88. Tener Dr.

ANSWER SHEET TO EXERCISE 4

1. Ⓐ Ⓑ Ⓒ Ⓓ Ⓔ   31. Ⓐ Ⓑ Ⓒ Ⓓ Ⓔ   61. Ⓐ Ⓑ Ⓒ Ⓓ Ⓔ
2. Ⓐ Ⓑ Ⓒ Ⓓ Ⓔ   32. Ⓐ Ⓑ Ⓒ Ⓓ Ⓔ   62. Ⓐ Ⓑ Ⓒ Ⓓ Ⓔ
3. Ⓐ Ⓑ Ⓒ Ⓓ Ⓔ   33. Ⓐ Ⓑ Ⓒ Ⓓ Ⓔ   63. Ⓐ Ⓑ Ⓒ Ⓓ Ⓔ
4. Ⓐ Ⓑ Ⓒ Ⓓ Ⓔ   34. Ⓐ Ⓑ Ⓒ Ⓓ Ⓔ   64. Ⓐ Ⓑ Ⓒ Ⓓ Ⓔ
5. Ⓐ Ⓑ Ⓒ Ⓓ Ⓔ   35. Ⓐ Ⓑ Ⓒ Ⓓ Ⓔ   65. Ⓐ Ⓑ Ⓒ Ⓓ Ⓔ
6. Ⓐ Ⓑ Ⓒ Ⓓ Ⓔ   36. Ⓐ Ⓑ Ⓒ Ⓓ Ⓔ   66. Ⓐ Ⓑ Ⓒ Ⓓ Ⓔ
7. Ⓐ Ⓑ Ⓒ Ⓓ Ⓔ   37. Ⓐ Ⓑ Ⓒ Ⓓ Ⓔ   67. Ⓐ Ⓑ Ⓒ Ⓓ Ⓔ
8. Ⓐ Ⓑ Ⓒ Ⓓ Ⓔ   38. Ⓐ Ⓑ Ⓒ Ⓓ Ⓔ   68. Ⓐ Ⓑ Ⓒ Ⓓ Ⓔ
9. Ⓐ Ⓑ Ⓒ Ⓓ Ⓔ   39. Ⓐ Ⓑ Ⓒ Ⓓ Ⓔ   69. Ⓐ Ⓑ Ⓒ Ⓓ Ⓔ
10. Ⓐ Ⓑ Ⓒ Ⓓ Ⓔ   40. Ⓐ Ⓑ Ⓒ Ⓓ Ⓔ   70. Ⓐ Ⓑ Ⓒ Ⓓ Ⓔ
11. Ⓐ Ⓑ Ⓒ Ⓓ Ⓔ   41. Ⓐ Ⓑ Ⓒ Ⓓ Ⓔ   71. Ⓐ Ⓑ Ⓒ Ⓓ Ⓔ
12. Ⓐ Ⓑ Ⓒ Ⓓ Ⓔ   42. Ⓐ Ⓑ Ⓒ Ⓓ Ⓔ   72. Ⓐ Ⓑ Ⓒ Ⓓ Ⓔ
13. Ⓐ Ⓑ Ⓒ Ⓓ Ⓔ   43. Ⓐ Ⓑ Ⓒ Ⓓ Ⓔ   73. Ⓐ Ⓑ Ⓒ Ⓓ Ⓔ
14. Ⓐ Ⓑ Ⓒ Ⓓ Ⓔ   44. Ⓐ Ⓑ Ⓒ Ⓓ Ⓔ   74. Ⓐ Ⓑ Ⓒ Ⓓ Ⓔ
15. Ⓐ Ⓑ Ⓒ Ⓓ Ⓔ   45. Ⓐ Ⓑ Ⓒ Ⓓ Ⓔ   75. Ⓐ Ⓑ Ⓒ Ⓓ Ⓔ
16. Ⓐ Ⓑ Ⓒ Ⓓ Ⓔ   46. Ⓐ Ⓑ Ⓒ Ⓓ Ⓔ   76. Ⓐ Ⓑ Ⓒ Ⓓ Ⓔ
17. Ⓐ Ⓑ Ⓒ Ⓓ Ⓔ   47. Ⓐ Ⓑ Ⓒ Ⓓ Ⓔ   77. Ⓐ Ⓑ Ⓒ Ⓓ Ⓔ
18. Ⓐ Ⓑ Ⓒ Ⓓ Ⓔ   48. Ⓐ Ⓑ Ⓒ Ⓓ Ⓔ   78. Ⓐ Ⓑ Ⓒ Ⓓ Ⓔ
19. Ⓐ Ⓑ Ⓒ Ⓓ Ⓔ   49. Ⓐ Ⓑ Ⓒ Ⓓ Ⓔ   79. Ⓐ Ⓑ Ⓒ Ⓓ Ⓔ
20. Ⓐ Ⓑ Ⓒ Ⓓ Ⓔ   50. Ⓐ Ⓑ Ⓒ Ⓓ Ⓔ   80. Ⓐ Ⓑ Ⓒ Ⓓ Ⓔ
21. Ⓐ Ⓑ Ⓒ Ⓓ Ⓔ   51. Ⓐ Ⓑ Ⓒ Ⓓ Ⓔ   81. Ⓐ Ⓑ Ⓒ Ⓓ Ⓔ
22. Ⓐ Ⓑ Ⓒ Ⓓ Ⓔ   52. Ⓐ Ⓑ Ⓒ Ⓓ Ⓔ   82. Ⓐ Ⓑ Ⓒ Ⓓ Ⓔ
23. Ⓐ Ⓑ Ⓒ Ⓓ Ⓔ   53. Ⓐ Ⓑ Ⓒ Ⓓ Ⓔ   83. Ⓐ Ⓑ Ⓒ Ⓓ Ⓔ
24. Ⓐ Ⓑ Ⓒ Ⓓ Ⓔ   54. Ⓐ Ⓑ Ⓒ Ⓓ Ⓔ   84. Ⓐ Ⓑ Ⓒ Ⓓ Ⓔ
25. Ⓐ Ⓑ Ⓒ Ⓓ Ⓔ   55. Ⓐ Ⓑ Ⓒ Ⓓ Ⓔ   85. Ⓐ Ⓑ Ⓒ Ⓓ Ⓔ
26. Ⓐ Ⓑ Ⓒ Ⓓ Ⓔ   56. Ⓐ Ⓑ Ⓒ Ⓓ Ⓔ   86. Ⓐ Ⓑ Ⓒ Ⓓ Ⓔ
27. Ⓐ Ⓑ Ⓒ Ⓓ Ⓔ   57. Ⓐ Ⓑ Ⓒ Ⓓ Ⓔ   87. Ⓐ Ⓑ Ⓒ Ⓓ Ⓔ
28. Ⓐ Ⓑ Ⓒ Ⓓ Ⓔ   58. Ⓐ Ⓑ Ⓒ Ⓓ Ⓔ   88. Ⓐ Ⓑ Ⓒ Ⓓ Ⓔ
29. Ⓐ Ⓑ Ⓒ Ⓓ Ⓔ   59. Ⓐ Ⓑ Ⓒ Ⓓ Ⓔ
30. Ⓐ Ⓑ Ⓒ Ⓓ Ⓔ   60. Ⓐ Ⓑ Ⓒ Ⓓ Ⓔ

(This page may be removed to mark answers.)

ANSWERS TO EXERCISE 4

1.	C	31.	A	61.	E
2.	D	32.	C	62.	C
3.	A	33.	B	63.	A
4.	B	34.	A	64.	D
5.	B	35.	E	65.	D
6.	C	36.	A	66.	C
7.	A	37.	B	67.	E
8.	C	38.	A	68.	D
9.	C	39.	E	69.	B
10.	E	40.	D	70.	B
11.	C	41.	C	71.	E
12.	E	42.	C	72.	C
13.	A	43.	E	73.	D
14.	D	44.	B	74.	D
15.	A	45.	E	75.	B
16.	B	46.	D	76.	B
17.	B	47.	E	77.	C
18.	D	48.	D	78.	A
19.	E	49.	C	79.	A
20.	C	50.	D	80.	A
21.	E	51.	E	81.	D
22.	B	52.	A	82.	B
23.	C	53.	D	83.	D
24.	E	54.	E	84.	E
25.	A	55.	A	85.	E
26.	D	56.	B	86.	C
27.	B	57.	E	87.	C
28.	B	58.	A	88.	E
29.	A	59.	C		
30.	D	60.	B		

If Your Score Was:
—70 or more correct you have an excellent score
—between 45 and 69 correct you have a good score
—44 or below correct you should practice more

EXERCISE 5.

TIME: 3 MINUTES

A	B	C	D	E
4800-4899 Brice	5300-5399 Brice	4700-4799 Brice	5100-5199 Brice	4400-4499 Brice
Covington	Plaza Dr.	Klondyke	Cooper Ave.	Raleigh
6400-6499 Fern	7300-7399 Fern	5600-5699 Fern	5500-5599 Fern	6000-6099 Fern
Clover Leaf	Granite Dr.	Rainbow Ct.	Harrisburg	Melbourne
2200-2299 Amhurst	0600-0699 Amhurst	1500-1599 Amhurst	3300-3399 Amhurst	1200-1299 Amhurst

TIME: 3 MINUTES

A	B	C	D	E
4800-4899 Brice	5300-5399 Brice	4700-4799 Brice	5100-5199 Brice	4400-4499 Brice
Covington	Plaza Dr.	Klondyke	Cooper Ave.	Raleigh
6400-6499 Fern	7300-7399 Fern	5600-5699 Fern	5500-5599 Fern	6000-6099 Fern
Clover Leaf	Granite Dr.	Rainbow Ct.	Harrisburg	Melbourne
2200-2299 Amhurst	0600-0699 Amhurst	1500-1599 Amhurst	3300-3399 Amhurst	1200-1299 Amhurst

1. 4800-4899 Brice
2. Granite Dr.
3. 5500-5599 Fern
4. Rainbow Ct.
5. 5100-5199 Brice
6. 5600-5699 Fern
7. Covington
8. Clover Leaf
9. 5300-5399 Brice
10. 2200-2299 Amhurst
11. Klondyke
12. 3300-3399 Amhurst
13. 6000-6099 Fern
14. 4400-4499 Brice
15. Melbourne
16. 1500-1599 Amhurst
17. Harrisburg
18. Cooper Ave.
19. 1200-1299 Amhurst
20. Plaza Dr.
21. Rainbow Ct.
22. Raleigh
23. Melbourne
24. 4700-4799 Brice
25. 6400-6499 Fern
26. Plaza Dr.
27. 5300-5399 Brice
28. 0600-0699 Amhurst
29. 7300-7399 Fern
30. Covington
31. Clover Leaf
32. Granite Dr.
33. Harrisburg
34. Raleigh
35. 5100-5199 Brice
36. 2200-2299 Amhurst
37. Klondyke
38. 4700-4799 Brice
39. 3300-3399 Amhurst
40. 6000-6099 Fern
41. Clover Leaf
42. Cooper Ave.
43. 5300-5399 Brice
44. 7300-7399 Fern
45. Rainbow Ct.
46. 5600-5699 Fern
47. 0600-0699 Amhurst
48. Harrisburg
49. 4800-4899 Brice
50. Covington
51. Plaza Dr.
52. 6400-6499 Fern
53. 2200-2299 Amhurst
54. 1200-1299 Amhurst
55. Granite Dr.
56. Cooper Ave.
57. 5500-5599 Fern
58. 4400-4499 Brice
59. 1200-1299 Amhurst
60. Klondyke
61. 5500-5599 Fern
62. 0600-0699 Amhurst
63. Rainbow Ct.
64. Melbourne
65. 4400-4499 Brice
66. 4800-4899 Brice
67. Klondyke
68. 5500-5599 Fern
69. 6400-6499 Fern
70. 1500-1599 Amhurst
71. Harrisburg
72. Plaza Dr.
73. 3300-3399 Amhurst
74. Cooper Ave.
75. Raleigh
76. 4700-4799 Brice
77. 6000-6099 Fern
78. 1500-1599 Amhurst
79. Granite Dr.
80. Klondyke
81. Covington
82. Raleigh
83. 5100-5199 Brice
84. 7300-7399 Fern
85. Clover Leaf
86. 5600-5699 Fern
87. 4700-4799 Brice
88. Melbourne

1. Covington
2. 5300-5399 Brice
3. 5600-5699 Fern
4. Plaza Dr.
5. Cooper Ave.
6. 2200-2299 Amhurst
7. 1200-1299 Amhurst
8. Granite Dr.
9. 4400-4499 Brice
10. 6400-6499 Fern
11. Clover Leaf
12. Rainbow Ct.
13. Raleigh
14. 4800-4899 Brice
15. 0600-0699 Amhurst
16. 7300-7399 Fern
17. Harrisburg
18. 6000-6099 Fern
19. 4700-4799 Brice
20. Cooper Ave.
21. Klondyke
22. 5500-5599 Fern
23. 5100-5199 Brice
24. 1500-1599 Amhurst
25. Rainbow Ct.
26. 6400-6499 Fern
27. Melbourne
28. 5600-5699 Fern
29. 5300-5399 Brice
30. Covington
31. 1200-1299 Amhurst
32. Raleigh
33. 0600-0699 Amhurst
34. 6400-6499 Fern
35. Plaza Dr.
36. Klondyke
37. Clover Leaf
38. 5500-5599 Fern
39. 2200-2299 Amhurst
40. 4700-4799 Brice
41. Cooper Ave.
42. 4800-4899 Brice
43. Granite Dr.
44. Harrisburg
45. Melbourne
46. 1500-1599 Amhurst
47. 5100-5199 Brice
48. Covington
49. Rainbow Ct.
50. 1200-1299 Amhurst
51. Raleigh
52. 3300-3399 Amhurst
53. Melbourne
54. 5600-5699 Fern
55. 5500-5599 Fern
56. Plaza Dr.
57. 5300-5399 Brice
58. Cooper Ave.
59. 6400-6499 Fern
60. 4800-4899 Brice
61. Klondyke
62. Granite Dr.
63. 7300-7399 Fern
64. 4400-4499 Brice
65. Clover Leaf
66. 3300-3399 Amhurst
67. Rainbow Ct.
68. 2200-2299 Amhurst
69. 5100-5199 Brice
70. 6000-6099 Fern
71. Plaza Dr.
72. Harrisburg
73. 4800-4899 Brice
74. 1500-1599 Amhurst
75. Melbourne
76. Rainbow Ct.
77. Harrisburg
78. 4700-4799 Brice
79. 6000-6099 Fern
80. Klondyke
81. Raleigh
82. 3300-3399 Amhurst
83. Clover Leaf
84. Granite Dr.
85. 0600-0699 Amhurst
86. 7300-7399 Fern
87. Covington
88. 4400-4499 Brice

ANSWER SHEET TO EXERCISE 5

(This page may be removed to mark answers.)

ANSWERS TO EXERCISE 5.

1.	A	31.	E	61.	C
2.	B	32.	E	62.	B
3.	C	33.	B	63.	B
4.	B	34.	A	64.	E
5.	D	35.	B	65.	A
6.	A	36.	C	66.	D
7.	E	37.	A	67.	C
8.	B	38.	D	68.	A
9.	E	39.	A	69.	D
10.	A	40.	C	70.	E
11.	A	41.	D	71.	B
12.	C	42.	A	72.	D
13.	E	43.	B	73.	A
14.	A	44.	D	74.	C
15.	B	45.	E	75.	E
16.	B	46.	C	76.	C
17.	D	47.	D	77.	D
18.	E	48.	A	78.	C
19.	C	49.	C	79.	E
20.	D	50.	E	80.	C
21.	C	51.	E	81.	E
22.	D	52.	D	82.	D
23.	D	53.	E	83.	A
24.	C	54.	C	84.	B
25.	C	55.	D	85.	B
26.	A	56.	B	86.	B
27.	E	57.	B	87.	A
28.	C	58.	D	88.	E
29.	B	59.	A		
30.	A	60.	A		

If Your Score Was:
—70 or more correct you have an excellent score
—between 45 and 69 correct you have a good score
—44 or below correct you should practice more

The Postal Exam Preparation Book 163

EXERCISE 6.

TIME: 3 MINUTES

A	B	C	D	E
4500-4599 Flint	3400-3499 Flint	4100-4199 Flint	4700-4799 Flint	3900-3999 Flint
Armstrong Dr.	Bridgeview	Knoll Rd.	Bingham	Pinecone Ave.
6700-6799 Simon	7200-7299 Simon	7000-7099 Simon	6400-6499 Simon	5200-5299 Simon
Bender Way	Jackson	Ford Ave.	Averley Dr.	Walnut Grove
1200-1299 Grant	3100-3199 Grant	2900-2999 Grant	0300-0399 Grant	1300-1399 Grant

TIME: 3 MINUTES

A	B	C	D	E
4500-4599 Flint	3400-3499 Flint	4100-4199 Flint	4700-4799 Flint	3900-3999 Flint
Armstrong Dr.	Bridgeview	Knoll Rd.	Bingham	Pinecone Ave.
6700-6799 Simon	7200-7299 Simon	7000-7099 Simon	6400-6499 Simon	5200-5299 Simon
Bender Way	Jackson	Ford Ave.	Averley Dr.	Walnut Grove
1200-1299 Grant	3100-3199 Grant	2900-2999 Grant	0300-0399 Grant	1300-1399 Grant

1. Walnut Grove
2. 1200-1299 Grant
3. 6400-6499 Simon
4. Bender Way
5. Jackson
6. 2900-2999 Grant
7. 4500-4599 Flint
8. Ford Ave.
9. Averley Dr.
10. Bridgeview
11. 4100-4199 Flint
12. 7200-7299 Simon
13. Bingham
14. 3100-3199 Grant
15. 6400-6499 Simon
16. Knoll Rd.
17. 3900-3999 Flint
18. Jackson
19. 1300-1399 Grant
20. Walnut Grove
21. Armstrong Dr.
22. 6700-6799 Simon
23. Averley Dr.
24. 4500-4599 Flint
25. 0300-0399 Grant
26. Pinecone Ave.
27. Bender Way
28. Pinecone Ave.
29. 1200-1299 Grant
30. 2900-2999 Grant
31. 7000-7099 Simon
32. Bridgeview
33. Jackson
34. 6400-6499 Simon
35. 1300-1399 Grant
36. Walnut Grove
37. 3400-3499 Flint
38. 4700-4799 Flint
39. 7200-7299 Simon
40. Pinecone Ave.
41. Jackson
42. 6400-6499 Simon
43. Armstrong Dr.
44. 1300-1399 Grant
45. 3900-3999 Flint
46. 4500-4599 Flint
47. Knoll Rd.
48. Ford Ave.
49. 4100-4199 Flint
50. 5200-5299 Simon
51. 4700-4799 Flint
52. Averley Dr.
53. Bridgeview
54. Knoll Rd.
55. 3100-3199 Grant
56. 7200-7299 Simon
57. 3400-3499 Flint
58. 2900-2999 Grant
59. 7000-7099 Simon
60. Pinecone Ave.
61. 6700-6799 Simon
62. Ford Ave.
63. Walnut Grove
64. Knoll Rd.
65. Bingham
66. 1200-1299 Grant
67. 6700-6799 Simon
68. 0300-0399 Grant
69. Bender Way
70. Armstrong Dr.
71. 3400-3499 Flint
72. 5200-5299 Simon
73. Bingham
74. 3900-3999 Flint
75. 4100-4199 Flint
76. Averley Dr.
77. 7200-7299 Simon
78. 7000-7099 Simon
79. 4700-4799 Flint
80. Bridgeview
81. 0300-0399 Grant
82. Bender Way
83. 3100-3199 Grant
84. Armstrong Dr.
85. 2900-2999 Grant
86. Ford Ave.
87. Bingham
88. 5200-5299 Simon

1. Pinecone Ave.
2. 4500-4599 Flint
3. 2900-2999 Grant
4. Armstrong Dr.
5. Averley Dr.
6. 6700-6799 Simon
7. 0300-0399 Grant
8. Knoll Rd.
9. Walnut Grove
10. 4100-4199 Flint
11. 3900-3999 Flint
12. 6400-6499 Simon
13. Bridgeview
14. 4700-4799 Flint
15. 7000-7099 Simon
16. Bingham
17. Bender Way
18. Ford Ave.
19. 1200-1299 Grant
20. 5200-5299 Simon
21. Jackson
22. 3400-3499 Flint
23. 7200-7299 Simon
24. 0300-0399 Grant
25. Averley Dr.
26. Walnut Grove
27. 6400-6499 Simon
28. 3100-3199 Grant
29. Jackson
30. Averley Dr.
31. 6700-6799 Simon
32. 4500-4599 Flint
33. 2900-2999 Grant
34. 4700-4799 Flint
35. Armstrong Dr.
36. Bridgeview
37. Knoll Rd.
38. Ford Ave.
39. 4100-4199 Flint
40. 4700-4799 Flint
41. 5200-5299 Simon
42. Bingham
43. 0300-0399 Grant
44. 3400-3499 Flint
45. Bender Way
46. Walnut Grove
47. 4700-4799 Flint
48. 1200-1299 Grant
49. 7200-7299 Simon
50. Pinecone Ave.
51. Ford Ave.
52. 1300-1399 Grant
53. Armstrong Dr.
54. 7000-7099 Simon
55. 0300-0399 Grant
56. Jackson
57. Bingham
58. Averley Dr.
59. 3900-3999 Flint
60. 6700-6799 Simon
61. 3100-3199 Grant
62. Bender Way
63. Bridgeview
64. 1300-1399 Grant
65. 4500-4599 Flint
66. 7200-7299 Simon
67. 2900-2999 Grant
68. Knoll Rd.
69. Pinecone Ave.
70. Walnut Grove
71. 5200-5299 Simon
72. 1200-1299 Grant
73. 1300-1399 Grant
74. Averley Dr.
75. Ford Ave.
76. 6400-6499 Simon
77. 3100-3199 Grant
78. Pinecone Ave.
79. Bingham
80. Bender Way
81. 4100-4199 Flint
82. Bridgeview
83. Jackson
84. 3900-3999 Flint
85. Armstrong Dr.
86. 7000-7099 Simon
87. 3400-3499 Flint
88. Knoll Rd.

ANSWER SHEET TO EXERCISE 6

1. Ⓐ Ⓑ Ⓒ Ⓓ Ⓔ	31. Ⓐ Ⓑ Ⓒ Ⓓ Ⓔ	61. Ⓐ Ⓑ Ⓒ Ⓓ Ⓔ	
2. Ⓐ Ⓑ Ⓒ Ⓓ Ⓔ	32. Ⓐ Ⓑ Ⓒ Ⓓ Ⓔ	62. Ⓐ Ⓑ Ⓒ Ⓓ Ⓔ	
3. Ⓐ Ⓑ Ⓒ Ⓓ Ⓔ	33. Ⓐ Ⓑ Ⓒ Ⓓ Ⓔ	63. Ⓐ Ⓑ Ⓒ Ⓓ Ⓔ	
4. Ⓐ Ⓑ Ⓒ Ⓓ Ⓔ	34. Ⓐ Ⓑ Ⓒ Ⓓ Ⓔ	64. Ⓐ Ⓑ Ⓒ Ⓓ Ⓔ	
5. Ⓐ Ⓑ Ⓒ Ⓓ Ⓔ	35. Ⓐ Ⓑ Ⓒ Ⓓ Ⓔ	65. Ⓐ Ⓑ Ⓒ Ⓓ Ⓔ	
6. Ⓐ Ⓑ Ⓒ Ⓓ Ⓔ	36. Ⓐ Ⓑ Ⓒ Ⓓ Ⓔ	66. Ⓐ Ⓑ Ⓒ Ⓓ Ⓔ	
7. Ⓐ Ⓑ Ⓒ Ⓓ Ⓔ	37. Ⓐ Ⓑ Ⓒ Ⓓ Ⓔ	67. Ⓐ Ⓑ Ⓒ Ⓓ Ⓔ	
8. Ⓐ Ⓑ Ⓒ Ⓓ Ⓔ	38. Ⓐ Ⓑ Ⓒ Ⓓ Ⓔ	68. Ⓐ Ⓑ Ⓒ Ⓓ Ⓔ	
9. Ⓐ Ⓑ Ⓒ Ⓓ Ⓔ	39. Ⓐ Ⓑ Ⓒ Ⓓ Ⓔ	69. Ⓐ Ⓑ Ⓒ Ⓓ Ⓔ	
10. Ⓐ Ⓑ Ⓒ Ⓓ Ⓔ	40. Ⓐ Ⓑ Ⓒ Ⓓ Ⓔ	70. Ⓐ Ⓑ Ⓒ Ⓓ Ⓔ	
11. Ⓐ Ⓑ Ⓒ Ⓓ Ⓔ	41. Ⓐ Ⓑ Ⓒ Ⓓ Ⓔ	71. Ⓐ Ⓑ Ⓒ Ⓓ Ⓔ	
12. Ⓐ Ⓑ Ⓒ Ⓓ Ⓔ	42. Ⓐ Ⓑ Ⓒ Ⓓ Ⓔ	72. Ⓐ Ⓑ Ⓒ Ⓓ Ⓔ	
13. Ⓐ Ⓑ Ⓒ Ⓓ Ⓔ	43. Ⓐ Ⓑ Ⓒ Ⓓ Ⓔ	73. Ⓐ Ⓑ Ⓒ Ⓓ Ⓔ	
14. Ⓐ Ⓑ Ⓒ Ⓓ Ⓔ	44. Ⓐ Ⓑ Ⓒ Ⓓ Ⓔ	74. Ⓐ Ⓑ Ⓒ Ⓓ Ⓔ	
15. Ⓐ Ⓑ Ⓒ Ⓓ Ⓔ	45. Ⓐ Ⓑ Ⓒ Ⓓ Ⓔ	75. Ⓐ Ⓑ Ⓒ Ⓓ Ⓔ	
16. Ⓐ Ⓑ Ⓒ Ⓓ Ⓔ	46. Ⓐ Ⓑ Ⓒ Ⓓ Ⓔ	76. Ⓐ Ⓑ Ⓒ Ⓓ Ⓔ	
17. Ⓐ Ⓑ Ⓒ Ⓓ Ⓔ	47. Ⓐ Ⓑ Ⓒ Ⓓ Ⓔ	77. Ⓐ Ⓑ Ⓒ Ⓓ Ⓔ	
18. Ⓐ Ⓑ Ⓒ Ⓓ Ⓔ	48. Ⓐ Ⓑ Ⓒ Ⓓ Ⓔ	78. Ⓐ Ⓑ Ⓒ Ⓓ Ⓔ	
19. Ⓐ Ⓑ Ⓒ Ⓓ Ⓔ	49. Ⓐ Ⓑ Ⓒ Ⓓ Ⓔ	79. Ⓐ Ⓑ Ⓒ Ⓓ Ⓔ	
20. Ⓐ Ⓑ Ⓒ Ⓓ Ⓔ	50. Ⓐ Ⓑ Ⓒ Ⓓ Ⓔ	80. Ⓐ Ⓑ Ⓒ Ⓓ Ⓔ	
21. Ⓐ Ⓑ Ⓒ Ⓓ Ⓔ	51. Ⓐ Ⓑ Ⓒ Ⓓ Ⓔ	81. Ⓐ Ⓑ Ⓒ Ⓓ Ⓔ	
22. Ⓐ Ⓑ Ⓒ Ⓓ Ⓔ	52. Ⓐ Ⓑ Ⓒ Ⓓ Ⓔ	82. Ⓐ Ⓑ Ⓒ Ⓓ Ⓔ	
23. Ⓐ Ⓑ Ⓒ Ⓓ Ⓔ	53. Ⓐ Ⓑ Ⓒ Ⓓ Ⓔ	83. Ⓐ Ⓑ Ⓒ Ⓓ Ⓔ	
24. Ⓐ Ⓑ Ⓒ Ⓓ Ⓔ	54. Ⓐ Ⓑ Ⓒ Ⓓ Ⓔ	84. Ⓐ Ⓑ Ⓒ Ⓓ Ⓔ	
25. Ⓐ Ⓑ Ⓒ Ⓓ Ⓔ	55. Ⓐ Ⓑ Ⓒ Ⓓ Ⓔ	85. Ⓐ Ⓑ Ⓒ Ⓓ Ⓔ	
26. Ⓐ Ⓑ Ⓒ Ⓓ Ⓔ	56. Ⓐ Ⓑ Ⓒ Ⓓ Ⓔ	86. Ⓐ Ⓑ Ⓒ Ⓓ Ⓔ	
27. Ⓐ Ⓑ Ⓒ Ⓓ Ⓔ	57. Ⓐ Ⓑ Ⓒ Ⓓ Ⓔ	87. Ⓐ Ⓑ Ⓒ Ⓓ Ⓔ	
28. Ⓐ Ⓑ Ⓒ Ⓓ Ⓔ	58. Ⓐ Ⓑ Ⓒ Ⓓ Ⓔ	88. Ⓐ Ⓑ Ⓒ Ⓓ Ⓔ	
29. Ⓐ Ⓑ Ⓒ Ⓓ Ⓔ	59. Ⓐ Ⓑ Ⓒ Ⓓ Ⓔ		
30. Ⓐ Ⓑ Ⓒ Ⓓ Ⓔ	60. Ⓐ Ⓑ Ⓒ Ⓓ Ⓔ		

(This page may be removed to mark answers.)

ANSWERS TO EXERCISE 6.

1.	E	31.	A	61.	B
2.	A	32.	A	62.	A
3.	C	33.	C	63.	B
4.	A	34.	D	64.	E
5.	D	35.	A	65.	A
6.	A	36.	B	66.	B
7.	D	37.	C	67.	C
8.	C	38.	C	68.	C
9.	E	39.	C	69.	E
10.	C	40.	D	70.	E
11.	E	41.	E	71.	E
12.	D	42.	D	72.	A
13.	B	43.	D	73.	E
14.	D	44.	B	74.	D
15.	C	45.	A	75.	C
16.	D	46.	E	76.	D
17.	A	47.	D	77.	B
18.	C	48.	A	78.	E
19.	A	49.	B	79.	D
20.	E	50.	E	80.	A
21.	B	51.	C	81.	C
22.	B	52.	E	82.	B
23.	B	53.	A	83.	B
24.	D	54.	C	84.	E
25.	D	55.	D	85.	A
26.	E	56.	B	86.	C
27.	D	57.	D	87.	B
28.	B	58.	D	88.	C
29.	B	59.	E		
30.	D	60.	A		

If Your Score Was:
—70 or more correct you have an excellent score
—between 45 and 69 correct you have a good score
—44 or below correct you should practice more

EXERCISE 7.

TIME: 3 MINUTES

A	B	C	D	E
1700-1799 Straton	2500-2599 Straton	2200-2299 Straton	1400-1499 Straton	1100-1199 Straton
Northern Dr.	Belmont Ln.	Meadowbrook	Lowry Ave.	Buckner
3300-3399 King	4000-4099 King	3700-3799 King	5500-5599 King	4900-4999 King
Prairie Dr.	Conifer Ct.	Juniper	Wright Ave.	Snyder Blvd.
8700-8799 Knox	8200-8299 Knox	7700-7799 Knox	7100-7199 Knox	7500-7599 Knox

TIME: 3 MINUTES

A	B	C	D	E
1700-1799 Straton	2500-2599 Straton	2200-2299 Straton	1400-1499 Straton	1100-1199 Straton
Northern Dr.	Belmont Ln.	Meadowbrook	Lowry Ave.	Buckner
3300-3399 King	4000-4099 King	3700-3799 King	5500-5599 King	4900-4999 King
Prairie Dr.	Conifer Ct.	Juniper	Wright Ave.	Snyder Blvd.
8700-8799 Knox	8200-8299 Knox	7700-7799 Knox	7100-7199 Knox	7500-7599 Knox

1. 4000-4099 King
2. 1700-1799 Straton
3. 7700-7799 Knox
4. Northern Dr.
5. Belmont Ln.
6. Conifer Ct.
7. 1400-1499 Straton
8. 3300-3399 King
9. Prairie Dr.
10. Meadowbrook
11. 2500-2599 Straton
12. 4900-4999 King
13. Buckner
14. Juniper
15. 7500-7599 Knox
16. 3700-3799 King
17. Lowry Ave.
18. 7500-7599 Knox
19. 1100-1199 Straton
20. Conifer Ct.
21. Buckner
22. 4900-4999 King
23. Prairie Dr.
24. Juniper
25. Snyder Blvd.
26. 7700-7799 Knox
27. 1700-1799 Straton
28. Meadowbrook
29. 2200-2299 Straton
30. 3300-3399 King
31. Northern Dr.
32. 8200-8299 Knox
33. 2500-2599 Straton
34. Lowry Ave.
35. 4900-4999 King
36. Belmont Ln.
37. Wright Ave.
38. 3700-3799 King
39. 7100-7199 Knox
40. 1400-1499 Straton
41. Snyder Blvd.
42. Northern Dr.
43. 1100-1199 Straton
44. 8700-8799 Knox
45. 4000-4099 King
46. Belmont Ln.
47. Prairie Dr.
48. Wright Ave.
49. 3700-3799 King
50. 2500-2599 Straton
51. 7700-7799 Knox
52. Meadowbrook
53. Lowry Ave.
54. Conifer Ct.
55. 8200-8299 Knox
56. Buckner
57. 5500-5599 King
58. 7500-7599 Knox
59. 1700-1799 Straton
60. 8700-8799 Knox
61. Wright Ave.
62. 3700-3799 King
63. 2200-2299 Straton
64. Meadowbrook
65. Snyder Blvd.
66. 3300-3399 King
67. 8700-8799 Knox
68. 1700-1799 Straton
69. Belmont Ln.
70. Juniper
71. 1100-1199 Straton
72. 7100-7199 Knox
73. 5500-5599 King
74. Prairie Dr.
75. Conifer Ct.
76. 7500-7599 Knox
77. 1400-1499 Straton
78. 8200-8299 Knox
79. 7100-7199 Knox
80. Wright Ave.
81. Juniper
82. Snyder Blvd.
83. 4000-4099 King
84. Northern Dr.
85. Lowry Ave.
86. 5500-5599 King
87. 2200-2299 Straton
88. Buckner

The Postal Exam Preparation Book 171

1. Meadowbrook
2. 1700-1799 Straton
3. 4000-4099 King
4. Lowry Ave.
5. Belmont Ln.
6. 8700-8799 Knox
7. 7500-7599 Knox
8. Buckner
9. 1400-1499 Straton
10. 5500-5599 King
11. 8200-8299 Knox
12. Northern Dr.
13. 3300-3399 King
14. Prairie Dr.
15. Conifer Ct.
16. 2200-2299 Straton
17. 7700-7799 Knox
18. 4900-4999 King
19. Snyder Blvd.
20. Meadowbrook
21. 7100-7199 Knox
22. 1100-1199 Straton
23. 3700-3799 King
24. 8200-8299 Knox
25. Wright Ave.
26. Conifer Ct.
27. Juniper
28. 2500-2599 Straton
29. Snyder Blvd.
30. 4000-4099 King
31. 7700-7799 Knox
32. Belmont Ln.
33. 2200-2299 Straton
34. 5500-5599 King
35. Lowry Ave.
36. Buckner
37. 1700-1799 Straton
38. Prairie Dr.
39. Wright Ave.
40. 4900-4999 King
41. 8200-8299 Knox
42. Northern Dr.
43. 7100-7199 Knox
44. 2200-2299 Straton
45. 1400-1499 Straton
46. 3300-3399 King
47. Juniper
48. 7500-7599 Knox
49. 3700-3799 King
50. 1100-1199 Straton
51. Belmont Ln.
52. 8700-8799 Knox
53. 2500-2599 Straton
54. 7100-7199 Knox
55. Northern Dr.
56. 5500-5599 King
57. Buckner
58. Conifer Ct.
59. Wright Ave.
60. 1100-1199 Straton
61. 4000-4099 King
62. 7500-7599 Knox
63. Meadowbrook
64. Lowry Ave.
65. Juniper
66. 2500-2599 Straton
67. Prairie Dr.
68. 4900-4999 King
69. Snyder Blvd.
70. 8200-8299 Knox
71. 3700-3799 King
72. 1400-1499 Straton
73. Meadowbrook
74. Juniper
75. 2500-2599 Straton
76. Buckner
77. Wright Ave.
78. 3300-3399 King
79. 7700-7799 Knox
80. Belmont Ln.
81. Prairie Dr.
82. Lowry Ave.
83. 1700-1799 Straton
84. 7500-7599 Knox
85. Northern Dr.
86. Snyder Blvd.
87. 8700-8799 Knox
88. Conifer Ct.

ANSWER SHEET TO EXERCISE 7

1. Ⓐ Ⓑ Ⓒ Ⓓ Ⓔ   31. Ⓐ Ⓑ Ⓒ Ⓓ Ⓔ   61. Ⓐ Ⓑ Ⓒ Ⓓ Ⓔ
2. Ⓐ Ⓑ Ⓒ Ⓓ Ⓔ   32. Ⓐ Ⓑ Ⓒ Ⓓ Ⓔ   62. Ⓐ Ⓑ Ⓒ Ⓓ Ⓔ
3. Ⓐ Ⓑ Ⓒ Ⓓ Ⓔ   33. Ⓐ Ⓑ Ⓒ Ⓓ Ⓔ   63. Ⓐ Ⓑ Ⓒ Ⓓ Ⓔ
4. Ⓐ Ⓑ Ⓒ Ⓓ Ⓔ   34. Ⓐ Ⓑ Ⓒ Ⓓ Ⓔ   64. Ⓐ Ⓑ Ⓒ Ⓓ Ⓔ
5. Ⓐ Ⓑ Ⓒ Ⓓ Ⓔ   35. Ⓐ Ⓑ Ⓒ Ⓓ Ⓔ   65. Ⓐ Ⓑ Ⓒ Ⓓ Ⓔ
6. Ⓐ Ⓑ Ⓒ Ⓓ Ⓔ   36. Ⓐ Ⓑ Ⓒ Ⓓ Ⓔ   66. Ⓐ Ⓑ Ⓒ Ⓓ Ⓔ
7. Ⓐ Ⓑ Ⓒ Ⓓ Ⓔ   37. Ⓐ Ⓑ Ⓒ Ⓓ Ⓔ   67. Ⓐ Ⓑ Ⓒ Ⓓ Ⓔ
8. Ⓐ Ⓑ Ⓒ Ⓓ Ⓔ   38. Ⓐ Ⓑ Ⓒ Ⓓ Ⓔ   68. Ⓐ Ⓑ Ⓒ Ⓓ Ⓔ
9. Ⓐ Ⓑ Ⓒ Ⓓ Ⓔ   39. Ⓐ Ⓑ Ⓒ Ⓓ Ⓔ   69. Ⓐ Ⓑ Ⓒ Ⓓ Ⓔ
10. Ⓐ Ⓑ Ⓒ Ⓓ Ⓔ   40. Ⓐ Ⓑ Ⓒ Ⓓ Ⓔ   70. Ⓐ Ⓑ Ⓒ Ⓓ Ⓔ
11. Ⓐ Ⓑ Ⓒ Ⓓ Ⓔ   41. Ⓐ Ⓑ Ⓒ Ⓓ Ⓔ   71. Ⓐ Ⓑ Ⓒ Ⓓ Ⓔ
12. Ⓐ Ⓑ Ⓒ Ⓓ Ⓔ   42. Ⓐ Ⓑ Ⓒ Ⓓ Ⓔ   72. Ⓐ Ⓑ Ⓒ Ⓓ Ⓔ
13. Ⓐ Ⓑ Ⓒ Ⓓ Ⓔ   43. Ⓐ Ⓑ Ⓒ Ⓓ Ⓔ   73. Ⓐ Ⓑ Ⓒ Ⓓ Ⓔ
14. Ⓐ Ⓑ Ⓒ Ⓓ Ⓔ   44. Ⓐ Ⓑ Ⓒ Ⓓ Ⓔ   74. Ⓐ Ⓑ Ⓒ Ⓓ Ⓔ
15. Ⓐ Ⓑ Ⓒ Ⓓ Ⓔ   45. Ⓐ Ⓑ Ⓒ Ⓓ Ⓔ   75. Ⓐ Ⓑ Ⓒ Ⓓ Ⓔ
16. Ⓐ Ⓑ Ⓒ Ⓓ Ⓔ   46. Ⓐ Ⓑ Ⓒ Ⓓ Ⓔ   76. Ⓐ Ⓑ Ⓒ Ⓓ Ⓔ
17. Ⓐ Ⓑ Ⓒ Ⓓ Ⓔ   47. Ⓐ Ⓑ Ⓒ Ⓓ Ⓔ   77. Ⓐ Ⓑ Ⓒ Ⓓ Ⓔ
18. Ⓐ Ⓑ Ⓒ Ⓓ Ⓔ   48. Ⓐ Ⓑ Ⓒ Ⓓ Ⓔ   78. Ⓐ Ⓑ Ⓒ Ⓓ Ⓔ
19. Ⓐ Ⓑ Ⓒ Ⓓ Ⓔ   49. Ⓐ Ⓑ Ⓒ Ⓓ Ⓔ   79. Ⓐ Ⓑ Ⓒ Ⓓ Ⓔ
20. Ⓐ Ⓑ Ⓒ Ⓓ Ⓔ   50. Ⓐ Ⓑ Ⓒ Ⓓ Ⓔ   80. Ⓐ Ⓑ Ⓒ Ⓓ Ⓔ
21. Ⓐ Ⓑ Ⓒ Ⓓ Ⓔ   51. Ⓐ Ⓑ Ⓒ Ⓓ Ⓔ   81. Ⓐ Ⓑ Ⓒ Ⓓ Ⓔ
22. Ⓐ Ⓑ Ⓒ Ⓓ Ⓔ   52. Ⓐ Ⓑ Ⓒ Ⓓ Ⓔ   82. Ⓐ Ⓑ Ⓒ Ⓓ Ⓔ
23. Ⓐ Ⓑ Ⓒ Ⓓ Ⓔ   53. Ⓐ Ⓑ Ⓒ Ⓓ Ⓔ   83. Ⓐ Ⓑ Ⓒ Ⓓ Ⓔ
24. Ⓐ Ⓑ Ⓒ Ⓓ Ⓔ   54. Ⓐ Ⓑ Ⓒ Ⓓ Ⓔ   84. Ⓐ Ⓑ Ⓒ Ⓓ Ⓔ
25. Ⓐ Ⓑ Ⓒ Ⓓ Ⓔ   55. Ⓐ Ⓑ Ⓒ Ⓓ Ⓔ   85. Ⓐ Ⓑ Ⓒ Ⓓ Ⓔ
26. Ⓐ Ⓑ Ⓒ Ⓓ Ⓔ   56. Ⓐ Ⓑ Ⓒ Ⓓ Ⓔ   86. Ⓐ Ⓑ Ⓒ Ⓓ Ⓔ
27. Ⓐ Ⓑ Ⓒ Ⓓ Ⓔ   57. Ⓐ Ⓑ Ⓒ Ⓓ Ⓔ   87. Ⓐ Ⓑ Ⓒ Ⓓ Ⓔ
28. Ⓐ Ⓑ Ⓒ Ⓓ Ⓔ   58. Ⓐ Ⓑ Ⓒ Ⓓ Ⓔ   88. Ⓐ Ⓑ Ⓒ Ⓓ Ⓔ
29. Ⓐ Ⓑ Ⓒ Ⓓ Ⓔ   59. Ⓐ Ⓑ Ⓒ Ⓓ Ⓔ
30. Ⓐ Ⓑ Ⓒ Ⓓ Ⓔ   60. Ⓐ Ⓑ Ⓒ Ⓓ Ⓔ

(This page may be removed to mark answers.)

ANSWERS TO EXERCISE 7.

1.	C	31.	C	61.	B
2.	A	32.	B	62.	E
3.	B	33.	C	63.	C
4.	D	34.	D	64.	D
5.	B	35.	D	65.	C
6.	A	36.	E	66.	B
7.	E	37.	A	67.	A
8.	E	38.	A	68.	E
9.	D	39.	D	69.	E
10.	D	40.	E	70.	B
11.	B	41.	B	71.	C
12.	A	42.	A	72.	D
13.	A	43.	D	73.	C
14.	A	44.	C	74.	C
15.	B	45.	D	75.	B
16.	C	46.	A	76.	E
17.	C	47.	C	77.	D
18.	E	48.	E	78.	A
19.	E	49.	C	79.	C
20.	C	50.	E	80.	B
21.	D	51.	B	81.	A
22.	E	52.	A	82.	D
23.	C	53.	B	83.	A
24.	B	54.	D	84.	E
25.	D	55.	A	85.	A
26.	B	56.	D	86.	E
27.	C	57.	E	87.	A
28.	B	58.	B	88.	B
29.	E	59.	D		
30.	B	60.	E		

If Your Score Was:
—70 or more correct you have an excellent score
—between 45 and 69 correct you have a good score
—44 or below correct you should practice more

EXERCISE 8.

TIME: 3 MINUTES

A	B	C	D	E
4700-4799 Bell	5900-5999 Bell	4000-4099 Bell	5200-5299 Bell	4100-4199 Bell
Belfair	Knottingham	Springer Ave.	Jersey St.	Silverton Ct.
7700-7799 Boyson	8000-8099 Boyson	8400-8499 Boyson	7100-7199 Boyson	7000-7099 Boyson
Eldorado Blvd.	Summit Ave.	Marine Dr.	Burwell	Almira Dr.
0200-0299 Foster	3500-3599 Foster	0900-0999 Foster	0100-0199 Foster	3600-3699 Foster

TIME: 3 MINUTES

A	B	C	D	E
4700-4799 Bell	5900-5999 Bell	4000-4099 Bell	5200-5299 Bell	4100-4199 Bell
Belfair	Knottingham	Springer Ave.	Jersey St.	Silverton Ct.
7700-7799 Boyson	8000-8099 Boyson	8400-8499 Boyson	7100-7199 Boyson	7000-7099 Boyson
Eldorado Blvd.	Summit Ave.	Marine Dr.	Burwell	Almira Dr.
0200-0299 Foster	3500-3599 Foster	0900-0999 Foster	0100-0199 Foster	3600-3699 Foster

1. Summit Ave.
2. 5200-5299 Bell
3. 8000-8099 Boyson
4. Belfair
5. Marine Dr.
6. 4700-4799 Bell
7. 7100-7199 Boyson
8. Knottingham
9. Jersey St.
10. Springer Ave.
11. Almira Dr.
12. 5900-5999 Bell
13. 0200-0299 Foster
14. 3600-3699 Foster
15. Eldorado Blvd.
16. 3500-3599 Foster
17. 5200-5299 Bell
18. 0100-1099 Foster
19. 7100-7199 Boyson
20. Summit Ave.
21. Silverton Ct.
22. Almira Dr.
23. 7700-7799 Boyson
24. Marine Dr.
25. 5900-5999 Bell
26. 0900-0999 Foster
27. Belfair
28. Springer Avve.
29. Eldorado Blvd.
30. 4700-4799 Bell

31. Burwell
32. 0200-0299 Foster
33. 7700-7799 Boyson
34. 0100-0199 Foster
35. Jersey St.
36. 4000-4099 Bell
37. 8000-8099 Boyson
38. 3600-3699 Foster
39. Burwell
40. 3500-3599 Foster
41. Knottingham
42. Almira Dr.
43. 8400-8499 Boyson
44. Springer Ave.
45. 0200-0299 Foster
46. 7100-7199 Boyson
47. Jersey St.
48. Eldorado Blvd.
49. 8000-8099 Boyson
50. Springer Ave.
51. 4000-4099 Bell
52. Silverton Ct.
53. 0900-0999 Foster
54. 8400-8499 Boyson
55. Marine Dr.
56. 3600-3699 Foster
57. 5200-5299 Bell
58. 4100-4199 Bell
59. 3500-3599 Foster
60. Summit Ave.

61. Belfair
62. 4000-4099 Bell
63. 7000-7099 Boyson
64. Knottingham
65. Burwell
66. 8400-8499 Boyson
67. 4700-4799 Bell
68. 5900-5999 Bell
69. Silverton Ct.
70. 0100-0199 Foster
71. Springer Ave.
72. Summit Ave.
73. 4100-4199 Bell
74. Marine Dr.
75. 7000-7099 Boyson
76. 0900-0999 Foster
77. Knottingham
78. 7700-7799 Boyson
79. 0200-0299 Foster
80. Eldorado Blvd.
81. Silverton Ct.
82. Burwell
83. 4100-4199 Bell
84. Belfair
85. Jersey St.
86. 7000-7099 Boyson
87. 8400-8499 Boyson
88. Almira Dr.

The Postal Exam Preparation Book 177

1. Almira Dr.
2. Jersey St.
3. 4700-4799 Bell
4. 7100-7199 Boyson
5. Eldorado Blvd.
6. 7700-7799 Boyson
7. 8400-8499 Boyson
8. Belfair
9. Springer Ave.
10. Burwell
11. Summit Ave.
12. 5900-5999 Bell
13. 0200-0299 Foster
14. 7000-7099 Boyson
15. Knottingham
16. 4000-4099 Bell
17. 0900-0999 Foster
18. Jersey St.
19. Marine Dr.
20. 3600-3699 Foster
21. 5200-5299 Bell
22. 4100-4199 Bell
23. 0100-0199 Foster
24. Silverton Ct.
25. 4000-4099 Bell
26. Summit Ave.
27. 7700-7799 Boyson
28. Burwell
29. 4700-4799 Bell
30. Belfair
31. Jersey St.
32. Eldorado Blvd.
33. 5200-5299 Bell
34. 8000-8099 Boyson
35. Knottingham
36. Springer Ave.
37. 4100-4199 Bell
38. 7100-7199 Boyson
39. Silverton Ct.
40. Summit Ave.
41. 4000-4099 Bell
42. Almira Dr.
43. 0200-0299 Foster
44. 7000-7099 Boyson
45. Eldorado Blvd.
46. 3500-3599 Foster
47. Marine Dr.
48. 8400-8499 Boyson
49. 0900-0999 Foster
50. Almira Dr.
51. Burwell
52. 8000-8099 Boyson
53. Knottingham
54. 7100-7199 Boyson
55. 4700-4799 Bell
56. Springer Ave.
57. Jersey St.
58. 4100-4199 Bell
59. Silverton Ct.
60. 7700-7799 Boyson
61. 5900-5999 Bell
62. Eldorado Blvd.
63. 0100-0199 Foster
64. 3500-3599 Foster
65. Belfair
66. Marine Dr.
67. 3600-3699 Foster
68. 4000-4099 Bell
69. 0900-0999 Foster
70. Springer Ave.
71. Jersey St.
72. 7000-7099 Boyson
73. Almira Dr.
74. 3600-3699 Foster
75. 0100-0199 Foster
76. Summit Ave.
77. Burwell
78. Almira Dr.
79. 8400-8499 Boyson
80. Belfair
81. 3500-3599 Foster
82. 5200-5299 Bell
83. Knottingham
84. Marine Dr.
85. Silverton Ct.
86. 0200-0299 Foster
87. 8000-8099 Boyson
88. 5900-5999 Bell

ANSWER SHEET TO EXERCISE 8

(This page may be removed to mark answers.)

ANSWERS TO EXERCISE 8.

1.	E	31.	D	61.	B
2.	D	32.	A	62.	A
3.	A	33.	D	63.	D
4.	D	34.	B	64.	B
5.	A	35.	B	65.	A
6.	A	36.	C	66.	C
7.	C	37.	E	67.	E
8.	A	38.	D	68.	C
9.	C	39.	E	69.	C
10.	D	40.	B	70.	C
11.	B	41.	C	71.	D
12.	B	42.	E	72.	E
13.	A	43.	A	73.	E
14.	E	44.	E	74.	E
15.	B	45.	A	75.	D
16.	C	46.	B	76.	B
17.	C	47.	C	77.	D
18.	D	48.	C	78.	E
19.	C	49.	C	79.	C
20.	E	50.	E	80.	A
21.	D	51.	D	81.	B
22.	E	52.	B	82.	D
23.	D	53.	B	83.	B
24.	E	54.	D	84.	C
25.	C	55.	A	85.	E
26.	B	56.	C	86.	A
27.	A	57.	D	87.	B
28.	D	58.	E	88.	B
29.	A	59.	E		
30.	A	60.	A		

If Your Score Was:
—70 or more correct you have an excellent score
—between 45 and 69 correct you have a good score
—44 or below correct you should practice more

What Follows After The Examination?

Once you have taken the exam, it will be a few weeks before your test results are mailed back to you. If you score was 70 or better, your name will be placed on the federal register; that which belongs to the Post Office that submitted the test. Your score is not transferable to other post offices that apply the exam. As a consequence, it is to your advantage to take as many of these exams as possible. The more scores outstanding on other registers, the better are your chances for employment.

When you are among those to be considered for a Clerk or Carrier position you will be notified via mail about the time and place of your interview. It is very important to convey the best impression you can of yourself to the interviewer. Dress well and be, if not early, prompt for your scheduled interview time. If you happen to have some references on hand from old or current jobs, it would not be a bad idea to bring them along too.

During the interview, if you can show an awareness of what the position you are interviewing for entails and have some general idea of how the Postal Service operates, you will be much further ahead of those who walk in unknowing and just want a job. Try to draw a parallel between your old job experiences and a Clerk or Carrier position; that would be looked upon favorably also. You do not want to paint an over-glorified picture of yourself, but if you are a hard worker, take pride in what you do, and put out that extra effort when needed, tell the person who is interviewing you. It gives him (the interviewer) an overall optimistic picture of you and your potential work performance.

It may take a few weeks before you are notified about the outcome of your interview. At this point, it would only be in order to extend the author's best of luck wishes to you. You have gone to a lot of hard work and time to find placement within the Postal Service. Once you are employed with the Postal Service the job satisfaction is great.

DISTRIBUTION CLERK MACHINE EXAM

This section is to be used in conjunction with the Clerk Carrier study guide for complete preparation for the Postal Distribution Clerk Machine (DCM) exam. All information found within the text of the Clerk-Carrier study guide will be on the DCM test, plus the number series exams included in this section..

TEST CONTENT

Numbers series tests really are not that difficult if you can quickly establish the pattern of numbers compiled. By studying a series of five or more numbers, a pattern should become evident so that the next two numbers in the sequence can be determined. As an example, look at the question below.

    2   4   6   8   10   12   ?   ?

It should be fairly obvious that there is an addition constant of +2 between each number. Therefore, the next two numbers in the sequence should be 14 and 16.

2 (+2) 4 (+2) 6 (+2) 8 (+2) 10 (+2) 12 (+2) 14 (+2) 16

Subtraction and multiplication number series are much the same as the prior example. An example of each is given below. Try to determine what the last two numbers are in each of the number sequences.

    23   20   17   14   11   8   ?   ?

    1   3   9   27   81   ?   ?

The first example shown is a subtraction number series. If you determined that there was a subtraction constant of -3 between numbers, you are right. So the last two numbers in the first sequence should be 5 and 2.

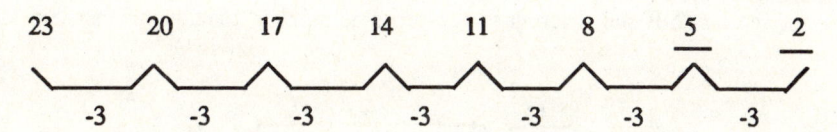

23 (-3) 20 (-3) 17 (-3) 14 (-3) 11 (-3) 8 (-3) 5 (-3) 2

The second example represents a multiplication number series. If you determined that there was a multiplication constant of 3 between the numbers in the sequence, you were right again. Therefore, the last two numbers in this series are 243 and 729.

1 (x3) 3 (x3) 9 (x3) 27 (x3) 81 (x3) 243 (x3) 729

The last kind of number series that will appear on the exam is an alternating number series. This kind of number sequence is a little more involved and consequently takes extra time to solve. The series involves alternating uses of addition and subtraction to create a pattern. The patterns may not be immediately evident but with a little diligence they should become apparent. Two examples are given below. Try to determine what the last two numbers are in each sequence.

    0   12   10   3   6   8   6   9   ?   ?

    0   16   17   4   18   19   8   20   ?   ?

The Postal Exam Preparation Book

If you guessed 12 and 4, and 21 and 12, respectively, you are right. You can see how these patterns can become a bit more complicated.

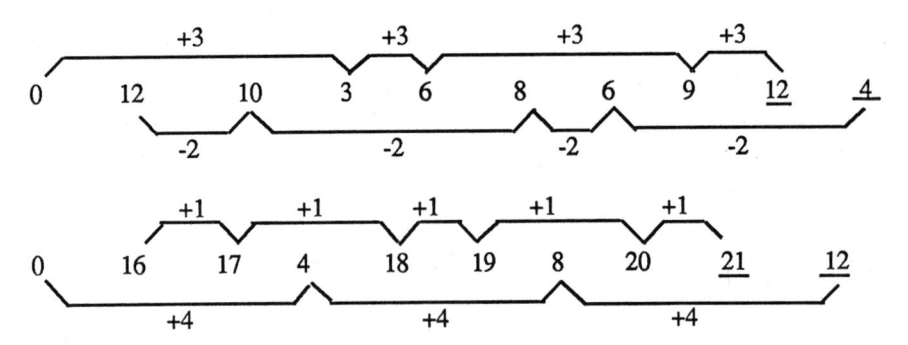

```
      +3        +3        +3        +3
    ⌢         ⌢         ⌢         ⌢
0  12  10  3  6  8  6  9  12  4
         ⌣        ⌣        ⌣        ⌣
         -2       -2       -2       -2
```

```
      +1       +1       +1       +1       +1
    ⌢        ⌢        ⌢        ⌢        ⌢
0  16  17  4  18  19  8  20  21  12
       ⌣          ⌣          ⌣
       +4         +4         +4
```

If a pattern in an alternating number series is not discernable, there is a method you can use to help. The first step involves determining the differences between each successive number in sequence. For example:

```
8   12   4   9   14   16   20   19   ?   ?
  +4   +4  +5   +5   +5   +2   -1
```

Note that there are two +4 and two +5 constants. the next step is to check these similar differences to see if, indeed, some kind of pattern can be established. Let's start with the +4 constant. The numbers involved are 8, 12, 16 and 20. What should become evident is that this series of four numbers represents an addition number series pattern. To better clarify the pattern, if you diagram it as shown below, it should alleviate some confusion.

```
8   12   4   9   14   16   20   19   ?   ?
  +4           +4           +4
```

If there were one more answer blank, the number 24 would be the right answer. However, the addition number series pattern already established does not encompass the two answer blanks. Now look at the remaining numbers: 4, 9, 14, and 19. Do you see a pattern emerge here? If you determined the series as another addition number series with +5 constant, you are correct.

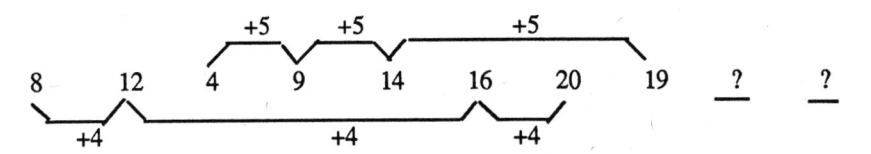

```
            +5    +5         +5
8   12   4   9   14   16   20   19   ?   ?
  +4           +4           +4
```

By blocking off the pattern of +5's the answer can be determined.

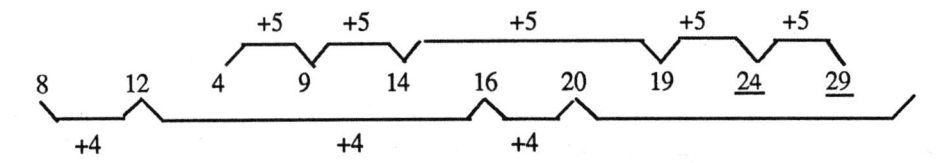

```
            +5    +5         +5         +5    +5
8   12   4   9   14   16   20   19   24   29
  +4           +4           +4
```

Since you are allotted only 20 minutes on the actual exam to complete 24 number series questions, time is of the essence. If an answer to an alternating number series question is not apparent within the scope of 30 seconds, skip the question and go on to the next one. If you have any time remaining after you have completed the test questions you know, return to those questions you skipped and try to solve them.

For your convenience, Number Series Exam I questions have been segregated into the four number series groups (i.e., addition, subtraction, multiplication and alternating). this should clue you in as to what kind of pattern to be searching for. Unfortunately, you are not given this luxury on the Numbers Series Exams II and III. On those exams the series will be relatively well mixed for variety. The answer sheets will provide the correct answers and the pattern to the number series. Thus you can see how the answer to the question was determined. A scale has been provided for determination of your performance on each exam.

NUMBER SERIES EXAM I

Time: 20 minutes

Addition Number Series

1.	7	10	13	16	19	22	___	___
2.	24	30	36	42	48	54	___	___
3.	18	27	36	45	54	63	___	___
4.	4	20	36	52	68	84	___	___
5.	13	15	17	19	21	21	___	___
6.	1	18	35	52	69	86	___	___

Subtraction Number Series

7.	14	12	10	8	6	4	___	___
8.	174	150	126	102	78	54	___	___
9.	45	40	35	30	25	20	___	___
10.	81	72	63	53	45	36	___	___
11.	163	149	135	121	107	93	___	___
12.	1205	1088	971	854	737	620	___	___

Multiplication Number Series

13.	2	4	8	16	32	___	___
14.	4	20	100	500	2500	___	___
15.	3	9	27	81	243	___	___
16.	1	7	49	343	___	___	
17.	6	12	24	48	96	___	___
18.	2	8	32	128	512	___	___

Alternating Number Series

19.	12	10	16	17	8	6	18	___	___
20.	7	11	3	8	13	15	19	18	___	___
21.	3	6	9	17	14	12	15	18	___	___
22.	30	20	25	28	30	35	26	40	___	___
23.	18	14	13	16	12	11	14	10	___	___
24.	36	42	35	28	45	21	14	7	___	___

-END-

The Postal Exam Preparation Book 185

ANSWERS TO NUMBER SERIES EXAM I

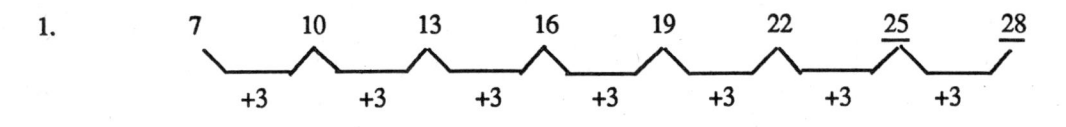

1. 7, 10, 13, 16, 19, 22, <u>25</u>, <u>28</u> (+3 each)

2. 24, 30, 36, 42, 48, 54, <u>60</u>, <u>66</u> (+6 each)

3. 18, 27, 36, 45, 54, 63, <u>72</u>, <u>81</u> (+9 each)

4. 4, 20, 36, 52, 68, 84, <u>100</u>, <u>116</u> (+16 each)

5. 13, 15, 17, 19, 21, 23, <u>25</u>, <u>27</u> (+2 each)

6. 1, 18, 35, 52, 69, 86, <u>103</u>, <u>120</u> (+17 each)

7. 14, 12, 10, 8, 6, 4, <u>2</u>, <u>0</u> (−2 each)

8. 174, 150, 126, 102, 78, 54, <u>30</u>, <u>6</u> (−24 each)

9. 45, 40, 35, 30, 25, 20, <u>15</u>, <u>10</u> (−5 each)

10. 81, 72, 63, 54, 45, 36, <u>27</u>, <u>18</u> (−9 each)

11. 163, 149, 135, 121, 107, 93, <u>79</u>, <u>65</u> (−14 each)

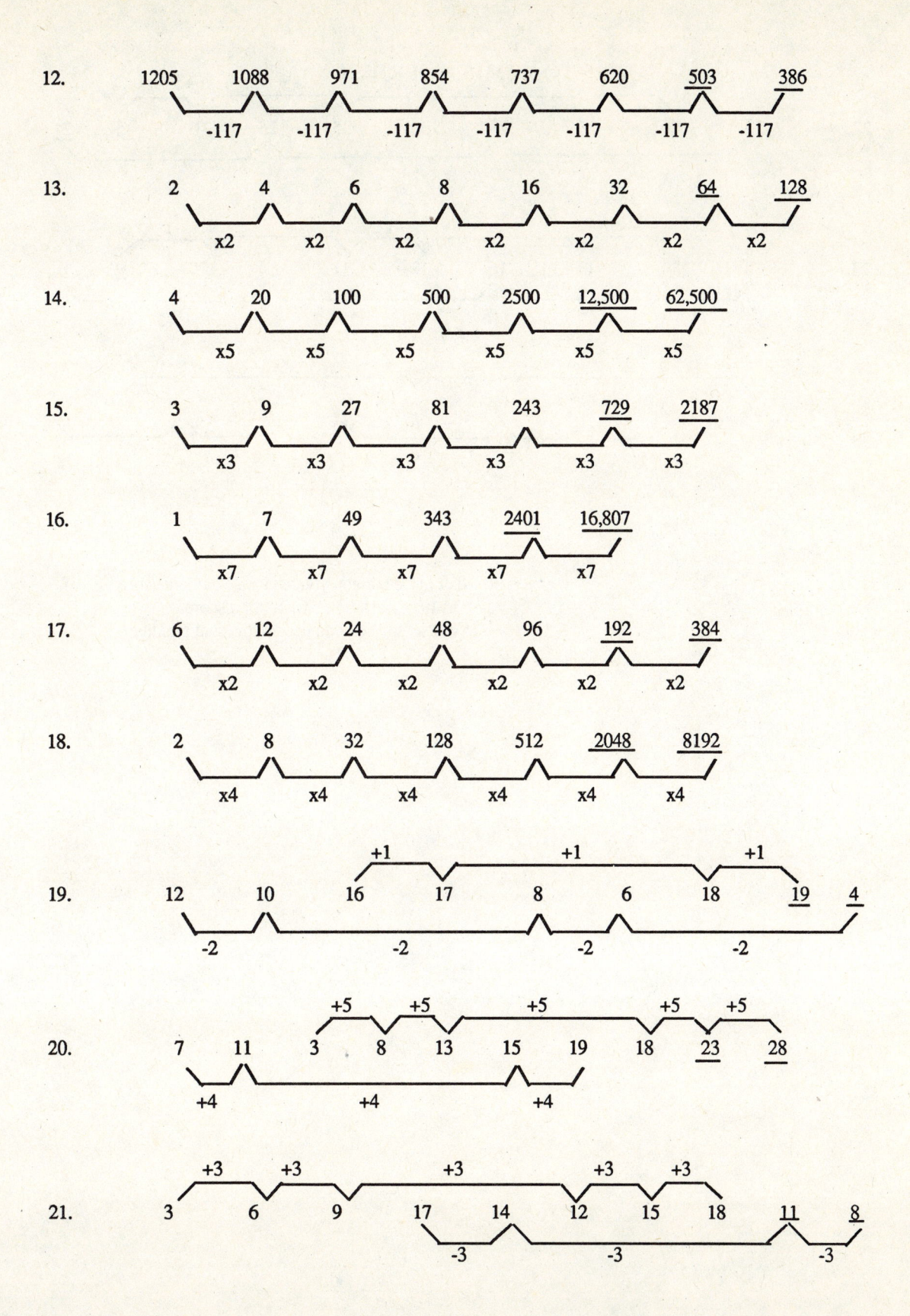

12. 1205 1088 971 854 737 620 503 386
    −117 −117 −117 −117 −117 −117 −117

13. 2 4 6 8 16 32 64 128
    ×2 ×2 ×2 ×2 ×2 ×2 ×2

14. 4 20 100 500 2500 12,500 62,500
    ×5 ×5 ×5 ×5 ×5 ×5

15. 3 9 27 81 243 729 2187
    ×3 ×3 ×3 ×3 ×3 ×3

16. 1 7 49 343 2401 16,807
    ×7 ×7 ×7 ×7 ×7

17. 6 12 24 48 96 192 384
    ×2 ×2 ×2 ×2 ×2 ×2

18. 2 8 32 128 512 2048 8192
    ×4 ×4 ×4 ×4 ×4 ×4

19. 12 10 16 17 8 6 18 19 4
    −2, +1, −2, +1, −2, +1, −2

20. 7 11 3 8 13 15 19 18 23 28
    +4, +5, +5, +4, +5, +4, +5, +5

21. 3 6 9 17 14 12 15 18 11 8
    +3, +3, +3, −3, +3, +3, −3, −3

The Postal Exam Preparation Book 187

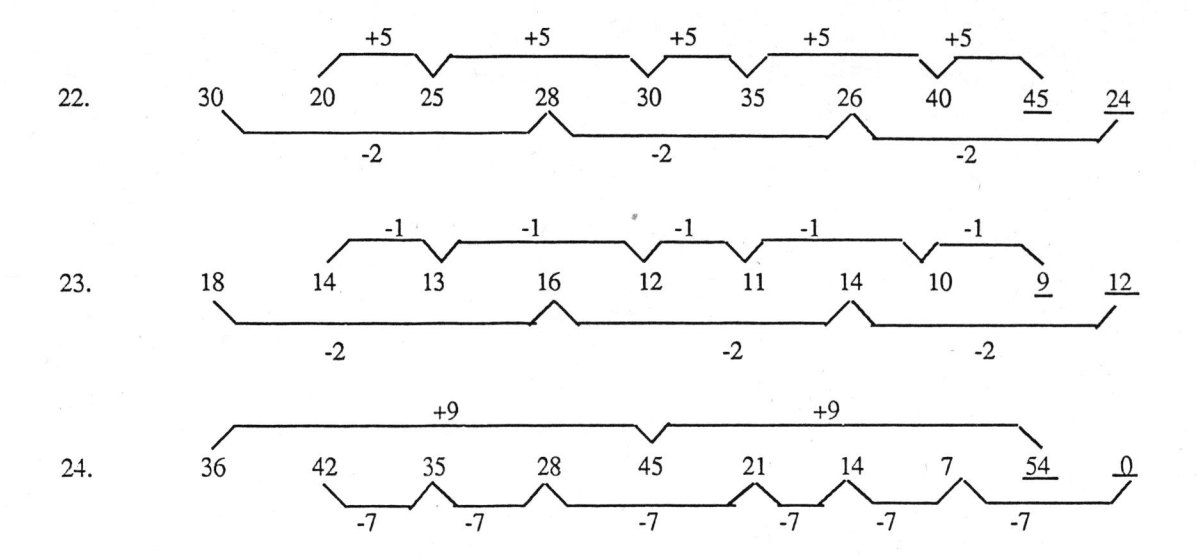

22. 30 20 25 28 30 35 26 40 45 24
     (+5, +5, +5, +5, +5 on top; -2, -2, -2 on bottom)

23. 18 14 13 16 12 11 14 10 9 12
     (-1, -1, -1, -1, -1 on top; -2, -2, -2 on bottom)

24. 36 42 35 28 45 21 14 7 54 0
     (+9, +9 on top; -7, -7, -7, -7, -7, -7 on bottom)

If your score was:
- 20 or more correct, you have an excellent score
- 16 to 19 correct, you have a good score
- 15 or less correct, you need additional practice

188 The Postal Exam Preparation Book

NUMBER SERIES EXAM II

Time: 20 minutes

#									
1.	12	16	20	24	28	—	—		
2.	1	4	16	64	256	—	—		
3.	21	20	18	24	15	28	—	—	
4.	17	27	37	32	47	57	67	30	— —
5.	3	6	12	24	48	—			
6.	29	7	23	13	17	19	11	25	— —
7.	18	12	20	28	21	36	44	— —	
8.	19	17	15	13	11	—			
9.	14	15	23	19	32	23	—	—	
10.	23	40	57	74	91	—	—		
11.	4	3	5	3	7	9	—	—	
12.	27	25	23	20	19	15	—	—	
13.	9	18	27	36	45	—	—		
14.	4	7	15	9	26	11	—	—	
15.	37	40	41	39	43	46	37	— —	
16.	1	7	6	14	36	28	—	—	
17.	15	20	25	30	35	40	—	—	
18.	1	21	9	19	17	17	25	— —	
19.	12	40	39	24	38	37	36	36	— —
20.	68	60	52	44	36	—	—		
21.	7	12	10	145	13	16	—	—	
22.	15	12	18	19	9	6	20	— —	
23.	4	12	36	108	—	—			
24.	8	7	6	7	8	5	4	— —	

The Postal Exam Preparation Book 189

ANSWERS TO NUMBER EXAM II

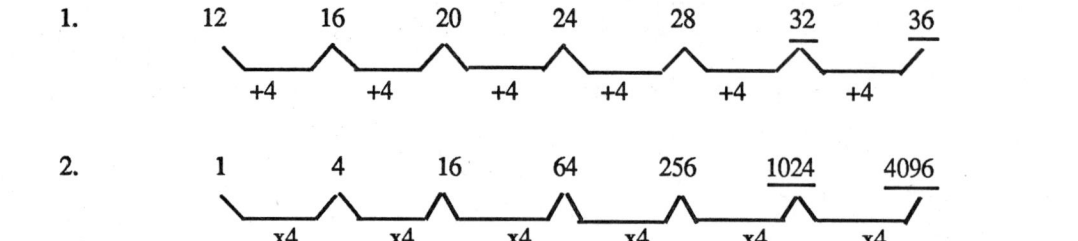

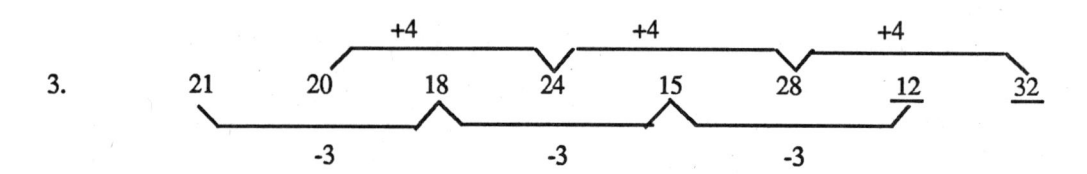

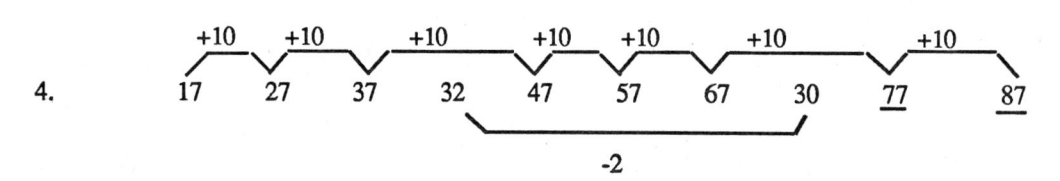

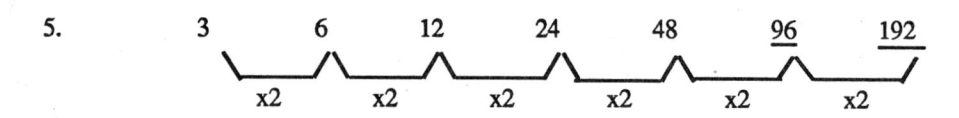

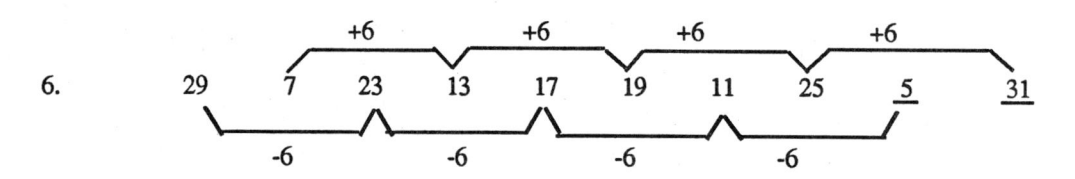

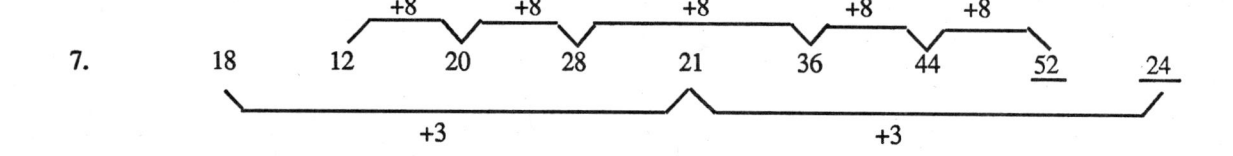

1. 12, 16, 20, 24, 28, **32**, **36** (+4 each)

2. 1, 4, 16, 64, 256, **1024**, **4096** (×4 each)

3. 21, 20, 18, 24, 15, 28, **12**, 32 (alternating −3 and +4)

4. 17, 27, 37, 32, 47, 57, 67, 30, **77**, **87** (+10 with −2 interruptions)

5. 3, 6, 12, 24, 48, **96**, **192** (×2 each)

6. 29, 7, 23, 13, 17, 19, 11, 25, **5**, **31** (alternating +6 and −6)

7. 18, 12, 20, 28, 21, 36, 44, **52**, 24 (alternating +8 and +3)

190 The Postal Exam Preparation Book

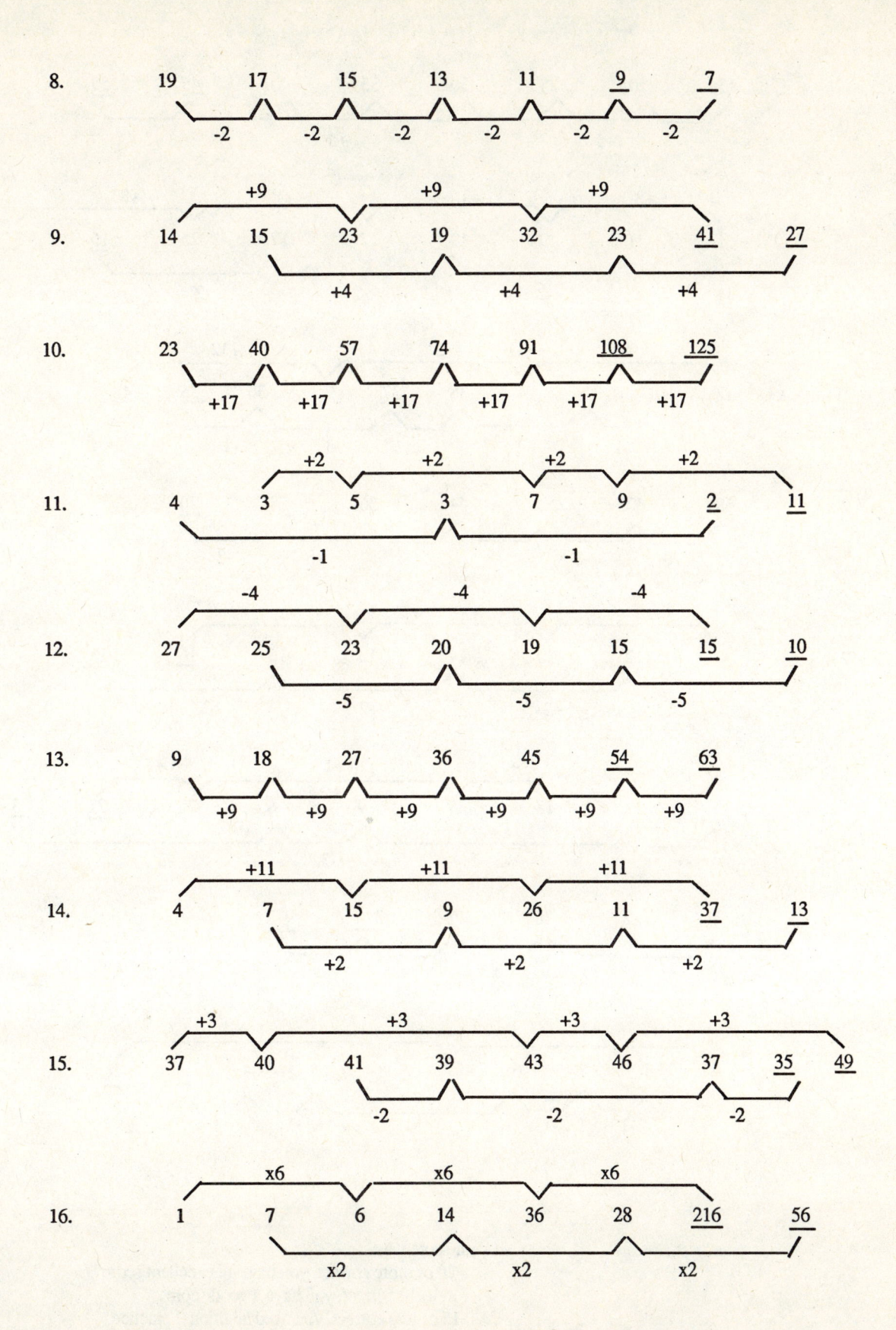

8. 19 17 15 13 11 9 7 (−2 each)

9. Top: +9, +9, +9
   14 15 23 19 32 23 41 27
   Bottom: +4, +4, +4

10. 23 40 57 74 91 108 125 (+17 each)

11. Top: +2, +2, +2, +2
    4 3 5 3 7 9 2 11
    Bottom: −1, −1

12. Top: −4, −4, −4
    27 25 23 20 19 15 15 10
    Bottom: −5, −5, −5

13. 9 18 27 36 45 54 63 (+9 each)

14. Top: +11, +11, +11
    4 7 15 9 26 11 37 13
    Bottom: +2, +2, +2

15. Top: +3, +3, +3, +3
    37 40 41 39 43 46 37 35 49
    Bottom: −2, −2, −2

16. Top: ×6, ×6, ×6
    1 7 6 14 36 28 216 56
    Bottom: ×2, ×2, ×2

The Postal Exam Preparation Book 191

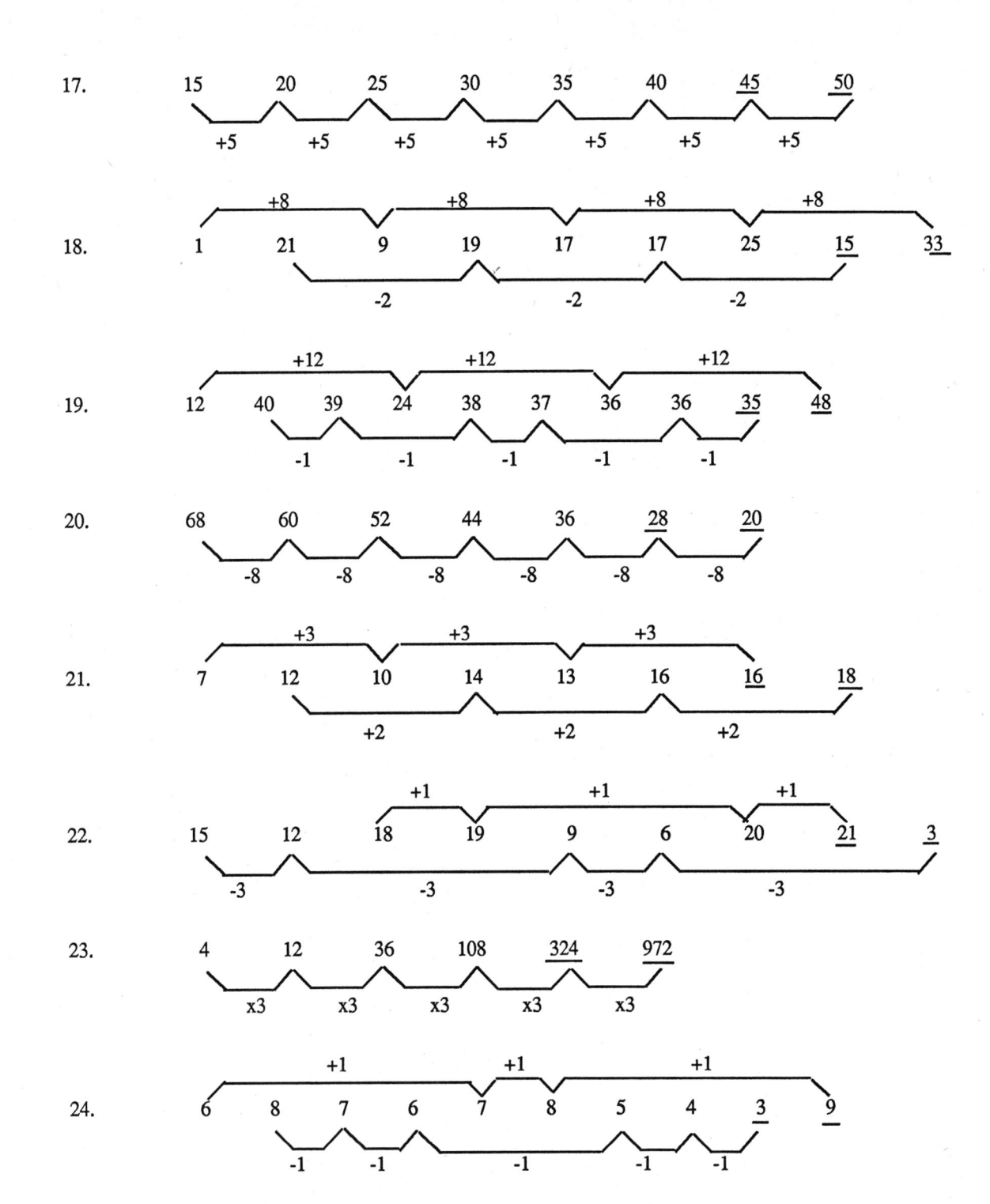

17. 15   20   25   30   35   40   <u>45</u>   <u>50</u>
(+5 between each)

18. 1   21   9   19   17   17   25   <u>15</u>   <u>33</u>
(alternating +8 and −2)

19. 12   40   39   24   38   37   36   36   <u>35</u>   <u>48</u>
(alternating +12 and −1)

20. 68   60   52   44   36   <u>28</u>   <u>20</u>
(−8 between each)

21. 7   12   10   14   13   16   <u>16</u>   <u>18</u>
(alternating +3 and +2)

22. 15   12   18   19   9   6   20   <u>21</u>   <u>3</u>
(alternating −3 and +1)

23. 4   12   36   108   <u>324</u>   <u>972</u>
(×3 between each)

24. 6   8   7   6   7   8   5   4   <u>3</u>   <u>9</u>
(alternating +1 and −1)

If your score was:
- 20 or more correct, you have an excellent score
- 16 to 19 correct, you have a good score
- 15 or less correct, you need additional practice

NUMBER SERIES EXAM III

Time: 20 minutes

1.	6	13	20	27	34	___	___		
2.	19	16	13	10	7	___	___		
3.	1	8	64	512	___	___			
4.	17	19	16	19	13	10	___	___	
5.	24	27	23	25	26	27	19	___	___
6.	16	12	15	14	18	21	___	___	
7.	3	21	147	___	___				
8.	1	8	17	26	7	35	44	___	___
9.	64	80	77	75	90	70	___	___	
10.	11	8	7	13	6	___	___		
11.	27	34	41	48	55	62	___	___	
12.	96	81	66	51	36	___	___		
13.	20	17	15	19	13	11	___	___	
14.	37	29	30	31	32	32	33	___	___
15.	48	58	60	63	72	68	___	___	
16.	6	10	27	22	48	34	69	___	___
17.	25	22	19	16	13	___	___		
18.	2	5	7	6	5	8	11	4	3	___	___
19.	20	16	12	8	___	___			
20.	1	2	4	8	16	___	___		
21.	14	21	3	28	35	13	___	___	
22.	12	11	9	14	10	9	19	24	___	___
23.	36	42	48	54	60	66	___	___	
24.	48	16	28	36	40	52	24	64	___	___

ANSWERS TO NUMBER SERIES EXAM III

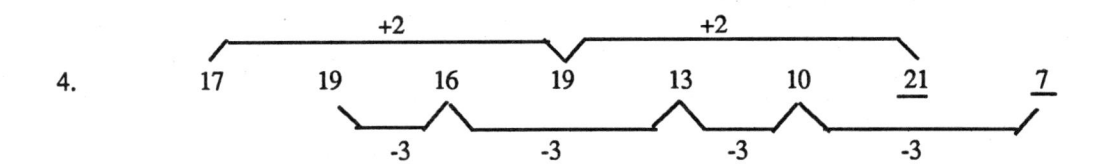

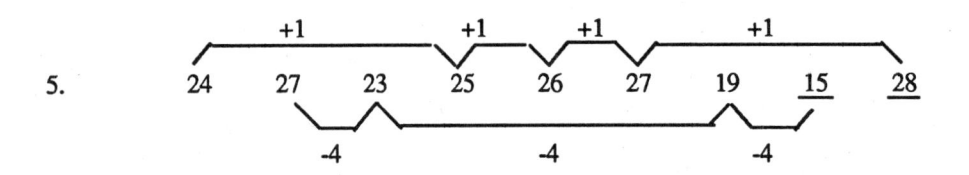

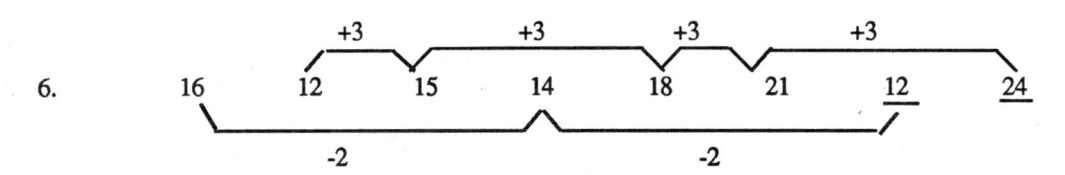

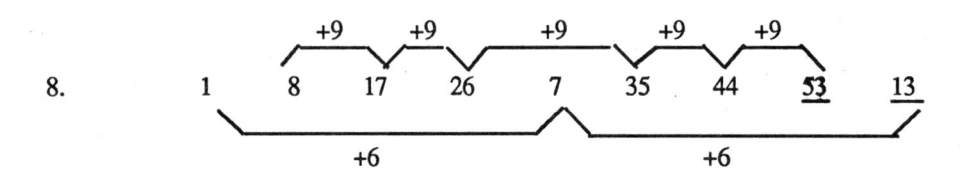

1. 6, 13, 20, 27, 34, __41__, __48__ (+7 each)

2. 19, 16, 13, 10, 7, __4__, __1__ (−3 each)

3. 1, 8, 64, 512, __4096__, __32,768__ (×8 each)

4. 17, 19, 16, 19, 13, 10, __21__, __7__ (alternating +2 and −3)

5. 24, 27, 23, 25, 26, 27, 19, __15__, __28__ (alternating +1 and −4)

6. 16, 12, 15, 14, 18, 21, __12__, __24__ (alternating +3 and −2)

7. 3, 21, 147, __1029__, __7203__ (×7 each)

8. 1, 8, 17, 26, 7, 35, 44, __53__, __13__ (+9 and +6 patterns)

9. 64 +13→ 80 −5→ 77 +13→ 75 −5→ 90 +13→ 70 −5→ 103 65

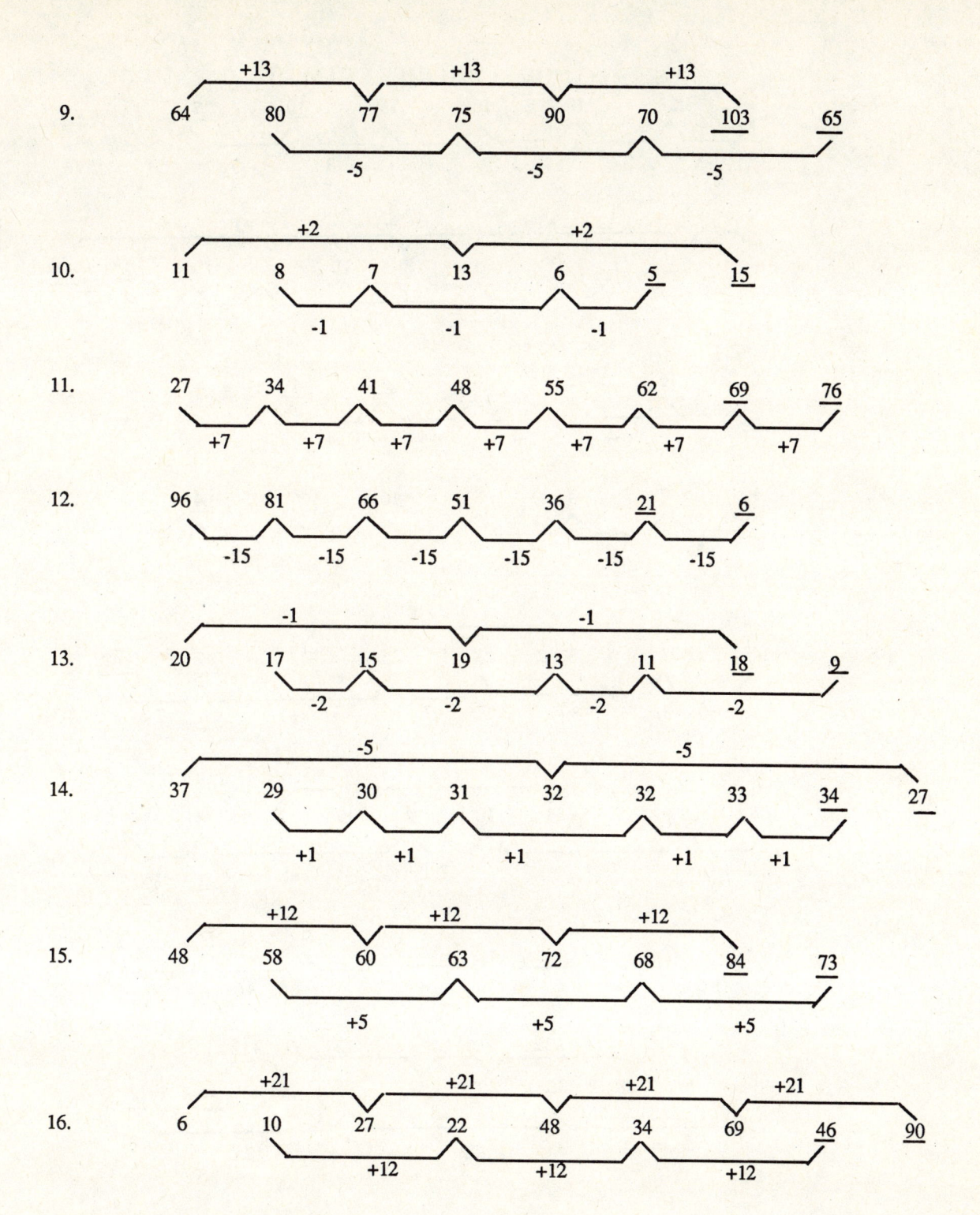

10. 11 +2→ 8 −1→ 7 +2→ 13 −1→ 6 −1→ 5 15

11. 27 +7 34 +7 41 +7 48 +7 55 +7 62 +7 69 +7 76

12. 96 −15 81 −15 66 −15 51 −15 36 −15 21 −15 6

13. 20 −1→ 17 −2→ 15 19 −2→ 13 −2→ 11 −2→ 18 9

14. 37 −5→ 29 +1 30 +1 31 +1 32 −5→ 32 +1 33 +1 34 27

15. 48 +12→ 58 +5 60 +12→ 63 +5 72 +12→ 68 +5 84 73

16. 6 +21→ 10 +12 27 +21→ 22 +12 48 +21→ 34 +12 69 +21→ 46 90

17. 25 22 19 16 13 10 7
     -3 -3 -3 -3 -3 -3

18.
    +3   +3   +3   +3
    2 5 7 6 5 8 11 4 3 2 14
         -1 -1   -1   -1 -1

19. 20 16 12 8 4 0
      -4 -4 -4 -4 -4

20. 1 2 4 8 16 32 64
     x2 x2 x2 x2 x2 x2

21.
                    +10
    14 21 3 28 35 13 42 49
      +7   +7   +7   +7   +7

22.
              +5   +5   +5
    12 11 9 14 10 9 19 24 8 7
      -1   -1   -1   -1   -1

23. 36 42 48 54 60 66 72 78
      +6 +6 +6 +6 +6 +6 +6

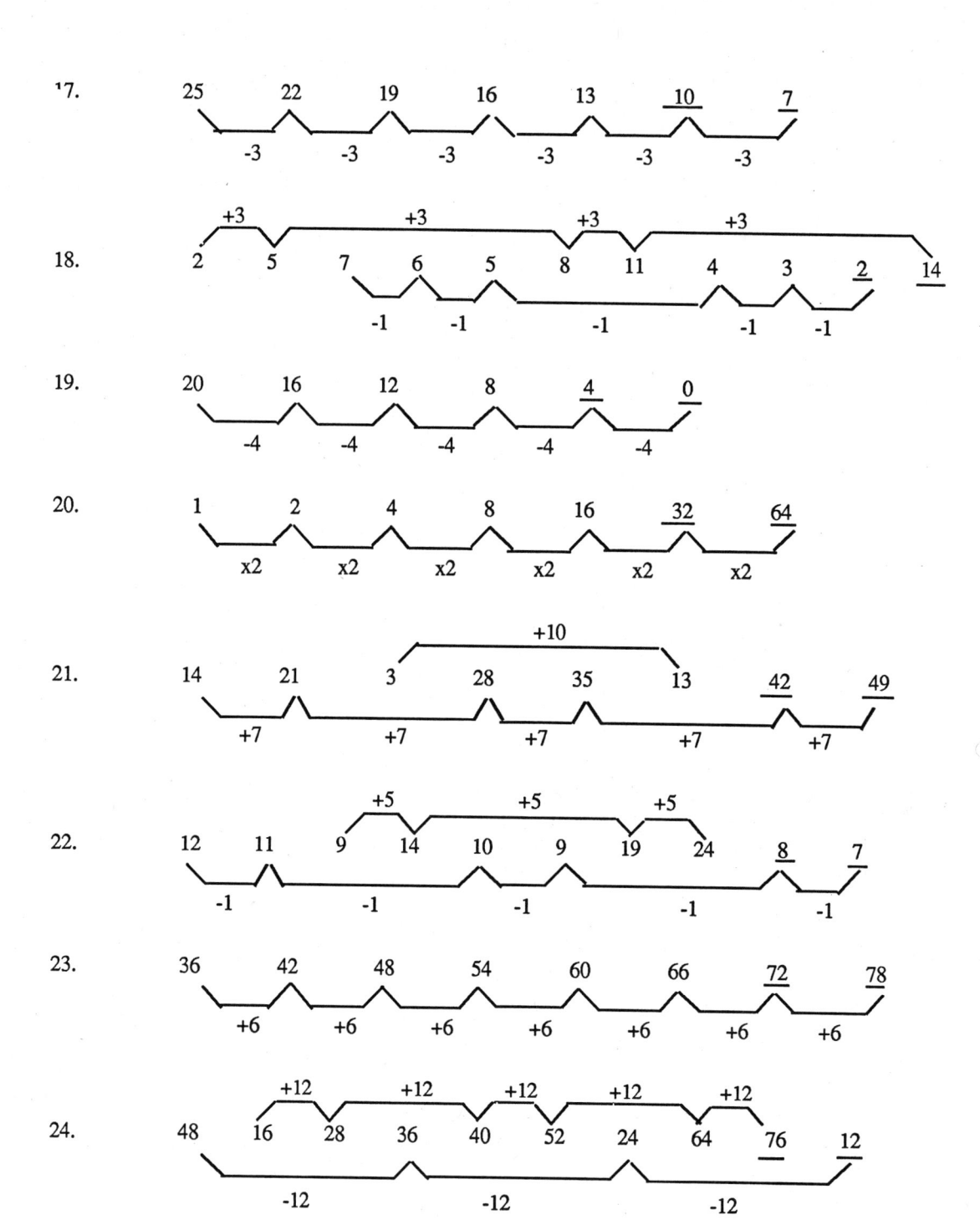

24.
          +12 +12 +12 +12 +12
    48 16 28 36 40 52 24 64 76 12
        -12   -12   -12

If your score was:
- 20 or more correct, you have an excellent score
- 16 to 19 correct, you have a good score
- 15 or less correct, you need additional practice

A Comprehensive Guide

For The

Postal Service

MAIL HANDLER

EXAM

GENERAL INFORMATION ABOUT THE TEST

The Mail Handler exam is divided into three sections. The first section of the test deals with Following Directions. You will be required to follow specific instructions from a test examiner and mark only answers he or she directs. Section Two of the exam deals with Address Comparison. In this section, you will compare pairs of addresses and determine if they are different or exactly alike. You will be given a very limited amount of time to do this section. The last portion of the test deals with Word Meaning. The test questions are sentences that each contain a single key word. You must identify the key word's meaning in each sentence from the choices given. Only one choice is synonymous to the key word. Each individual section in this guide is elaborated on at the beginning of the practice exercises provided.

Before you go any further in this book, it is suggested that you find yourself a place that is completely free of any distractions, has adequate overhead lighting and a comfortable desk and chair. It is not important where you go to satisfy these requirements; what is important is that you simulate examination room conditions as closely as possible. Thus, you will have a reasonable idea of what to expect when taking the actual test and become comfortable with that atmosphere.

FOLLOWING DIRECTIONS

This part of the exam is designed to determine how well you follow directions. How you perform here has bearing on the amount of time and effort required by the Post Office personnel to train you for a specific job. Obviously, a person that needs to be told only once how to do something would stand a better chance of being hired than someone who needs directions repeated. This is not a difficult test to do, particularly if you pay full attention to the examiner's every direction. You will be given an ample amount of time between directions to respond on your answer sheet. This is not a time oriented section, but rather it is just a matter of keeping up with the examiner's instructions as they are given.

A friend or relative will be needed to play the part of the test examiner. He or she will be responsible for reading the directions orally to you at a rate of 75 to 80 words per minute, pausing where indicated in the text. As a suggestion, have whoever you choose to help you, read with a timer until they have a general idea of what the rate of 75 to 80 words per minute is like. Pauses between directions should be timed also.

When you are ready to do one of the four exercises provided in this book, tear out those pages with the directions and give them to the person assisting you. You should be left with only the samples and answer sheets on which to mark your responses. Once a direction has been read by the examiner, it cannot be repeated. If you happen to miss part of a direction or do not understand the direction completely, do not attempt to guess the correct answer. Guessing on this part of the Mail Handler exam will probably hurt your test score more than help it. Just pass over that question and listen more closely to the next direction given. Most importantly, do not panic if a question has to be skipped. Overlooking one or two questions will not substantially affect your test score.

There are more answer blanks provided than there are directions on the exam so a great deal of your answer sheet will remain blank after you have completed the test. Also, your answers will tend to skip around on the answer sheet. Typically, question number 1 would correspond with answer blank number 1, question number 2 with answer blank number 2, etc. On this particular test, however, question number 1 may direct you to darken a particular letter in answer blank number 82, question number 2 may concern answer blank number 25, etc.

This is the major reason why it is suggested not to do any guessing if a question is not completely heard or understood; there are too many possibilities to consider. The correct answers to practice exams are posted at the end of each exercise. A scale has also been provided to rank your proficiency at following directions.

FOLLOWING DIRECTIONS / TEST I

NOTE TO PERSON ASSISTING IN THIS EXERCISE:
Remove from this test guide those pages of this exercise that comprise the directions (this page and the reverse). The test applicant should be left with only the samples and the answer sheet.

Directions are to be read orally, at the suggested rate of 75-80 words per minute, pausing only where indicated in parentheses. Read as clearly and concisely as possible; once a statement has been read, it cannot be repeated.

Examine Sample 1. (Pause 2-3 seconds). If more than two months begin with the letter J, as in jack, go to number 15 on your answer sheet and darken the letter B, as in boy. (Pause 7 seconds). Otherwise, darken the letter C, as in cat, at number 5 on your answer sheet. (Pause 7 seconds).

Examine Sample 2. (Pause 2-3 seconds). Write the number 17 in the smallest circle shown. Darken the resulting number-letter combination on your answer sheet only if there are two larger circles shown in the sample. (Pause 10 seconds). Otherwise, write the number 16 in square D, as in dog, and darken that number-letter combination on your answer sheet. (Pause 10 seconds).

Examine Sample 3. (Pause 2-3 seconds). This sample illustrates the respective number of routes originating from each of three postal substations in a metropolitan area. Select the largest substation in terms of number of routes and write the letter C, as in cat, beside it. (Pause 7 seconds). Darken the resulting number-letter combination on your answer sheet. (Pause 7 seconds).

Examine Sample 3 again. (Pause 2-3 seconds). If the Chaney Street station has more routes than the Myers Boulevard station, write the letter B, as in boy, beside the Clifford Avenue station. (Pause 5 seconds). If not, write the letter A, as in apple, beside the Myers Boulevard station (Pause 5 seconds). Darken the number-letter combination you have selected on your answer sheet. (Pause 7 seconds).

Examine Sample 4. (Pause 2-3 seconds). If the third number is greater than the second number, but less than the fifth number, write the letter A, as in apple, beside 42. (Pause 5 seconds). Otherwise, write the letter D, as in dog, beside the fourth number. (Pause 5 seconds). Darken the number-letter combination that you have selected on your answer sheet. (Pause 7 seconds).

Examine Sample 3 again. (Pause 2-3 seconds). Darken the letter D, as in dog, on number 9 of your answer sheet if the Chaney Street substation has the smallest number of routes. (Pause 7 seconds). Otherwise, go to number 82 on your answer sheet and darken the letter D, as in dog. (Pause 7 seconds).

Examine Sample 4 again. (Pause 2-3 seconds). If there are any numbers greater than 53, but less than 70, write the letter B, as in boy, beside that number and darken the resulting number-letter combination on your answer sheet. (Pause 7 seconds). Otherwise, write the letter E, as in elephant, beside the second number of the sample and darken that number-letter combination on your answer sheet. (Pause 10 seconds).

Examine Sample 5. (Pause 2-3 seconds). This sample shows four numbers, each representing a combined zip code and route direct number. The first five digits of each number identifies the zip code and the last two digits represent intercity route numbers. If all of the zip codes in Sample 5 are the same and there is not a route number higher than 50, darken the letter A, as in apple, on number 50 of your answer sheet. (Pause 10 seconds). Otherwise, darken the letter C, as in cat, on number 49 of your answer sheet. (Pause 7 seconds).

Examine Sample 6. (Pause 2-3 seconds). Write the letter A, as in apple, beside the lowest number if the first number in the sample is less than the last number in the sample, and if there is a number greater than 91. (Pause 7 seconds). Otherwise, write the letter E, as in elephant, beside the number 30. (Pause 5 seconds). Darken the number-letter combination you have selected on your answer sheet. (Pause 7 seconds).

Examine Sample 6 again. (Pause 2-3 seconds). Write the letter B, as in boy, beside the number 84 if the preceding number is less than 84. (Pause 5 seconds). Otherwise, write the letter C, as in cat, beside 84. (Pause 5 seconds). Darken the number- letter combination you have chosen on your answer sheet. (Pause 7 seconds).

Examine Sample 6 one more time. (Pause 2-3 seconds). If there is a number which is greater than 43, yet less than 53, write the letter D, as in dog, beside it. Darken that number-letter combination on your answer sheet. (Pause 10 seconds). If not, go to number 14 on your answer sheet and darken the letter B, as in boy. (Pause 7 seconds).

Examine Sample 7. (Pause 2-3 seconds). If Los Angeles is located in Florida, and Washington, D.C. is in California, write the number 16 on the line beside the letter E, as in elephant. (Pause 5 seconds). If the preceding statement is false, write the number 16 beside the letter E, as in elephant, anyway and darken the resulting number-letter combination on your answer sheet. (Pause 10 seconds).

Examine Sample 8. (Pause 2-3 seconds). Each of the five boxes show the starting and finishing times of five rural routes on a particular day. The time at the top is the rural carriers' starting time and the time listed below shows when they finished for the day. Find the carrier that spends the longest time on his route and write the number 10 beside the letter representing the carrier in question. (Pause 10 seconds). Darken your answer sheet with the number-letter combination you just made. (Pause 7 seconds).

Examine Sample 8 again. (Pause 2-3 seconds). If Carrier A, as in apple, finished for the day before Carrier B, as in boy, write the number 2 beside the letter A, as in apple. (Pause 5 seconds). Otherwise, find which one of the carriers had the latest starting time and write the number 7 beside the letter representing that carrier. (Pause 7 seconds). Darken the number-letter combination you have chosen on your answer sheet. (Pause 7 seconds).

Examine Sample 8 one more time. (Pause 2-3 seconds). Write the number 11 beside the letter representing the carrier with the second latest finishing time. (Pause 7 seconds). Darken that number-letter combination on your answer sheet. (Pause 7 seconds).

Examine Sample 9. (Pause 2-3 seconds). Write the letter E, as in elephant, beside the number that is in the circle and darken your answer with the resulting number-letter combination. (Pause 5 seconds). If there is no circle present, write the number 47 beside the letter within the rectangel and darken that number-letter combinationon your answer sheet. (Pause 10 seconds).

Examine Sample 10. (Pause 2-3 seconds). If any one of the statues shown in the sample is not located in the western part of the United States, go to number 36 on your answer sheet and darken the letter E, as in elephant. (Pause 7 seconds). Otherwise, go to number 3 on your answer sheet and darken the letter B, as in boy. (Paue 7 seconds).

Examine Sample 10 again. (Pause 2-3 seconds). If any of the states listed begin with the letter C, as in cat, go to number 49 on your answer sheet and darken the letter C, as in cat. (Pause 7 seconds).

Examine Sample 11. (Pause 2-3 seconds.) If 9 is greater than 7, and 20 is less than 21, write the number 60 on the line beside D, as in dog, and darken that number-letter combination on your answer sheet. (Pause 10 seconds.) Otherwise go to number 23 on your answer sheet and darken the letter B, as in boy.

Examine Sample 12. (Pause 2-3 seconds). Find the number that is greater than 13 and less than 64, and go to that number on your answer sheet and darken the letter C, as in cat. (Pause 10 seconds).

Examine Sample 13. (Pause 2-3 seconds). Choose the number that is shown in identically sized shapes and go to that number on you answer sheet and darken the letter E, as in elephant. (Pause 10 seconds).

Examine Sample 14. (Pause 2-3 seconds). If 40 is less than 69 and greater than 15, go to 40 on your answer sheet and darken the letter A, as in apple. (Pause 7 seconds). If not, write the letter C, as in cat, beside the number 15 in the sample. (Pause 5 seconds). Darken that number-letter combination on your answer sheet. (Pause 7 seconds).

-END OF TEST-

FOLLOWING DIRECTIONS / TEST I SAMPLES

1. March : December : November : July : January

2. (A)   (C)   [D]   [E]   (B)

3. [Myers Blvd 32_ routes]   [Clifford Ave 45_ routes]   [Chaney St 9_routes]

4. 42_   1_   50_   73_   79_

5. 9837841   9837810   9837814   9837813

6. 43_   27_   84_   91_   30_   52_

7. _____B   _____E

8. [7:30AM 2:45PM _A] [7:00AM 2:15PM _B] [6:00AM 4:00PM _C] [6:45AM 3:30PM _D] [7:00AM 3:00PM _E]

9. [B_]   [12_]   /\A_/\   /\47_/\

10. California : Oregon : Alaska : Florida : Washington

11. _____D

12. 13   51   64   65   80

13. [20]   (6)   [20]   (6)

14. _A   15_   69_   40_   _C

The Postal Exam Preparation Book 201

ANSWER SHEET TO FOLLOWING DIRECTIONS / TEST I

(This page may be removed to mark answers.)

FOLLOWING DIRECTIONS / TEST I ANSWERS

12	E		16	E
5	C		10	C
17	B		7	A
45	C		11	D
32	A		47	B
42	A		36	E
9	D		49	C
1	E		60	D
50	A		51	C
30	E		20	E
84	B		40	A
52	D			

If your score was:
- —19 or more correct, you have an excellent score
- —14 to 18 correct, you have a good score
- —13 or less correct, you should practice more.

FOLLOWING DIRECTIONS / TEST II

NOTE TO PERSON ASSISTING IN THIS EXERCISE:
Remove from this test guide those pages of this exercise that comprise the directions (this page and the reverse). The test applicant should be left with only the samples and the answer sheet.

Directions are to be read orally, at the suggested rate of 75-80 words per minute, pausing only where indicated in parentheses. Read as clearly and concisely as possible; once a statement has been read, it cannot be repeated.

Examine Sample 1. (Pause 2-3 seconds) The figures shown represent postal drop boxes, each showing respective collection times. Write the letter B, as in boy, in the box that has the earliest collection time. (Pause 5 seconds). Examine the numbers that represent the minutes of the collection time you have selected. Go to that number on your answer sheet and darken that letter- number combination on your answer sheet.. (Pause 7 seconds).

Examine Sample 2. (Pause 2-3 seconds). If 30 is more than 27, and 40 is less than 41, write the letter C, as in cat, beside number 5 in the sample. (Pause 5 seconds). If not, write the letter E, as in elephant, beside number 16. (Pause 5 seconds). Darken the selected number-letter combination on your answer sheet.. (Pause 7 seconds).

Examine Sample 2 again. (Pause 2-3 seconds). Write the letter E, as in elephant, beside 16 if 16 is greater than 7. (Pause 5 seconds). Otherwise, write an A, as in apple, beside number 7. (Pause 5 seconds). Darken your chosen number-letter combination on your answer sheet. (Pause 7 seconds).

Examine Sample 3. (Pause 2-3 seconds). There are three squares and two circles of different proportions. In the second to the largest square write the number 75. (Pause 7 seconds). Darken that number-letter combination on your answer sheet. (Pause 7 seconds).

Examine Sample 3 again. (Pause 2-3 seconds). If 10 divided by 5 equals 3, then write the number 76 in Square C, as in cat. (Pause 5 seconds). If not, write the number 81 in the larger circle. (Pause 5 seconds). Darken the number-letter combination you have selected on your answer sheet. (Pause 7 seconds).

Examine Sample 4. (Pause 2-3 seconds). Write the letter A, as in apple, beside the second largest number and the letter D, as in dog, beside the largest number. (Pause 10 seconds). Of the remaining two numbers, write the letter E, as in elephant, beside the smallest number of the two. (Pause 5 seconds). Darken that number-letter combination on your answer sheet. (Pause 7 seconds).

Examine Sample 5. (Pause 2-3 seconds). The three boxes shown in this sample represent different classes of mail; each are assigned a letter to reference them. If Box D, as in dog, is a cheaper means of mailing advertisements than Box A, as in apple, find number 15 on your answer sheet and darken the letter D, as in dog. (Pause 7 seconds). If Box D, as in dog, is a more expensive means of mailing advertisements, then find number 3 on your answer sheet and darken the letter A, as in apple. (Pause 7 seconds).

Examine Sample 6. (Pause 2-3 seconds). This sample illustrates five numbers each representing the length of a different mail route in terms of mileage. Write the letter C, as in cat, beside the third longest route, if it is over 25 miles in length. (Pause 5 seconds). Otherwise, write the letter A, as in apple, beside the smallest route. (Pause 5 seconds). Darken the number-letter combination you have chosen on your answer sheet. (Pause 7 seconds).

Examine Sample 6 again. (Pause 2-3 seconds). Pick out the route that is more than 14 miles long, yet less than 40 miles long. (Pause 5 seconds). Write the letter A, as in apple, beside it. (Pause 5 seconds). Darken the resulting number-letter combination on your answer sheet. (Pause 7 seconds).

Examine Sample 6 one more time. (Pause 2-3 seconds). If the longest mail route is exactly 37 miles more than the smallest route, go to number 3 on your answer sheet and darken the letter C, as in cat. (Pause 10 seconds). If it is not exactly 37 miles longer, then find number 8 on your answer sheet and darken the letter E, as in elephant. (Pause 10 seconds).

Examine Sample 7. (Pause 2-3 seconds). Write the letter B, as in boy, in the triangular shape and the letter C, as in cat, in the circular shape. (Pause 10 seconds). If the trapezoid shape represented by the number 24 has more sides than a square, darken the number-letter combination that is shown in the triangular shape on your answer sheet. (Pause 10 seconds). Otherwise, darken the number-letter combination on your answer sheet that is shown in the circular shape. (Pause 10 seconds).

Examine Sample 8. (Pause 2-3 seconds). This sample has five different numbers shown. Each number represents the number of parcels that each route has had to deliver on a particular day. Consider 72 the largest number and 9 the smallest number. If the second largest number is more than 50, then write the letter C, as in cat, beside number 12. (Pause 5 seconds). Darken the number-letter combination you have made on your answer sheet. (Pause 7 seconds). If the second smallest number of parcels is less than 11, write the letter E, as in elephant, beside 45 and darken that number-letter combination on your answer sheet. (Pause 10 seconds). If none of the previous statements are true then write the letter C, as in cat, beside the number 9 and darken your answer sheet accordingly. (Pause 10 seconds).

Examine Sample 9. (Pause 2-3 seconds). Write the number 20 beside letter B, as in boy, if Chicago is located in Alaska. (Pause 5 seconds). If not, write the number 6 beside letter C, as in cat, and darken that number-letter combination on your answer sheet. (Pause 10 seconds).

Examine Sample 9 again. (Pause 2-3 seconds). If the product of 3 times 3 is greater than the sum of 4 plus 4, then write the number 17 beside the letter E, as in elephant. (Pause 7 seconds). Otherwise, write the number 82 beside the letter E, as in elephant. (Pause 5 seconds). Darken your answer sheet with the number-letter comination that you have chosen. (Pause 7 seconds.)

Examine Sample 10. (Pause2-3 seconds). Sample 10 shows five mail volume index figures. Index numbers located in the upper portion of each circle indicate an above-average mail volume. Index numbers located in the lower portion of each circle indicate a below-average index figure. If Circle C, as in cat, and E, as elephant, each illustrate a below-average index figure, find number 27 on your answer sheet and darken the letter D, as in dog. (Pause 10 seconds). However, if Circle A, as in apple, and C, as in cat, show above-average figures, find number 14 on your answer sheet and darken the letter A, as in apple. (Pause 10 seconds).

Examine Sample 11. (Pause 2-3 seconds). If 30 is greater than 31, write the number 30 on the line beside letter C, as in cat.. Darken that number-letter comination on your answer sheet.. (Pause 10 seconds). If not, then write the number 30 on the line beside the letter B, as in boy, and darken your answer sheet accordingly. (Pause 10 seconds).

Examine Sample 9 again. (Pause 2-3 seconds). Go to the fourth letter form the right side of the sample and write the number 32 beside it. (Pause 5 seconds). Darken this number-letter combination on your answer sheet. (Pause 7 seconds).

Examine Sample 11 again. (Pause 2-3 seconds). Write the letter C, as in cat, beside 30. Darken that number-letter combination on your answer sheet only if 30 is the largest number present in the sample. (Pause 10 seconds). Otherwise, write the letter A, as in apple, beside 48. Darken your answer on the answer sheet. (Pause 7 seconds).

Examine Sample 12. (Pause 2-3 seconds). This sample has four pairs of numbers each measuring the quantity of letter dropped in a test collection box on four consecutive Mondays. The first number in each pair represents the number of out-of-town letters and the second number represents the number of local delivery letters. If there are more out-of-town letters than there are local letters in each of the pairs and the testing is conducted on Tuesday, go to number 93 on your answer sheet and darken the letter A, as in apple. (Pause 7 seconds). Otherwise, go to number 69 on your answer sheet and darken the letter B, as in boy. (Pause 7 seconds.)

-END OF TEST-

FOLLOWING DIRECTIONS / TEST II SAMPLES

1. [1:10PM]   [1:45PM]   [10:45PM]

2.   5_   7_   16_

3. [_A]   [_B]   [_C]   (_D)   (_E)

4. 47___   52___   46___   2___

5. [First Class A]   [Second Class C]   [Third Class D]

6. 4_   13_   41_   40_   24__

7. [□21_]   [△22_]   [○23_]   [▱24_]

8. 12___   18___   9___   72___   45___

9. _B   _D   _X   _E   _C

10. (A^{83})   (B$_{46}$)   (C^{15})   (D$_{10}$)   (E^{26})

11. A__   30__   C__   31__   B__   48__

12. 70/10   87/14   90/3   88/69

ANSWER SHEET TO FOLLOWING DIRECTIONS / TEST 2

1. Ⓐ Ⓑ Ⓒ Ⓓ Ⓔ   33. Ⓐ Ⓑ Ⓒ Ⓓ Ⓔ   65. Ⓐ Ⓑ Ⓒ Ⓓ Ⓔ
2. Ⓐ Ⓑ Ⓒ Ⓓ Ⓔ   34. Ⓐ Ⓑ Ⓒ Ⓓ Ⓔ   66. Ⓐ Ⓑ Ⓒ Ⓓ Ⓔ
3. Ⓐ Ⓑ Ⓒ Ⓓ Ⓔ   35. Ⓐ Ⓑ Ⓒ Ⓓ Ⓔ   67. Ⓐ Ⓑ Ⓒ Ⓓ Ⓔ
4. Ⓐ Ⓑ Ⓒ Ⓓ Ⓔ   36. Ⓐ Ⓑ Ⓒ Ⓓ Ⓔ   68. Ⓐ Ⓑ Ⓒ Ⓓ Ⓔ
5. Ⓐ Ⓑ Ⓒ Ⓓ Ⓔ   37. Ⓐ Ⓑ Ⓒ Ⓓ Ⓔ   69. Ⓐ Ⓑ Ⓒ Ⓓ Ⓔ
6. Ⓐ Ⓑ Ⓒ Ⓓ Ⓔ   38. Ⓐ Ⓑ Ⓒ Ⓓ Ⓔ   70. Ⓐ Ⓑ Ⓒ Ⓓ Ⓔ
7. Ⓐ Ⓑ Ⓒ Ⓓ Ⓔ   39. Ⓐ Ⓑ Ⓒ Ⓓ Ⓔ   71. Ⓐ Ⓑ Ⓒ Ⓓ Ⓔ
8. Ⓐ Ⓑ Ⓒ Ⓓ Ⓔ   40. Ⓐ Ⓑ Ⓒ Ⓓ Ⓔ   72. Ⓐ Ⓑ Ⓒ Ⓓ Ⓔ
9. Ⓐ Ⓑ Ⓒ Ⓓ Ⓔ   41. Ⓐ Ⓑ Ⓒ Ⓓ Ⓔ   73. Ⓐ Ⓑ Ⓒ Ⓓ Ⓔ
10. Ⓐ Ⓑ Ⓒ Ⓓ Ⓔ   42. Ⓐ Ⓑ Ⓒ Ⓓ Ⓔ   74. Ⓐ Ⓑ Ⓒ Ⓓ Ⓔ
11. Ⓐ Ⓑ Ⓒ Ⓓ Ⓔ   43. Ⓐ Ⓑ Ⓒ Ⓓ Ⓔ   75. Ⓐ Ⓑ Ⓒ Ⓓ Ⓔ
12. Ⓐ Ⓑ Ⓒ Ⓓ Ⓔ   44. Ⓐ Ⓑ Ⓒ Ⓓ Ⓔ   76. Ⓐ Ⓑ Ⓒ Ⓓ Ⓔ
13. Ⓐ Ⓑ Ⓒ Ⓓ Ⓔ   45. Ⓐ Ⓑ Ⓒ Ⓓ Ⓔ   77. Ⓐ Ⓑ Ⓒ Ⓓ Ⓔ
14. Ⓐ Ⓑ Ⓒ Ⓓ Ⓔ   46. Ⓐ Ⓑ Ⓒ Ⓓ Ⓔ   78. Ⓐ Ⓑ Ⓒ Ⓓ Ⓔ
15. Ⓐ Ⓑ Ⓒ Ⓓ Ⓔ   47. Ⓐ Ⓑ Ⓒ Ⓓ Ⓔ   79. Ⓐ Ⓑ Ⓒ Ⓓ Ⓔ
16. Ⓐ Ⓑ Ⓒ Ⓓ Ⓔ   48. Ⓐ Ⓑ Ⓒ Ⓓ Ⓔ   80. Ⓐ Ⓑ Ⓒ Ⓓ Ⓔ
17. Ⓐ Ⓑ Ⓒ Ⓓ Ⓔ   49. Ⓐ Ⓑ Ⓒ Ⓓ Ⓔ   81. Ⓐ Ⓑ Ⓒ Ⓓ Ⓔ
18. Ⓐ Ⓑ Ⓒ Ⓓ Ⓔ   50. Ⓐ Ⓑ Ⓒ Ⓓ Ⓔ   82. Ⓐ Ⓑ Ⓒ Ⓓ Ⓔ
19. Ⓐ Ⓑ Ⓒ Ⓓ Ⓔ   51. Ⓐ Ⓑ Ⓒ Ⓓ Ⓔ   83. Ⓐ Ⓑ Ⓒ Ⓓ Ⓔ
20. Ⓐ Ⓑ Ⓒ Ⓓ Ⓔ   52. Ⓐ Ⓑ Ⓒ Ⓓ Ⓔ   84. Ⓐ Ⓑ Ⓒ Ⓓ Ⓔ
21. Ⓐ Ⓑ Ⓒ Ⓓ Ⓔ   53. Ⓐ Ⓑ Ⓒ Ⓓ Ⓔ   85. Ⓐ Ⓑ Ⓒ Ⓓ Ⓔ
22. Ⓐ Ⓑ Ⓒ Ⓓ Ⓔ   54. Ⓐ Ⓑ Ⓒ Ⓓ Ⓔ   86. Ⓐ Ⓑ Ⓒ Ⓓ Ⓔ
23. Ⓐ Ⓑ Ⓒ Ⓓ Ⓔ   55. Ⓐ Ⓑ Ⓒ Ⓓ Ⓔ   87. Ⓐ Ⓑ Ⓒ Ⓓ Ⓔ
24. Ⓐ Ⓑ Ⓒ Ⓓ Ⓔ   56. Ⓐ Ⓑ Ⓒ Ⓓ Ⓔ   88. Ⓐ Ⓑ Ⓒ Ⓓ Ⓔ
25. Ⓐ Ⓑ Ⓒ Ⓓ Ⓔ   57. Ⓐ Ⓑ Ⓒ Ⓓ Ⓔ   89. Ⓐ Ⓑ Ⓒ Ⓓ Ⓔ
26. Ⓐ Ⓑ Ⓒ Ⓓ Ⓔ   58. Ⓐ Ⓑ Ⓒ Ⓓ Ⓔ   90. Ⓐ Ⓑ Ⓒ Ⓓ Ⓔ
27. Ⓐ Ⓑ Ⓒ Ⓓ Ⓔ   59. Ⓐ Ⓑ Ⓒ Ⓓ Ⓔ   91. Ⓐ Ⓑ Ⓒ Ⓓ Ⓔ
28. Ⓐ Ⓑ Ⓒ Ⓓ Ⓔ   60. Ⓐ Ⓑ Ⓒ Ⓓ Ⓔ   92. Ⓐ Ⓑ Ⓒ Ⓓ Ⓔ
29. Ⓐ Ⓑ Ⓒ Ⓓ Ⓔ   61. Ⓐ Ⓑ Ⓒ Ⓓ Ⓔ   93. Ⓐ Ⓑ Ⓒ Ⓓ Ⓔ
30. Ⓐ Ⓑ Ⓒ Ⓓ Ⓔ   62. Ⓐ Ⓑ Ⓒ Ⓓ Ⓔ   94. Ⓐ Ⓑ Ⓒ Ⓓ Ⓔ
31. Ⓐ Ⓑ Ⓒ Ⓓ Ⓔ   63. Ⓐ Ⓑ Ⓒ Ⓓ Ⓔ   95. Ⓐ Ⓑ Ⓒ Ⓓ Ⓔ
32. Ⓐ Ⓑ Ⓒ Ⓓ Ⓔ   64. Ⓐ Ⓑ Ⓒ Ⓓ Ⓔ

(This page may be removed to mark answers.)

FOLLOWING DIRECTIONS / TEST II ANSWERS

10	B		9	C
5	C		6	C
16	E		17	E
75	B		14	A
81	D		27	B
2	E		83	A
15	D		30	B
4	A		32	D
24	A		48	A
3	C		69	B
23	C		14	C

If your score was:
—19 or more correct, you have an excellent score
—14 to 18 correct, you have a good score
—13 or less correct, you should practice more.

FOLLOWING DIRECTIONS / TEST III

NOTE TO PERSON ASSISTING IN THIS EXERCISE:
Remove from this test guide those pages of this exercise that comprise the directions (this page and the reverse). The test applicant should be left with only the samples and the answer sheet.

Directions are to be read orally, at the suggested rate of 75-80 words per minute, pausing only where indicated in parentheses. Read as clearly and concisely as possible; once a statement has been read, it cannot be repeated.

Examine Sample 1. (Pause 2-3 seconds). If any of the numbers shown are greater than 122, go to number 22 on your answer sheet and darken the letter D, as in dog. (Pause 7 seconds). If not, go to number 23 on your answer sheet and darken the letter A, as in apple. (Pause 7 seconds).

Examine Sample 2. (Pause 2-3 seconds). Write the letter E, as in elephant, on the line provided only if the number shown is less than 51. (Pause 5 seconds). If the number shown is greater than or equal to 51, write the letter B, as in boy, on the line provided. (Pause 5 seconds). Darken the number-letter combination you have selected on your answer sheet. (Pause 7 seconds).

Examine Sample 3. (Pause 2-3 seconds). Write the number 67 on the shortest line shown. (Pause 5 seconds). Write the number 68 on the longest line shown. (Pause 5 seconds). Now, darken both of the number-letter combinations you have made on your answer sheet. (Pause 12 seconds).

Examine Sample 3 again. (Pause 2-3 seconds). If any part of the statement that I am about to read is false, write the number 2 on line A, as in apple. (Pause 3 seconds). There are seven days in a week, four weeks in a month, and 12 months in a year. (Pause 5 seconds). However, if any of the statement is true, write the number one on line A, as in apple. (Pause 3 seconds). Darken the number-letter combination you have selected for line A, as in apple, on your answer sheet. (Pause 7 seconds).

Examine Sample 4. (Pause 2-3 seconds). Write the letter B, as in boy, beside the highest number shown within a geometric shape. (Pause 5 seconds). Darken the resulting number-letter combination on your answer sheet. (Pause 7 seconds).

Examine Sample 4 again. (Pause 2-3 seconds). Now, write the letter C, as in cat, beside the highest number shown in the sample. (Pause 5 seconds). Darken that number-letter combination on your answer sheet. (Pause 7 seconds).

Examine Sample 4 one more time. (Pause 2-3 seconds). Write the letter D, as in dog, in the circular shape and darken that number-letter combination on your answer sheet. (Pause 10 seconds).

Examine Sample 5. (Pause 2-3 seconds). This sample is a record of the time that Mr. John Smith returned from his mail route. We will assume that Mr. Smith left the office at the same time each morning to begin his route. (Pause 3 seconds). If Mr. Smith's delivery time is improving as the week progresses, go to number 86 on your answer sheet and darken the letter E, as in elephant. (Pause 10 seconds). If, on the other hand, Mr. Smith seems to be taking more time to deliver his mail as the week progresses, go to number 89 on your answer sheet and darken the letter B, as in boy. (Pause 7 seconds).

If 40 is less than 40.5, but greater than 39, go to number 11 on your answer sheet and darken the letter D, as in dog. (Pause 7 seconds). Otherwise, go to number 15 on your answer sheet and darken the letter E, as in elephant. (Pause 7 seconds).

Examine Sample 6. (Pause 2-3 seconds). On the line provided write the number of letters that are needed to spell the word "Wednesday". (Pause 10 seconds). Darken the number-letter combination you have made on your answer sheet. (Pause 7 seconds).

Examine Sample 7. (Pause 2-3 seconds). Write the number 53 beside the letter A, as in apple. (Pause 5 seconds). If there are more than six letters shown in Sample 7, then darken the number-letter combination you have made on your answer sheet. (Pause 10 seconds). If not, write the number 57 beside the letter C, as in cat, and darken that number-letter combination on your answer sheet. (Pause 7 seconds).

If New York, New York is north of Miami, Florida, and Boston, Massachusetts, is east of San Francisco, California, go to number 38 on your answer sheet and darken the letter D, as in dog. (Pause 10 seconds). If any part of the previous statement is incorrect, go to number 36 on your answer sheet and darken the letter B, as in boy. (Pause 7 seconds).

Examine Sample 8. (Pause 2-3 seconds). Write the number 42 beside the letter B, as in boy. (Pause 5 seconds). Write the number 52 beside the letter D, as in dog. (Pause 5 seconds). Darken the number-letter combinations you have just made on your answer sheet. (Pause 10 seconds).

Examine Sample 9. (Pause 2-3 seconds). Write the letter A, as in apple, in the circle on the left side. (Pause 5 seconds). Write the letter D, as in dog, in the other circle. (Pause 5 seconds). Now, write the number 17 in Circle D, as in dog, and the number 18 in Circle A, as in apple. (Pause 10 seconds). On your answer sheet, darken both number-letter combinations shown in each of the circles. (Pause 10 seconds).

Examine Sample 9 again. (Pause 2-3 seconds). If Circle A, as in apple, and D, as in dog, are the same size and interconnected, go to number 63 on your answer sheet and darken the letter E, as in elephant. (Pause 7 seconds). If the circles are not interconnected, go to number 23 on your answer sheet and darken the letter C, as in cat. (Pause 7 seconds).

Examine Sample 10. (Pause 2-3 seconds). Write the letter A, as in apple, on the line provided. (Pause 5 seconds). Select the second highest number from the sequence shown and write it beside the letter you have just written. (Pause 7 seconds). Darken the resulting number-letter combination on your answer sheet. (Pause 7 seconds).

Examine Sample 10 again. (Pause 2-3 seconds). Select the highest number from the sequence shown. Go to that number on your answer sheet. (Pause 5 seconds). Darken the letter E, as in elephant. (Pause 5 seconds).

Examine Sample 11. (Pause 2-3 seconds). Select the largest number shown, and completely circle it and the letter above it. (Pause 7 seconds). Examine the last two digits of the number you have circled. Go to that number on your answer sheet. (Pause 5 seconds). Darken the letter shown in your circle. (Pause 5 seconds).

Examine Sample 11 again. (Pause 2-3 seconds). If the number below D, as in dog, is less than the number below C, as in cat, go to number 54 on your answer sheet, and darken the letter A, as in apple. (Pause 10 seconds). If not, go to 54 on your answer sheet and darken the letter B, as in boy. (Pause 7 seconds).

If 5 is greater than 4, but less than 6, darken the letter D, as in dog, at number 15 of your answer sheet. (Pause 7 seconds). If not, darken the letter C, as in cat, at number 55 on your answer sheet. (Pause 7 seconds).

If 40 is greater than 25 plus 15, go to number 71 on your answer sheet and darken the letter E as in elephant. (Pause 7 seconds). If not, go to number 71 on your answer sheet anyway and darken the letter B, as in boy. (Pause 7 seconds).

Examine Sample 10 again. (Pause 2-3 seconds). If there are more than 5 numbers in the sample, go to number 33 on your answer sheet and darken the letter B, as in boy (Pause 7 seconds). If otherwise, go to number 41 on your answer sheet and darken the letter A, as in apple. (Pause 7 seconds).

Examine Sample 1 again. (Pause 2-3 seconds). If any of the 3 numbers shown is greater than 145, go to number 3 on your answer sheet and darken the letter D, as in dog. (Pause 7 seconds). Otherwise, go to number 95 on your answer sheet and darken the letter E, as in elephant. (Pause 5 seconds).

-END OF TEST-

FOLLOWING DIRECTIONS / TEST III SAMPLES

1.   147   122   130

2.   50____

3.   0————A
                  0——————C
                  0——E

4.   [74_]   (72_)   △75_   77_   76_

5.   4:05PM   4:15PM   4:25PM   4:35PM   5:00PM
      Monday   Tuesday Wednesday Thursday   Friday

6.   _____A

7. ____A____X____L____C____F____I

8.   B____   D____

9.   ◯   ▭   ◯

10.   14   28   17   33   ____

11.   A   B   C   D
     .045 .054 .07   .45

ANSWER SHEET TO FOLLOWING DIRECTIONS / TEST III

(This page may be removed to mark answers.)

The Postal Exam Preparation Book

FOLLOWING DIRECTIONS / TEST III ANSWERS

22	D	42 B,	52 D
50	E	17 D,	18 A
67	E, 68 C	23	C
1	A	28	A
75	B	33	E
77	C	45	D
72	D	54	B
89	B	15	D
11	D	71	B
9	A	41	A
57	C	3	D
38	D		

If your score was:
— 19 or more correct, you have an excellent score
— 14 to 18 correct, you have a good score
— 13 or less correct, you should practice more.

The Postal Exam Preparation Book 221

FOLLOWING DIRECTIONS / TEST 4.

NOTE TO PERSON ASSISTING IN THIS EXERCISE:
Remove from this test guide those pages of this exercise that comprise the directions (this page and the reverse). The test applicant should be left with only the samples and the answer sheet.

Directions are to be read orally, at the suggested rate of 75-80 words per minute, pausing only where indicated in parentheses. Read as clearly and concisely as possible; once a statement has been read, it cannot be repeated.

Examine Sample 1. (Pause 2-3 seconds). Write the letter D, as in dog, beside the lowest number in the series of numbers shown. (Pause 5 seconds). Write the letter C, as in cat, beside the highest number in the series only if it is higher than 20. (Pause 5 seconds). Darken both the number-letter combinations you have just made on your answer sheet. (Pause 10 seconds).

Examine Sample 2. (Pause 2-3 seconds). If 20 is less than 20.5, but greater than 20.1 write the letter E, as in elephant, in the smallest circle shown. (Pause 5 seconds). Otherwise, write the letter A, as in apple, in the largest circle shown. (Pause 5 seconds). Darken the number-letter combination you have selected on your answer sheet. (Pause 7 seconds).

Examine Sample 2 again. (Pause 2-3 seconds). Write the letter B, as in boy, in the one shaped that is unlike the other four shapes in the sample. (Pause 5 seconds). Darken the resulting number-letter combination on your answer sheet. (Pause 7 seconds).

Examine Sample 3. (Pause 2-3 seconds). Each of the figures shown in the sample represents different postal substations and their respective deadlines for overnight express mail. Select the substation that has the latest deadline. Go to number 53 on your answer sheet and darken in the letter that corresponds to that station. (Pause 10 seconds).

Examine Sample 3 again. (Pause 2-3 seconds). Select the substation that has the earliest deadline. Go to number 54 on your answer sheet and darken in the letter that corresponds to that station. (Pause 10 seconds).

Examine Sample 4. (Pause 2-3 seconds). Select the third number in the series and go to that number on your answer sheet. Darken in the letter C, as in cat. (Pause 7 seconds).

Examine Sample 4 again. (Pause 2-3 seconds). Starting from the right, select the second number in the series. Go to that number on your answer sheet and darken the letter D, as in dog. (Pause 7 seconds).

Examine Sample 5. (Pause 2-3 seconds). On your answer sheet, go to both the numbers shown in the two smaller circles, and darken the letter E, as in elephant, at each corresponding number. (Pause 12 seconds).

Examine Sample 6. (Pause 2-3 seconds). This sample illustrates five boxes with their respective weight in pounds. Since the second box weighs more than the first box, write the letter C, as in cat, in the fourth box. (Pause 5 seconds). Darken that number-letter combination on your answer sheet. (Pause 7 seconds).

Examine Sample 6 again. (Pause 2-3 seconds). If the third box is the heaviest parcel and the fifth box is the lightest parcel, write the letter E, as in elephant, in the first box and darken that number-letter combination on your answer sheet. (Pause 10 seconds). Otherwise, write the letter D, as in dog, in the second parcel and darken your answer sheet with that number- letter combination. (Pause 10 seconds).

Examine Sample 7. (Pause 2-3 seconds). If 28 is greater than the sum of 20 plus 9, write the number 16 beside the letter E, as in elephant. (Pause 5 seconds). However, if 28 is not greater than the sum of 20 plus 9, write the number 55 beside the letter C, as in cat. (Pause 5 seconds). Darken the number-letter combination you have selected as correct on your answer sheet. (Pause 7 seconds).

Examine Sample 7 again. (Pause 2-3 seconds). If there are more than two days in a week, write the number 80 beside the letter A, as in apple. (Pause 5 seconds). If not, write the number 13 beside the letter E, as in elephant. Darken the number-letter combination you have chosen as correct on your answer sheet. (Pause 7 seconds).

Examine Sample 8. (Pause 2-3 seconds). Write the letter A, as in apple, beside 35. (Pause 5 seconds). Write the number 33 beside the letter D, as in dog, if 33 is less than 35. (Pause 5 seconds). Now, go to number 10 on your answer sheet and darken the letter D, as in dog. (Pause 7 seconds).

Examine Sample 9. (Pause 2-3 seconds). This sample illustrates three mail drop boxes and their respective collection times. Select the mail drop with the earliest collection time and darken the letter that represents it on number 5 of your answer sheet. (Pause 10 seconds).

Examine Sample 9 again. (Pause 2-3 seconds). Select the mail drop that is picked up at the latest time. Go to number 17 on your answer sheet and darken the letter E, as in elephant, not C, as in cat. (Pause 10 seconds).

The Postal Exam Preparation Book 223

Examine Sample 9 one more time. (Pause 2-3 seconds). If Box C, as in cat, is collected later than Box E, as in elephant, and Box D, as in dog, is collected later than Box C, as in cat, go to number 4 on your answer sheet and darken the letter A, as in apple. (Pause 10 seconds). Otherwise, go to number 9 on your answer sheet and darken the letter A, as in apple. (Pause 7 seconds).

Examine Sample 10. (Pause 2-3 seconds). The three boxes shown in the sample illustrate the first two numbers of zip codes. Consider, as a general rule, the higher the zip code number, the further west the destination. (Pause 3 seconds). Select the box that has the greatest chance to be delivered in the eastern United States and write the letter D, as in dog, beside that box. (Pause 5 seconds). Now, darken that number-letter combination on your answer sheet. (Pause 7 seconds).

Examine Sample 10 again. (Pause 2-3 seconds). Select the box that has the greatest chance to be delivered in the midwestern United States and write the letter D, as in dog, beside it. (Pause 5 seconds). Darken that number-letter combination on your answer sheet. (Pause 7 seconds).

If there are not exactly 50 states in the United States, darken the letter B, as in boy, on number 27 of your answer sheet. (Pause 7 seconds). Otherwise, go to number 82 on your answer sheet and darken the letter C, as in cat. (Pause 5 seconds).

If 6 is less than 36 and 8 plus 2 is greater than 11, go to number 47 on your answer sheet and darken the letter A, as in apple. (Pause 7 seconds). If the statement just given is wrong, go to number 48 on your answer sheet and darken the letter A, as in apple. (Pause 7 seconds).

Examine Sample 11. (Pause 2-3 seconds). Each of the five numbers shown represents the total number of deliveries for five different routes. Select the route with the largest number of deliveries and write the letter A, as in apple, to the right side of that number. (Pause 5 seconds). With regard to the same route, using the last two numbers of the delivery count, go to that number on your answer sheet and darken the letter A, as in apple. (Pause 10 seconds).

Examine Sample 11 again. (Pause 2-3 seconds). If any of the routes have more than 1059 stops, go to number 11 on your answer sheet and darken the letter B, as in boy. (Pause 7 seconds). Otherwise, go to number 94 on your answer sheet and darken the letter C, as in cat. (Pause 7 seconds).

Examine Sample 11 one more time. (Pause 2-3 seconds). Write the letter C, as in cat, above the route with 700 total deliveries. (Pause 5 seconds). Write the letter E, as in elephant, above the route with 640 total deliveries. (Pause 5 seconds). Write the letter C, as in cat, above the route with 930 total deliveries. (Pause 5 seconds). Darken the letter E, as in elephant, on number 64 of your answer sheet if the letter E, as in elephant, is assigned to the smallest of the three routes you have just assigned letters. (Pause 10 seconds). Otherwise, go to number 25 on your answer sheet and darken letter E, as in elephant. (Pause 7 seconds).

-END OF TEST-

FOLLOWING DIRECTIONS / TEST IV SAMPLES

1.   4____   8____   12____   15____   16____   30____

2.   (2)__   (1)__   (3)__   (5)__   [8]__

3.   3:00PM [A]   4:45PM [C]   5:30PM [B]

4.   2   15   20   13   59   78

5.   (11)   (40)   (12)   (41)

6.   [48_]   [50_]   [53_]   [3_]   [7_]

7.   ____A   ____C   ____E

8.   ____35   ____D

9.   D [12:10PM]   E [1:30PM]   C [5:30PM]

10.   [12]   [52]   [73]

11.   700   1095   640   250   930

The Postal Exam Preparation Book 225

ANSWER SHEET TO FOLLOWING DIRECTIONS / TEST IV

(This page may be removed to mark answers.)

The Postal Exam Preparation Book 227

FOLLOWING DIRECTIONS / TEST IV ANSWERS

4	D,	30 C	10	D	
2	A		5	D	
8	B		17	E	
53	B		9	A	
54	A		12	D	
20	C		52	D	
59	D		82	C	
40	E,	41 E	48	A	
3	C		95	A	
50	D		11	B	
55	C		64	E	
80	A				

If your score was:
—19 or more correct, you have an excellent score
—14 to 18 correct, you have a good score
—13 or less correct, you should practice more.

ADDRESS COMPARISON

Of the three sections in the Mail Handler exam, most people think that the Address Comparison section is the easiest to complete. However, there is only a limited amount of time allowed (6 minutes) to complete the 95 questions. Therefore, it is important to spend as little time as possible on each question, and yet, be thorough enough to select the correct answer without guessing.

The test, in general, provides 95 pairs of addresses. You need to determine if each pair of addresses given is different or exactly alike. The answer sheet to this test will have two choices from which you may select. Answer Ⓐ will be darkened if the pair of addresses shown are exactly alike. Answer Ⓓ will be shaded if the addresses are different. The ten pairs of sample addresses that follow will lend a general understanding of how this test is constructed. Take no more than 30 seconds to complete the samples.

1.	40407 Hayworth Ave.	44007 Hayworth Ave.	Ⓐ	Ⓓ
2.	Chatowaga Blvd. S.	Chatowega Blvd. S.	Ⓐ	Ⓓ
3.	Phoenix, Arizona 80553	Phoenix, Arizona 80553	Ⓐ	Ⓓ
4.	New York, NY 05130	New Haven, CT 05130	Ⓐ	Ⓓ
5.	Newport, KY	Newport, KY	Ⓐ	Ⓓ
6.	498 W 12th Ave.	498 12th Ave. W.	Ⓐ	Ⓓ
7.	1156 Beaumont Cr.	1156 Beaumont Cr.	Ⓐ	Ⓓ
8.	Roanoke, VA 32075	Roanoke, VA 32075	Ⓐ	Ⓓ
9.	4200 3rd St. Apt 2400	2400 3rd ST. Apt 4200	Ⓐ	Ⓓ
10.	Reno, NV	Reno, NV	Ⓐ	Ⓓ

Only pairs number 3, 5, 7, 8, and 10 are exactly alike and should have the answer Ⓐ darkened. Answer Ⓓ would be darkened for the remaining pairs (1, 2, 4, 6, and 9). If you missed any of these samples, review the pairs and determine what was overlooked.

As you can see, subtle differences in either the number or the spelling can be unrecognizable at first glance. You must pay particular attention to street or city names that may sound the same; often, the spelling is made different by the transposition of one or more adjacent numbers or letters.

You may have noticed while working on the sample exercises that a straight edge or ruler could have helped reduce confusion. Unfortunately, such aids are not allowed in the examination room. In fact, you are only allowed a pencil during the examination.

One helpful trick to reduce the confusion while comparing a set of addresses is to place your index finger on one column of addresses and your little finger on the other column. As you proceed with each pair, move your fingers in unison down the page. This does essentially the same thing as a straight edge. Using this method makes it substantially easier to focus your attention on just the two addresses you are comparing. You also save precious time by not having to search for where you left off in order to mark your answer sheet.

Four practice exercises are provided in this book. Tear the answer sheets out of the book for your convenience in marking and to help you get an idea of how things will be in the actual exam. You should use a kitchen timer or have someone time you for the allotted six minutes as you work each exercise. This will protect you from the unnecessary distraction of timing yourself. When time is called, do not work any further on the exercise. If you were to continue, you would lose the true sense of what will be required of you on the actual exam.

A scale is provided at the end of each exercise to allow you to determine your standings. Simply count the number of correct answers you have made and determine where you fall on the scale.

ADDRESS COMPARISON / TEST I

TIME: 6 MINUTES

1.	Burien Ave.	Burein Avenue
2.	12137 Hrtford Dr.	12317 Hartford Dr.
3.	Marguriete Pl.	Margurete Pl.
4.	4731 E. 19th St.	4731 E. 19th St.
5.	Truman W.	Trueman W.
6.	45-D Levenworth Ave.	45-D Levenworth Ave.
7.	Cottage Blvd.	Hut Blvd.
8.	753 Pinecone	753 Pinecone
9.	Ft. Worth, TX	Ft. Apache, AR
10.	Oakland, CA 94371	Oakland, CA 94371
11.	Deception Pass	Deseption Pass
12.	20-L Hogan Ln.	20-L Hogan Ln.
13.	4536 SW 103rd St.	4536 NW 103rd St.
14.	Hutchinson Blvd.	Hutchenson Blvd.
15.	30785 Elliot Bay Rd.	30785 Elliot Bay Rd.
16.	Sparks, NV	Sparks, NY
17.	Springfield, MO 97132	Springfield, MO 97132
18.	Coos Lane	Coos Ln.
19.	Evergreen, ND	Evergrein, MD
20.	Butt, MT 05317	Butte, MT 03517
21.	41-RT 3 Colo, IA	41-RT 3 Colo, IA
22.	Highland Pl.	Highland Place
23.	478 Beach Dr.	478 Beach Dr.
24.	22 Falcon W.	33 Falcon W.
25.	Anderson Heights	Andersin Heights
26.	Falcon Hills Rd.	Eagle Hills Rd.
27.	3249 Brice Pl.	3249 Brice Pl.
28.	42-A Savon Dr.	42-D Savon Dr.
29.	Jamestown, NJ	Jameston, NJ
30.	Victoria, BC 090	Victoria, BC 090
31.	359119 Galloway Ln.	359119 Galloway Ln.
32.	Rome, Georgia 31152	Rome, Georgia 31152
33.	Phinney Place	Phiney Place
34.	Constantine Rd.	Constantine Rd.
35.	44-AB Wilkes Dr.	44-AB Wilikes Dr.
36.	Ft. Collins, Colo.	Ft. Collins, CO
37.	2780 ST. John Rd.	2780 ST. Johns Rd.
38.	Livingston Blvd.	Livingston Blvd.
39.	Bloomington, Ill 61653	Bloomington, Ill 61563
40.	4802-E Blaine	4802-W Blaine
41.	Dallas, TX 25109	Dallas, TX 25108
42.	3103 Porter Way	3103 Porter Way
43.	Snohomish, WA	Snohamish, VA
44.	2516 Johnson Pl.	2516 Johnston Pl.
45.	32-D Jensen Way	354 Jensen Way
46.	4012 Rolling Oaks Rd.	4012 Rolling Oaks Rd.
47.	3710 Harsten Blvd.	3710 Harsten Blvd.
48.	Ankorage, AL	Anchorage, AK
49.	Petersville, KY 45108	Petersville, KY 45108
50.	3845 Reid Dr.	3844 Reid Dr.
51.	401-A Westin Pl.	401-A Westin Pl.

The Postal Exam Preparation Book 233

52.	20121 Dakota Point	20211 Dakota Point
53.	Faunterloy Center	Founterloy Center
54.	4013 Brussels Dr.	4013 Brussels Dr.
55.	Stovington, Conn.	Stovers, CO 43212
56.	12 Ash Place	12 Ash Pl.
57.	9040 Country Ln.	9040 Country Ln.
58.	Marguriette Ave.	Marguriete Ave.
59.	7140 Constitution Dr.	140 Constitution Pl.
60.	30-R Bloomfield Apts.	30-R Bloomfield Apts.
61.	4099 Harbel Rd.	4099 Harbel Rd.
62.	W. Palm Beach, CA.	Palm Beach, CA
63.	Phoenix, Ariz	Phoenix, AR 85021
64.	4037 Nipsic Pl.	4037 Nipsic Pl.
65.	1109 Tangerine Dr.	1109 Tangerine Dr.
66.	20A Abernathy Ct.	20A Abernathy Ct.
67.	Newberry, W. VA	Newberry, W. VA
68.	3401 E. 19th St.	3401 E. 20th St.
69.	1280 12th Ave.	1280 13th Ave.
70.	7800 Forest Ridge	7800 Forest Ridge
71.	Montgomery Pl.	Montgomery Pl.
72.	10 Pierce Grahm Cr.	10 Pierce Grahm Cr.
73.	New York, NY 11940	New York, NY 19140
74.	7780 Proxmire Rd.	8077 Proxmire Rd.
75.	1341 Ivy Terrace	1341 Ivy Terrace
76.	257 Rampert Dr.	275 Ramport Dr.
77.	Newport, WA 99510	Newport, PA 99510
78.	1144 60th St. SW	4411 60th St. NW
79.	117 Chespeke Ct.	117 Chesepeak Ct.
80.	Willow Way E.	Willow Way E.
81.	3030 Prairie Pl.	3030 Prairie Pl.
82.	1212 Seneca Point	2121 Seneca Court
83.	7999 Mercury Blvd.	7999 Mercury Blvd.
84.	Waterloo, IA 50578	Waterloo, IA 50758
85.	14818 1st Ave.	14818 2nd Ave.
86.	S. 120th Pl.	S. 120th Pl.
87.	South Port, KY 98451	South Port, WY 98950
88.	Twelve Oaks, MI	Twelve Oaks, MI
89.	4045 S. Duff St.	4045 N. Duff St.
90.	1391 Fremont Pkwy	1931 Freemont Pksy
91.	Terrington Park	Terrington Park
92.	Essex, MD	Essex, MD
93.	Covings, NM 53845	Sante Fe, NM
94.	Bessert Dr.	Bessert Dr.
95.	30921 W. Hamilton	93021 W. Hamilton

-END OF TEST-

ANSWER SHEET TO ADDRESS COMPARISON / TEST I

1. Ⓐ Ⓓ	33. Ⓐ Ⓓ	65. Ⓐ Ⓓ
2. Ⓐ Ⓓ	34. Ⓐ Ⓓ	66. Ⓐ Ⓓ
3. Ⓐ Ⓓ	35. Ⓐ Ⓓ	67. Ⓐ Ⓓ
4. Ⓐ Ⓓ	36. Ⓐ Ⓓ	68. Ⓐ Ⓓ
5. Ⓐ Ⓓ	37. Ⓐ Ⓓ	69. Ⓐ Ⓓ
6. Ⓐ Ⓓ	38. Ⓐ Ⓓ	70. Ⓐ Ⓓ
7. Ⓐ Ⓓ	39. Ⓐ Ⓓ	71. Ⓐ Ⓓ
8. Ⓐ Ⓓ	40. Ⓐ Ⓓ	72. Ⓐ Ⓓ
9. Ⓐ Ⓓ	41. Ⓐ Ⓓ	73. Ⓐ Ⓓ
10. Ⓐ Ⓓ	42. Ⓐ Ⓓ	74. Ⓐ Ⓓ
11. Ⓐ Ⓓ	43. Ⓐ Ⓓ	75. Ⓐ Ⓓ
12. Ⓐ Ⓓ	44. Ⓐ Ⓓ	76. Ⓐ Ⓓ
13. Ⓐ Ⓓ	45. Ⓐ Ⓓ	77. Ⓐ Ⓓ
14. Ⓐ Ⓓ	46. Ⓐ Ⓓ	78. Ⓐ Ⓓ
15. Ⓐ Ⓓ	47. Ⓐ Ⓓ	79. Ⓐ Ⓓ
16. Ⓐ Ⓓ	48. Ⓐ Ⓓ	80. Ⓐ Ⓓ
17. Ⓐ Ⓓ	49. Ⓐ Ⓓ	81. Ⓐ Ⓓ
18. Ⓐ Ⓓ	50. Ⓐ Ⓓ	82. Ⓐ Ⓓ
19. Ⓐ Ⓓ	51. Ⓐ Ⓓ	83. Ⓐ Ⓓ
20. Ⓐ Ⓓ	52. Ⓐ Ⓓ	84. Ⓐ Ⓓ
21. Ⓐ Ⓓ	53. Ⓐ Ⓓ	85. Ⓐ Ⓓ
22. Ⓐ Ⓓ	54. Ⓐ Ⓓ	86. Ⓐ Ⓓ
23. Ⓐ Ⓓ	55. Ⓐ Ⓓ	87. Ⓐ Ⓓ
24. Ⓐ Ⓓ	56. Ⓐ Ⓓ	88. Ⓐ Ⓓ
25. Ⓐ Ⓓ	57. Ⓐ Ⓓ	89. Ⓐ Ⓓ
26. Ⓐ Ⓓ	58. Ⓐ Ⓓ	90. Ⓐ Ⓓ
27. Ⓐ Ⓓ	59. Ⓐ Ⓓ	91. Ⓐ Ⓓ
28. Ⓐ Ⓓ	60. Ⓐ Ⓓ	92. Ⓐ Ⓓ
29. Ⓐ Ⓓ	61. Ⓐ Ⓓ	93. Ⓐ Ⓓ
30. Ⓐ Ⓓ	62. Ⓐ Ⓓ	94. Ⓐ Ⓓ
31. Ⓐ Ⓓ	63. Ⓐ Ⓓ	95. Ⓐ Ⓓ
32. Ⓐ Ⓓ	64. Ⓐ Ⓓ	

(This page may be removed to mark answers.)

The Postal Exam Preparation Book

ADDRESS COMPARISON / TEST I ANSWERS

1.	D	33.	D	65.	A
2.	D	34.	A	66.	A
3.	D	35.	D	67.	A
4.	A	36.	D	68.	D
5.	D	37.	D	69.	D
6.	A	38.	A	70.	A
7.	D	39.	D	71.	A
8.	A	40.	D	72.	A
9.	D	41.	D	73.	D
10.	A	42.	A	74.	D
11.	D	43.	D	75.	A
12.	A	44.	D	76.	D
13.	D	45.	D	77.	D
14.	D	46.	A	78.	D
15.	A	47.	A	79.	D
16.	D	48.	D	80.	A
17.	A	49.	A	81.	A
18.	D	50.	D	82.	D
19.	D	51.	A	83.	A
20.	D	52.	D	84.	D
21.	A	53.	D	85.	D
22.	D	54.	A	86.	A
23.	A	55.	D	87.	D
24.	D	56.	D	88.	A
25.	D	57.	A	89.	D
26.	D	58.	D	90.	D
27.	A	59.	D	91.	A
28.	D	60.	A	92.	A
29.	D	61.	A	93.	D
30.	A	62.	D	94.	A
31.	A	63.	D	95.	D
32.	A	64.	A		

If your score was:
—87 or more correct, you have an excellent score
—between 55 and 86 correct, you have a good score
—below 54 correct, you should practice more.

The Postal Exam Preparation Book 237

ADDRSESS COMPARISON / TEST II

TIME: 6 MINUTES

1.	2103 Highland Ave	3102 Highland Ave.
2.	4609 Simpson Pkwy	4609 Simson Parkway
3.	404-C Trenton Park	404-C Trentan Park
4.	Bowling Green, KY	Bowling Green, KY
5.	New Haven, CT 07510	New Haven, CT 07510
6.	Covington Cove SW	SW Covington Cove
7.	St. Louis, MO 44881	St. Louis, MO 88441
8.	Yuma, AZ	Yuma, AZ
9.	Santa Cruz, CA 99580	Santa Clara, NM 99580
10.	Erwin Point Dr.	Erwin Point Dr.
11.	Petersberg Ave. NE	21 Petersberg Ave. NE
12.	47109 Nome St.	47109 Nome St.
13.	558 E. 16th St.	558 W. 16th St.
14.	89D Turner Blvd.	89D Turner Blvd
15.	Harrisburg, PA 01184	Harrington, PA 01184
16.	Reno, Nevada 42851	Reno, Nevada 42851
17.	77 E. Fleming Rd.	77 E. Fleming Rd.
18.	Farmington Hills, CT	303 Farmington, Hills, CT
19.	1685 Jensen Way	1685 Jensen Way
20.	SW Tiffany Ct.	SW Tiffany Ct.
21.	3287 Front St.	3287 Front St.
22.	31-D McAllen Rd.	31-D McAllen Rd.
23.	791 Penny Square	719 Penny Square
24.	NE Pinchont View	NE Pinchant View
25.	2413 Wheaton Way	2413 Wheaton Way
26.	443 E. 102nd Ave.	443 E. 107th St.
27.	Elsinore Blvd.	Elsinore Blvd
28.	Montgomery Place S.	Montgomery Place S.
29.	742 Callahan Pl.	742 Calahan Pl.
30.	66 Tremont St.	99 Tremont St.
31.	Pershing Blvd. Apt. 37	Pershing Blvd. Apt. 37
32.	11 Finland Ave.	11 Finland Ave.
33.	Atlanta, GA 01789	Atlanta, GA 01789
34.	Gainesville, Fla. 22190	Gainesville, Fla. 22190
35.	2140 E. Carlson	2140 E. Carlson
36.	40301 SW Seneca	40301 NE Seneca
37.	Fremont, NE 57510	Freemont, NE 57510
38.	2020 N. Parkington	2020 N. Parkington
39.	47-D Spruce	47-D Spruce
40.	Suite N Columbia Square	Suite N Columbia Sq.
41.	Waco, TX	Waco, TX
42.	278 Fontain Dr.	278 Fountain Dr.
43.	521 Essex Blvd.	521 Crown Blvd.
44	1449 Bloomington St.	1449 Bloomington St.
45.	332 Edgingston Way	322 Edgingston Way
46.	Hazelwood Pkwy.	Hazelwood Pkwy.
47.	Island Lake Dr.	Island Lake Dr.
48.	29471 Chicago St.	29417 Chicago St.
49.	774 NE 42nd Ave.	774 NE 42nd Ave.

50.	Little Rock, Ark.	Little Stone, Ark.
51.	Norfolk, VA 11191	Norfolk, VA 11197
52.	3050 Lebaron Way	412 NW 19th ST.
53.	4640 NW 11th St.	46 N Cable St.
54.	7793 Halverson Dr.	7793 Halverson Dr.
55.	12-A Nordstrom Way	12-A Nordstrom Way
56.	Presley Ct.	Presley Ct.
57.	Z44 E. 22nd	Z44 E. 22nd
58.	2020 Ramport St.	202 Ramport St.
59.	Forsythe Ln.	Forsithe Ln.
60.	12178 Knoll Dr.	12178 Knoll Rd.
61.	E. 40th Place	S. 40th Place
62.	3047 Evansdale W.	3047 Evansdale W.
63.	SW Hampshire Ln.	SW Hampshire Ln.
64.	23 Flamingo Dr.	23 Flamingo St.
65.	Boise, ID 47814	Boise, ID 47814
66.	4700 Kitsap Way	7400 Kitsap Way
67.	Chepowacket Blvd.	Chepowackat Blvd.
68.	1010 Tanner St.	42 Sloan Ct.
69.	Greensboro, NC 21478	Greensbor, NC 21478
70.	Palo Alto, CA	Palo Alto, CA
71.	38841 Padock S.	38814 Padock St.
72.	2511 Cascade Trail	2511 Cascade Trail
73.	2324 Parker Place	2423 Parker Place
74.	South Shore, WA 99944	South Shore, WA 99944
75.	1710 Symington Ct.	1710 Symington Ct.
76.	Fairbanks, Alaska	Fairbanks, Alaska
77.	SE Karrington Blvd.	SE Karry Blvd.
78.	11111 Tisdale Ln.	1111 Tisdale Ln.
79.	3781 Livingston Sq.	3781 Livingston Sq.
80.	Brockton, Mass. 01171	Brockton, Mas. 01171
81.	734 A Twin Bay	734 B Twin Bay
82.	4000 Elsinora Beach	4000 Elsinore Beach
83.	308 Frampton Ave.	308 Frampton Ave.
84.	7901 Havelin Blvd.	7091 Havelin Blvd.
85.	Portland, ME 00521	Portland, ME 05021
86.	Sweitzer Way	Sweitzer Way
87.	44331 Bellingham	43431 Bellingham
88.	807 Terryington Ave.	807 Terryington Ave.
89.	Paradise Valley, AZ	Paridise Valley, AZ
90.	1201 Westin Lake Dr.	1201 Westin Lake Dr.
91.	4100 Hildalgo Park	4100 Hildalgo Park
92.	17181 Austin Center	17181 Astin Center
93.	2510 Stephenson Ave.	2510 Stephensen Ave.
94.	Reno, NV	Reno, NV
95.	2222 Hoffman Dr.	2222 Hoffman Dr.

-END OF TEST-

ANSWER SHEET TO ADDRESS COMPARISON / TEST II

1. Ⓐ Ⓓ		33. Ⓐ Ⓓ		65. Ⓐ Ⓓ	
2. Ⓐ Ⓓ		34. Ⓐ Ⓓ		66. Ⓐ Ⓓ	
3. Ⓐ Ⓓ		35. Ⓐ Ⓓ		67. Ⓐ Ⓓ	
4. Ⓐ Ⓓ		36. Ⓐ Ⓓ		68. Ⓐ Ⓓ	
5. Ⓐ Ⓓ		37. Ⓐ Ⓓ		69. Ⓐ Ⓓ	
6. Ⓐ Ⓓ		38. Ⓐ Ⓓ		70. Ⓐ Ⓓ	
7. Ⓐ Ⓓ		39. Ⓐ Ⓓ		71. Ⓐ Ⓓ	
8. Ⓐ Ⓓ		40. Ⓐ Ⓓ		72. Ⓐ Ⓓ	
9. Ⓐ Ⓓ		41. Ⓐ Ⓓ		73. Ⓐ Ⓓ	
10. Ⓐ Ⓓ		42. Ⓐ Ⓓ		74. Ⓐ Ⓓ	
11. Ⓐ Ⓓ		43. Ⓐ Ⓓ		75. Ⓐ Ⓓ	
12. Ⓐ Ⓓ		44. Ⓐ Ⓓ		76. Ⓐ Ⓓ	
13. Ⓐ Ⓓ		45. Ⓐ Ⓓ		77. Ⓐ Ⓓ	
14. Ⓐ Ⓓ		46. Ⓐ Ⓓ		78. Ⓐ Ⓓ	
15. Ⓐ Ⓓ		47. Ⓐ Ⓓ		79. Ⓐ Ⓓ	
16. Ⓐ Ⓓ		48. Ⓐ Ⓓ		80. Ⓐ Ⓓ	
17. Ⓐ Ⓓ		49. Ⓐ Ⓓ		81. Ⓐ Ⓓ	
18. Ⓐ Ⓓ		50. Ⓐ Ⓓ		82. Ⓐ Ⓓ	
19. Ⓐ Ⓓ		51. Ⓐ Ⓓ		83. Ⓐ Ⓓ	
20. Ⓐ Ⓓ		52. Ⓐ Ⓓ		84. Ⓐ Ⓓ	
21. Ⓐ Ⓓ		53. Ⓐ Ⓓ		85. Ⓐ Ⓓ	
22. Ⓐ Ⓓ		54. Ⓐ Ⓓ		86. Ⓐ Ⓓ	
23. Ⓐ Ⓓ		55. Ⓐ Ⓓ		87. Ⓐ Ⓓ	
24. Ⓐ Ⓓ		56. Ⓐ Ⓓ		88. Ⓐ Ⓓ	
25. Ⓐ Ⓓ		57. Ⓐ Ⓓ		89. Ⓐ Ⓓ	
26. Ⓐ Ⓓ		58. Ⓐ Ⓓ		90. Ⓐ Ⓓ	
27. Ⓐ Ⓓ		59. Ⓐ Ⓓ		91. Ⓐ Ⓓ	
28. Ⓐ Ⓓ		60. Ⓐ Ⓓ		92. Ⓐ Ⓓ	
29. Ⓐ Ⓓ		61. Ⓐ Ⓓ		93. Ⓐ Ⓓ	
30. Ⓐ Ⓓ		62. Ⓐ Ⓓ		94. Ⓐ Ⓓ	
31. Ⓐ Ⓓ		63. Ⓐ Ⓓ		95. Ⓐ Ⓓ	
32. Ⓐ Ⓓ		64. Ⓐ Ⓓ			

(This page may be removed to mark answers.)

The Postal Exam Preparation Book

ADDRESS COMPARISON / TEST II ANSWERS

1.	D	33.	A	65.	A
2.	D	34.	A	66.	D
3.	D	35.	A	67.	D
4.	A	36.	D	68.	D
5.	A	37.	D	69.	D
6.	D	38.	A	70.	A
7.	D	39.	A	71.	D
8.	A	40.	D	72.	A
9.	D	41.	A	73.	D
10.	A	42.	D	74.	A
11.	D	43.	D	75.	A
12.	A	44.	A	76.	A
13.	D	45.	D	77.	D
14.	A	46.	A	78.	D
15.	D	47.	A	79.	A
16.	A	48.	D	80.	D
17.	A	49.	A	81.	D
18.	D	50.	D	82.	D
19.	A	51.	D	83.	A
20.	A	52.	D	84.	D
21.	A	53.	D	85.	D
22.	A	54.	A	86.	A
23.	D	55.	A	87.	D
24.	D	56.	A	88.	A
25.	A	57.	A	89.	D
26.	D	58.	D	90.	A
27.	A	59.	D	91.	A
28.	A	60.	D	92.	D
29.	D	61.	D	93.	D
30.	D	62.	A	94.	A
31.	A	63.	A	95.	A
32.	A	64.	D		

If your score was:
- —87 or more correct, you have an excellent score
- —between 55 and 86 correct, you have a good score
- —below 54 correct, you should practice more.

The Postal Exam Preparation Book 243

ADDRESS COMPARISON / TEST III

TIME: 6 MINUTES

1.	1216 W. 6th Ave.	1216 S. 6th Ave.
2.	2020 Poplar Bluff Dr.	2020 Popular Bluff Dr.
3.	1402 Wasau Terrace	1402 Wasau Terrace
4.	Eau Claire, Wis. 76944	Eau Clare, Wis 76944
5.	7088 Benton Ave.	7088 Benton Ave.
6.	Pocatello, ID 86713	Pocatello, ID 87613
7.	113-D Rochestor Blvd.	113-D Rochestor Blvd.
8.	8755 Ironwood Dr.	8755 NE Ironwood Dr.
9.	6467 Ramsey Lane S.	6467 Ramsey Lane S.
10.	Salida, Colo. 78435	Salada, Colo. 78435
11.	5000 Natchez	5000 Natchez
12.	Chillicothe, MO 54311	Chilliclothe, MO 54311
13.	4039 Vicksburg St.	4039 Vicksburg St.
14.	50571 Coleman Dr.	50751 Coleman Dr.
15.	Tucumcari, NM 60681	Tucumcary, NM 60681
16.	7135 Roswell Way	7135 Rosewell Way
17.	970 Odessa Ave.	970 Odessa Ave.
18.	Amarillo, Texas 49873	Amabrillo, Texas 49873
19.	1023 Buffalo Pass	1023 Buffalo Pass
20.	Hannibal, MO 45555	Hanninbol, MO 45555
21.	60741 Ottumwa Dr.	67041 Ottumwa Dr.
22.	1010 Remington Cr.	1010 Remington Cr.
23.	W. Palm Beach, Fla.	E. Palm Beach, Fla.
24.	80473 McComb Ave.	80473 MacComb Ave.
25.	1519 67th St. NW	1519 67th St. W.
26.	2040 Albert Lane	2040 Albert Lane
27.	Prescott, Ariz 84988	Prescott, Ariz 84998
28.	1795 Casper Place	1795 Casper Place
29.	603 Craig	603 Craig
30.	4111 Montrose Ave.	4111 Montrose Dr.
31.	15990 Humboldt NE	15909 Humboldt NE
32.	Pierre, SD 77135	Pierre SD 77185
33.	4030 Cookie Pk.	4030 Cooke Pk.
34.	Missoula, MT 88803	Missoula, MD 88803
35.	33810 Mitchell Dr.	33810 Mitchell Dr.
36.	44-C Shenandoah Apts.	44-C Senandoah Apts.
37.	4848 Roanoke Dr.	4848 Roanoke Dr.
38.	Alpena, Mich. 38911	Alpena, Mich. 38911
39.	47811 Sherbrook	47881 Sherbrook
40.	32323 Roman Circle	32323 Romon Circle
41.	Charlotte, NC 12443	Charlette, NC 12443
42.	412 Peterbouroghs	412 Peterboroughs
43.	7651 Corbin St.	7651 Corbin St.
44.	3044 Violet Dr. NW	3404 Violet Dr. NW
45.	450-B Deer Park	450-B Deer Pk
46.	31571 Barrington Ave.	31571 Barrington Ave.
47.	3215 Dundee Dr.	3215 Dundee Dr.
48.	747 Kane St.	747 Kane St.
49.	3011 Foxhill Ave.	3011 Foxhill Ave.
50.	1205 Helm	1502 Helm

51.	1414 Millbern Rd.	1414 Millburn Rd.
52.	7350 Holdridge Dr.	7350 Holdridge Dr.
53.	351 Belvidere Pt.	315 Belvidere Pt.
54.	80913 Sullivan Pl.	80913 N Sullivan Pl.
55.	10009 Callahan Ln.	10009 Callahan Ln.
56.	2023 Gardner Blvd.	2023 Gardner Blvd.
57.	440-442 Greenwood Apts.	440-442 Greenwood Apts.
58.	1199 Hawley Ave.	1999 Hawley Ave.
59.	3000 Scribner Dr.	3000 Scribner Dr.
60.	4458 Countryside Ct.	4458 Countryside Court
61.	Chicago, Ill 60691	Chicago, ID 60691
62.	3008 Ivanhoe Ave.	3080 Ivanhoe Ave.
63.	7777 Kirchoff	9999 Kirchoff
64.	13133 Schaumburgh Dr.	13133 Schaumburgh Dr.
65.	1705 E. Addison Blvd.	1705 S. Addison Blvd.
66.	104 Glen Ellyn	104 Glenn Ellyn
67.	12-E Barber Corners	12-E Barbara Corners
68.	99661 Westmont Ave.	99661 Westmont Ave.
69.	7001 Liberty View	7001 Liberty View
70.	125 88th St. NE	125 88th Dr. NE
71.	Wytheville, VA 15891	Wytheville, VA 15891
72.	8903 Wheaton Way	8309 Wheaton Way
73.	79900 Indian Hts. SW	79900 Indian Hts. SW
74.	345 Lambert Lane	345 Lamburt Lane
75.	4646 Camalot Dr.	6464 Camalot Dr.
76.	8873 Stickney Blvd.	8873 Stickney Blvd.
77.	31371 Hammond Dr.	33171 Hammond Dr.
78.	304 Wilmette Ridge	304 Wilmette Ridge
79.	Bend, Ore. 80077	Bend, Oregon 80077
80.	Springfield, OH 39411	springfield, OH 39441
81.	7979 Baldwin Pt.	7979 Baldwin Pt.
82.	14001 Prospect Dr.	1401 Prospect Dr.
83.	307 Elm St.	307 Elm St.
84.	409 Kittyhawk Pl.	409 Kityhawk Pl.
85.	16073 Algoquin Ave.	16073 Algoquin Dr.
86.	2000 Euclid Blvd.	4000 Euclid Blvd.
87.	7581 Lincolnshire Dr.	7581 Lincolnshire Dr.
88.	180-D Turnball Woods	180-D Turnball Woods
89.	3042 Hintz St.	3042 Hienz St.
90.	393 Twin Orchard Ln.	393 Twin Orchid Ln.
91.	150 Central Ave.	150 Central Ave.
92.	6167 Hoffman Estates	6716 Hoffman Estates
93.	4311 Devon Dr.	4311 Devon Dr. S
94.	2222 Nickols Ave.	2222 Nickols Ave.
95.	111 82nd St.	111 82nd St.

-END OF TEST-

ANSWER SHEET TO ADDRESS COMPARISON / TEST III

1. Ⓐ Ⓓ	33. Ⓐ Ⓓ	65. Ⓐ Ⓓ
2. Ⓐ Ⓓ	34. Ⓐ Ⓓ	66. Ⓐ Ⓓ
3. Ⓐ Ⓓ	35. Ⓐ Ⓓ	67. Ⓐ Ⓓ
4. Ⓐ Ⓓ	36. Ⓐ Ⓓ	68. Ⓐ Ⓓ
5. Ⓐ Ⓓ	37. Ⓐ Ⓓ	69. Ⓐ Ⓓ
6. Ⓐ Ⓓ	38. Ⓐ Ⓓ	70. Ⓐ Ⓓ
7. Ⓐ Ⓓ	39. Ⓐ Ⓓ	71. Ⓐ Ⓓ
8. Ⓐ Ⓓ	40. Ⓐ Ⓓ	72. Ⓐ Ⓓ
9. Ⓐ Ⓓ	41. Ⓐ Ⓓ	73. Ⓐ Ⓓ
10. Ⓐ Ⓓ	42. Ⓐ Ⓓ	74. Ⓐ Ⓓ
11. Ⓐ Ⓓ	43. Ⓐ Ⓓ	75. Ⓐ Ⓓ
12. Ⓐ Ⓓ	44. Ⓐ Ⓓ	76. Ⓐ Ⓓ
13. Ⓐ Ⓓ	45. Ⓐ Ⓓ	77. Ⓐ Ⓓ
14. Ⓐ Ⓓ	46. Ⓐ Ⓓ	78. Ⓐ Ⓓ
15. Ⓐ Ⓓ	47. Ⓐ Ⓓ	79. Ⓐ Ⓓ
16. Ⓐ Ⓓ	48. Ⓐ Ⓓ	80. Ⓐ Ⓓ
17. Ⓐ Ⓓ	49. Ⓐ Ⓓ	81. Ⓐ Ⓓ
18. Ⓐ Ⓓ	50. Ⓐ Ⓓ	82. Ⓐ Ⓓ
19. Ⓐ Ⓓ	51. Ⓐ Ⓓ	83. Ⓐ Ⓓ
20. Ⓐ Ⓓ	52. Ⓐ Ⓓ	84. Ⓐ Ⓓ
21. Ⓐ Ⓓ	53. Ⓐ Ⓓ	85. Ⓐ Ⓓ
22. Ⓐ Ⓓ	54. Ⓐ Ⓓ	86. Ⓐ Ⓓ
23. Ⓐ Ⓓ	55. Ⓐ Ⓓ	87. Ⓐ Ⓓ
24. Ⓐ Ⓓ	56. Ⓐ Ⓓ	88. Ⓐ Ⓓ
25. Ⓐ Ⓓ	57. Ⓐ Ⓓ	89. Ⓐ Ⓓ
26. Ⓐ Ⓓ	58. Ⓐ Ⓓ	90. Ⓐ Ⓓ
27. Ⓐ Ⓓ	59. Ⓐ Ⓓ	91. Ⓐ Ⓓ
28. Ⓐ Ⓓ	60. Ⓐ Ⓓ	92. Ⓐ Ⓓ
29. Ⓐ Ⓓ	61. Ⓐ Ⓓ	93. Ⓐ Ⓓ
30. Ⓐ Ⓓ	62. Ⓐ Ⓓ	94. Ⓐ Ⓓ
31. Ⓐ Ⓓ	63. Ⓐ Ⓓ	95. Ⓐ Ⓓ
32. Ⓐ Ⓓ	64. Ⓐ Ⓓ	

(This page may be removed to mark answers.)

The Postal Exam Preparation Book

ADDRESS COMPARISON / TEST III ANSWERS

1.	D	33.	D	65.	D
2.	D	34.	D	66.	D
3.	A	35.	A	67.	D
4.	D	36.	D	68.	A
5.	A	37.	A	69.	A
6.	D	38.	A	70.	D
7.	A	39.	D	71.	A
8.	D	40.	D	72.	D
9.	A	41.	D	73.	A
10.	D	42.	D	74.	D
11.	A	43.	A	75.	D
12.	D	44.	D	76.	A
13.	A	45.	D	77.	D
14.	D	46.	A	78.	A
15.	D	47.	A	79.	D
16.	D	48.	A	80.	D
17.	A	49.	A	81.	A
18.	D	50.	D	82.	D
19.	A	51.	D	83.	A
20.	D	52.	A	84.	D
21.	D	53.	D	85.	D
22.	A	54.	D	86.	D
23.	D	55.	A	87.	A
24.	D	56.	A	88.	A
25.	D	57.	A	89.	D
26.	A	58.	D	90.	D
27.	D	59.	A	91.	A
28.	A	60.	D	92.	D
29.	A	61.	D	93.	D
30.	D	62.	D	94.	A
31.	D	63.	D	95.	A
32.	D	64.	A		

If your score was:
  —87 or more correct, you have an excellent score
  —between 55 and 86 correct, you have a good score
  —below 54 correct, you should practice more.

The Postal Exam Preparation Book

ADDRESS COMPARISON / TEST IV

TIME: 6 MINUTES

1.	4138 West Dupage Dr.	4813 West Dupage Dr.
2.	3500 St. Andrews Pl.	3500 St. Andrews Pl.
3.	5132 Kirkland Blvd.	5132 Kirkland St.
4.	407 Bryant Ave.	407 Bryant Ave.
5.	1115 Oak Brook Terrace	1115 Oak Brook Terrace
6.	43812 Wicker Park	43812 Wecker Park
7.	Worcester, Mass. 05899	Worchester, Mass. 05899
8.	Evansvill, IND 59433	Evansville ID 59433
9.	17-A Legion Park N	17-A Legion Park N
10.	4040 Delwood Hts.	40404 Delwood Hts.
11.	3221 Plainfield Rd.	3221 Planefield Rd.
12.	10083 Payton Blvd.	10803 Payton Blvd.
13.	312 SW Pioneer Ave.	312 NW Pioneer Ave.
14.	88888 Omega Place	77777 Omega Place
15.	10355 Herrick Dr.	10355 Herrick Dr.
16.	1616 Cloverdale St.	1616 Cloverdale St.
17.	30857 S. Grey St.	30857 S. Gray St.
18.	4170 Cape Canavrol Dr.	4170 Cape Canaverol Dr.
19.	7003 NW Bethany Ave.	7003 NW Bethany Ave.
20.	105 5th St.	105 5th St.
21.	3070 Granger Blvd.	3070 Granger Blvd.
22.	111 Brewster Dr.	111 Brewster Dr.
23.	308 Beverly Way	308 Beaverly Way
24.	16 N Reinburg	16 N Reinburg
25.	79003 Potawatomie Dr.	79003 Potawatomie Dr.
26.	4315 Caldwell Cr.	4315 Niles Cr.
27.	745 Wauconda Dr.	745 Wauconda Dr.
28.	301 Henderson Rd.	103 Henerson Rd.
29.	40-D Talcott	40-D Talcot
30.	Loyola Uni., Chicago, Ill	Loyola Uni., Chicago, Ill
31.	10101 Clayburn Dr.	1010 Clayburn Dr.
32.	478 Jewell Blvd.	477 Jewell Blvd.
33.	Superior, Wis. 40334	Superior, Wis. 40334
34.	Raleigh, NC 10773	Raliegh, NC 10773
35.	708 Twin Heritage	708 Twin Haritage
36.	331 Times	331 Time Dr.
37.	1117 Schiller Park	1117 Shiller Park
38.	8899 Toronto Ave.	9988 Toronto Ave.
39.	390 Kensington Dr.	390 Kensington Dr.
40.	4012 Calvin	4021 Calvin
41.	900 Cambrian Ave.	9000 Cambrian Ave.
42.	7680 Whitney Dr.	7680 Whitney Dr.
43.	853 N. Dalton	853 N. Dalton
44.	8990 Pacific Ave.	8990 Pacific Ave.
45.	4201 Juniper Ct.	4201 Jupiter Ct.
46.	909 Walbash Way	990 Walbash Way
47.	1305-M Maple Brook	1305-M Maple Brook
48.	7070 Crawford Dr.	7070 Crawford Park
49.	105 Butterfield	105 Butterfield
50.	66 66th Ave. SW	66 56th Ave. SW
51.	10035 Harper Dr.	1305 Harper Dr.

52.	Houston, Texas 79944	Houston, Texas 99744
53.	707 Smith Ave.	707 Smith Ave.
54.	8848 Plum Grove	8848 Plum Grove
55.	6677 Pickney Ln.	6677 Pickny Ln.
56.	716 Kelsy Bay Rd.	716 Kelsey Bay Rd.
57.	800 Larkin Dr.	800 Larkin Dr.
58.	606 Geneva Way	606 Geneva Pkwy
59.	7071 McNally Ct.	707 McNally Ct.
60.	434 63rd NE	434 63rd Ave.
61.	311 Betsey Ross Dr.	311 Betsy Ross Dr.
62.	100 Dempster	1000 Dempster
63.	4433 Granville Blvd.	4433 Granville Blvd.
64.	903 Collins Rd.	903 Collins Rd.
65.	40 Hirchwood Ave.	400 Birchwood Ave.
66.	Baltimore, MD 04356	Baltimore, MO 04356
67.	Ashland, KY 54568	Ashlake, KY 54568
68.	7890 Rolling Meadows	7890 Rollins Dr.
69.	3300 Vincent Bay	3300 Vincent Bay
70.	1213 Purnell Dr.	1213 Purnell Ave.
71.	13 Phipps Park	13 Phipps Park
72.	7878 Delta Way	8787 Delta Way
73.	434 135th Place	434 135th Place
74.	2045 Fairmont	2045 Faremont
75.	66801 Josephine	66801 Joplin
76.	31 Old Dutch Rd.	31 Old Dutch Rd.
77.	4177 Pershing Ct.	4177 Pershing Ct.
78.	730 International Ln.	730 International Ln.
79.	1515 Aptakistic Pk	1515 Aptackistic Pk
80.	411 Shadow Glen Dr.	411 Shadow Glen Dr.
81.	3007 Holiday Ln.	3007 N. Holliday Ln.
82.	4071 NW Grace	4017 NE Grace
83.	71781 Ardmore Trail	71718 Ardmore Trail
84.	Rock Island, Ill 60677	Rock Island, Ill 66077
85.	4173 Paulsen Dr.	4173 Paulsen Dr.
86.	130 Bartlett View	130 Bartlett View
87.	111 63rd Place	111 SW 52nd St.
88.	78022 Western Ln.	78202 Western Ln.
89.	9003 Harvey Rd.	903 Harvey Rd.
90.	414 Rice St.	414 Rice St.
91.	5058 Midway Dr.	50588 Midway Dr.
92.	Lancaster, PA 35077	Lancaster, PA 35011
93.	334 Archer Blvd.	334 Archer Blvd.
94.	Shreveport, LA 38922	Schreveport, LA 38922
95.	42 Wittle Dr.	42 Wittle Dr.

-END OF TEST-

ANSWER SHEET TO ADDRESS COMPARISON / TEST IV

NOTE
(THIS PAGE MAY BE REMOVED TO MARK ANSWERS)

1. Ⓐ Ⓓ	33. Ⓐ Ⓓ	65. Ⓐ Ⓓ	
2. Ⓐ Ⓓ	34. Ⓐ Ⓓ	66. Ⓐ Ⓓ	
3. Ⓐ Ⓓ	35. Ⓐ Ⓓ	67. Ⓐ Ⓓ	
4. Ⓐ Ⓓ	36. Ⓐ Ⓓ	68. Ⓐ Ⓓ	
5. Ⓐ Ⓓ	37. Ⓐ Ⓓ	69. Ⓐ Ⓓ	
6. Ⓐ Ⓓ	38. Ⓐ Ⓓ	70. Ⓐ Ⓓ	
7. Ⓐ Ⓓ	39. Ⓐ Ⓓ	71. Ⓐ Ⓓ	
8. Ⓐ Ⓓ	40. Ⓐ Ⓓ	72. Ⓐ Ⓓ	
9. Ⓐ Ⓓ	41. Ⓐ Ⓓ	73. Ⓐ Ⓓ	
10. Ⓐ Ⓓ	42. Ⓐ Ⓓ	74. Ⓐ Ⓓ	
11. Ⓐ Ⓓ	43. Ⓐ Ⓓ	75. Ⓐ Ⓓ	
12. Ⓐ Ⓓ	44. Ⓐ Ⓓ	76. Ⓐ Ⓓ	
13. Ⓐ Ⓓ	45. Ⓐ Ⓓ	77. Ⓐ Ⓓ	
14. Ⓐ Ⓓ	46. Ⓐ Ⓓ	78. Ⓐ Ⓓ	
15. Ⓐ Ⓓ	47. Ⓐ Ⓓ	79. Ⓐ Ⓓ	
16. Ⓐ Ⓓ	48. Ⓐ Ⓓ	80. Ⓐ Ⓓ	
17. Ⓐ Ⓓ	49. Ⓐ Ⓓ	81. Ⓐ Ⓓ	
18. Ⓐ Ⓓ	50. Ⓐ Ⓓ	82. Ⓐ Ⓓ	
19. Ⓐ Ⓓ	51. Ⓐ Ⓓ	83. Ⓐ Ⓓ	
20. Ⓐ Ⓓ	52. Ⓐ Ⓓ	84. Ⓐ Ⓓ	
21. Ⓐ Ⓓ	53. Ⓐ Ⓓ	85. Ⓐ Ⓓ	
22. Ⓐ Ⓓ	54. Ⓐ Ⓓ	86. Ⓐ Ⓓ	
23. Ⓐ Ⓓ	55. Ⓐ Ⓓ	87. Ⓐ Ⓓ	
24. Ⓐ Ⓓ	56. Ⓐ Ⓓ	88. Ⓐ Ⓓ	
25. Ⓐ Ⓓ	57. Ⓐ Ⓓ	89. Ⓐ Ⓓ	
26. Ⓐ Ⓓ	58. Ⓐ Ⓓ	90. Ⓐ Ⓓ	
27. Ⓐ Ⓓ	59. Ⓐ Ⓓ	91. Ⓐ Ⓓ	
28. Ⓐ Ⓓ	60. Ⓐ Ⓓ	92. Ⓐ Ⓓ	
29. Ⓐ Ⓓ	61. Ⓐ Ⓓ	93. Ⓐ Ⓓ	
30. Ⓐ Ⓓ	62. Ⓐ Ⓓ	94. Ⓐ Ⓓ	
31. Ⓐ Ⓓ	63. Ⓐ Ⓓ	95. Ⓐ Ⓓ	
32. Ⓐ Ⓓ	64. Ⓐ Ⓓ		

(This page may be removed to mark answers.)

ADDRESS COMPARISON / TEST IV ANSWERS

1.	D	33.	A	65.	D
2.	A	34.	D	66.	D
3.	D	35.	D	67.	D
4.	A	36.	D	68.	D
5.	A	37.	D	69.	A
6.	D	38.	D	70.	D
7.	D	39.	A	71.	A
8.	D	40.	D	72.	D
9.	A	41.	D	73.	A
10.	D	42.	A	74.	D
11.	D	43.	A	75.	D
12.	D	44.	A	76.	A
13.	D	45.	D	77.	A
14.	D	46.	D	78.	A
15.	A	47.	A	79.	D
16.	A	48.	D	80.	A
17.	D	49.	A	81.	D
18.	D	50.	D	82.	D
19.	A	51.	D	83.	D
20.	A	52.	D	84.	D
21.	A	53.	A	85.	A
22.	A	54.	A	86.	A
23.	D	55.	D	87.	D
24.	A	56.	D	88.	D
25.	A	57.	A	89.	D
26.	D	58.	D	90.	A
27.	A	59.	D	91.	D
28.	D	60.	D	92.	D
29.	D	61.	D	93.	A
30.	A	62.	D	94.	D
31.	D	63.	A	95.	A
32.	D	64.	A		

If your score was:
—87 or more correct, you have an excellent score
—between 55 and 86 correct, you have a good score
—below 54 correct, you should practice more

WORD MEANING / TEST I

(NOTE: FOR ASSISTANCE ON WORD MEANING TEST, REFER TO THE VOCABULARY SECTION OF THE RURAL CARRIER TEST)

TIME: 20 MINUTES

1. Many people believed that the whole family was "insane". Insane most nearly means
    - A. tranquil
    - B. quiet
    - C. joyous
    - D. deranged
    - E. eloquent

2. Even after the difficult surgery, he is showing remarkable signs of "recuperation". Recuperation most nearly means
    - A. improvement
    - B. degeneration
    - C. stagnation
    - D. hospitality
    - E. learning

3. It is not often that you run into a person that claims he or she has "supernatural" powers. Supernatural most nearly means
    - A. a problem
    - B. preternatural
    - C. indifferent
    - D. individual
    - E. lackluster

4. Once a week the grocery store down the block has a good "bargain" on bakery and dairy products. Bargain most nearly means
    - A. price hike
    - B. deal
    - C. demand
    - D. monopoly
    - E. meal

5. My wife is very "sentimental" about the family's photo album. Sentimental most nearly means
    - A. impartial
    - B. sensitive
    - C. vindictive
    - D. futile
    - E. beneficial

6. The car was completely "demolished" after it struck a tree on the side of the road. Demolished most nearly means
    - A. destroyed
    - B. cleaned
    - C. stripped
    - D. vandalized
    - E. absorbed

7. The hobo was just about to "pilfer" his sleeping companion's shoes when he noticed the shoe laces were tied in a million knots. He reluctantly gave up the idea. Pilfer most nearly means
    - A. assist
    - B. endure
    - C. steal
    - D. help
    - E. pivot

8. She was nearly "hysterical" with laughter after the comedian told his final joke for the night. Hysterical most nearly means
    A. dehydrated
    B. hostile
    C. perplexed
    D. unemotional
    E. wild

9. Black holes in outer space still remain a "mystery" among scientists. Mystery most nearly means
    A. puzzle
    B. myth
    C. legend
    D. museum
    E. problem

10. It is embarassing to be "tardy" for work. Tardy most nearly means
    A. early
    B. drunk
    C. late
    D. tired
    E. irritable

11. The next play was "crucial" for the team because points were needed and there was not enough time for another play. Crucial most nearly means
    A. easy
    B. unimportant
    C. crude
    D. simple
    E. critical

12. Water was leaking through a small "fissure" in the boat. Fissure most nearly means
    A. elongation
    B. bump
    C. depression
    D. planking
    E. crack

13. "Keepsakes" are a nice way of remembering past vacations. Keepsakes most nearly mean
    A. crossword puzzles
    B. souvenirs
    C. games
    D. expensive records
    E. recommendations

14. Most children have a constant "craving" for sweets. Craving most nearly means
    A. dislike
    B. indigestion
    C. objection
    D. agreement
    E. desire

15. Flooding can become a problem when the ground is "saturated" and heavier than normal rainfall continues. Saturated most nearly means
    A. electrified
    B. salt laden
    C. soaked
    D. acidic
    E. aeriated

16. Some people display an extra ordinary ability to memorize "trivial" things. Trivial most nearly means
     A. insignificant
     B. important
     C. complicated
     D. dynamic
     E. historical

17. The largest "advantage" of hydroelectricity over coal is cost per kilowatt; hydroelectricity is cheaper for the consumer. Advantage most nearly means
     A. drawback
     B. problem
     C. deficiency
     D. superiority
     E. adversity

18. Commercial airline pilots undergo "intensive" training before they are issued a license. Intensive most nearly means
     A. lax
     B. moderate
     C. obscure
     D. navigational
     E. extensive

19. It was not hard to tell who the "culprit" was when the evidence was examined. Culprit most nearly means
     A. offender
     B. innocent
     C. judge
     D. chairman
     E. stenographer

20. The new kid that moved here from New York seems to be really "amiable". Amiable most nearly means
     A. different
     B. friendly
     C. distressed
     D. belligerent
     E. unhappy

21. Mules have a habit of being "obstinate" every now and then. Obstinate most nearly means
     A. manageable
     B. stubborn
     C. tired
     D. demanding
     E. unsteady

22. It has been said that there is no "limit" to what one can learn. Limit most nearly means
     A. time
     B. problem
     C. path
     D. boundary
     E. infinity

23. The instructor was very "candid" with his pupils about his views on absences. Candid most nearly means
     A. straight forward
     B. indirect
     C. subtle
     D. subdued
     E. general

24. Scuba diving isn't as fun when the water is "turbid". Turbid most nearly means
    A. cold
    B. choppy
    C. warm
    D. salty
    E. cloudy

25. It is best to approach something that you are unsure of with some degree of "prudence". Prudence most nearly means
    A. absentmindedness
    B. prowess
    C. judiciousness
    D. rashness
    E. hindsight

26. The English "language" has a large number of slang words in it. Language most nearly means
    A. tradition
    B. speech
    C. custom
    D. aspect
    E. expression

27. It was a "futile" effort to try to put out the fire with the winds as strong as they were. Futile most nearly means
    A. useless
    B. effectual
    C. convenient
    D. insane
    E. concentrated

28. "Leisure" time is important to people who work long and hard hours. Leisure most nearly means
    A. part time work
    B. retirement benefits
    C. spare time
    D. recognition
    E. notoriety

29. It was apparent that he was an "affluent" citizen by the fact that he owned two Rolls Royces. Affluent most nearly means
    A. impoverished
    B. poor
    C. desperate
    D. sincere
    E. rich

30. Muscles tend to "fatigue" after a thorough workout. Fatigue most nearly means
    A. tire
    B. strengthen
    C. bulge
    D. perspire
    E. expand

31. Speeding is "illegal". Illegal most nearly means
    A. permitted
    B. favorable
    C. tolerated
    D. against the law
    E. condoned

32. The house's exterior looked like it had been "neglected" for years; it desperately needed another coat of paint. Neglected most nearly means
    A. attended to
    B. maintained
    C. ignored
    D. preserved
    E. sustained

33. Nighttime television soap operas seem to be "popular" these days. Popular most nearly means
    A. unfavorable
    B. desirable
    C. despised
    D. obnoxious
    E. offensive

34. Politicians frequently make "absurd" promises. Absurd most nearly means
    A. unreasonable
    B. believeable
    C. special
    D. meaningful
    E. memorable

35. The carpenter barely made enough money for his family to "subsist" on. Subsist most nearly means
    A. live
    B. ponder
    C. vacation
    D. travel
    E. entertain

-END OF TEST-

ANSWER SHEET TO WORD MEANING / TEST I

1.	Ⓐ Ⓑ Ⓒ Ⓓ Ⓔ	19.	Ⓐ Ⓑ Ⓒ Ⓓ Ⓔ
2.	Ⓐ Ⓑ Ⓒ Ⓓ Ⓔ	20.	Ⓐ Ⓑ Ⓒ Ⓓ Ⓔ
3.	Ⓐ Ⓑ Ⓒ Ⓓ Ⓔ	21.	Ⓐ Ⓑ Ⓒ Ⓓ Ⓔ
4.	Ⓐ Ⓑ Ⓒ Ⓓ Ⓔ	22.	Ⓐ Ⓑ Ⓒ Ⓓ Ⓔ
5.	Ⓐ Ⓑ Ⓒ Ⓓ Ⓔ	23.	Ⓐ Ⓑ Ⓒ Ⓓ Ⓔ
6.	Ⓐ Ⓑ Ⓒ Ⓓ Ⓔ	24.	Ⓐ Ⓑ Ⓒ Ⓓ Ⓔ
7.	Ⓐ Ⓑ Ⓒ Ⓓ Ⓔ	25.	Ⓐ Ⓑ Ⓒ Ⓓ Ⓔ
8.	Ⓐ Ⓑ Ⓒ Ⓓ Ⓔ	26.	Ⓐ Ⓑ Ⓒ Ⓓ Ⓔ
9.	Ⓐ Ⓑ Ⓒ Ⓓ Ⓔ	27.	Ⓐ Ⓑ Ⓒ Ⓓ Ⓔ
10.	Ⓐ Ⓑ Ⓒ Ⓓ Ⓔ	28.	Ⓐ Ⓑ Ⓒ Ⓓ Ⓔ
11.	Ⓐ Ⓑ Ⓒ Ⓓ Ⓔ	29.	Ⓐ Ⓑ Ⓒ Ⓓ Ⓔ
12.	Ⓐ Ⓑ Ⓒ Ⓓ Ⓔ	30.	Ⓐ Ⓑ Ⓒ Ⓓ Ⓔ
13.	Ⓐ Ⓑ Ⓒ Ⓓ Ⓔ	31.	Ⓐ Ⓑ Ⓒ Ⓓ Ⓔ
14.	Ⓐ Ⓑ Ⓒ Ⓓ Ⓔ	32.	Ⓐ Ⓑ Ⓒ Ⓓ Ⓔ
15.	Ⓐ Ⓑ Ⓒ Ⓓ Ⓔ	33.	Ⓐ Ⓑ Ⓒ Ⓓ Ⓔ
16.	Ⓐ Ⓑ Ⓒ Ⓓ Ⓔ	34.	Ⓐ Ⓑ Ⓒ Ⓓ Ⓔ
17.	Ⓐ Ⓑ Ⓒ Ⓓ Ⓔ	35.	Ⓐ Ⓑ Ⓒ Ⓓ Ⓔ
18.	Ⓐ Ⓑ Ⓒ Ⓓ Ⓔ		

(This page may be removed to mark answers.)

The Postal Exam Preparation Book

WORD MEANING / TEST I ANSWERS

1.	D		19.	A
2.	A		20.	B
3.	B		21.	B
4.	B		22.	D
5.	B		23.	A
6.	A		24.	E
7.	C		25.	C
8.	E		26.	B
9.	A		27.	A
10.	C		28.	C
11.	E		29.	E
12.	E		30.	A
13.	B		31.	D
14.	E		32.	C
15.	C		33.	B
16.	A		34.	A
17.	D		35.	A
18.	E			

If your score was:

—31 or more correct, you have an excellent score
—25 to 30 correct, you have a good score
—24 or less correct, you should practice more.

The Postal Exam Preparation Book 263

WORD MEANING / TEST II

TIME: 20 MINUTES

1. Grandma and Grandpa were "delighted" to see the entire family get together for Thanksgiving dinner. Delighted most nearly means
   - A. upset
   - B. happy
   - C. quiescent
   - D. sad
   - E. confused

2. When someone does an outstanding job they should be "complimented" for it. Complimented most nearly means
   - A. cursed
   - B. yelled at
   - C. dismissed
   - D. lamented
   - E. commended

3. The weatherman was "perplexed" when it was sunny after he and his associates predicted rain for the day. Perplexed most nearly means
   - A. puzzled
   - B. amused
   - C. unhappy
   - D. disenchanted
   - E. indifferent

4. The policeman felt "lethargic" in the morning before he had his morning cup of coffee. Lethargic most nearly means
   - A. alert
   - B. awake
   - C. energetic
   - D. drowsy
   - E. coherent

5. As April 15 draws nearer, certified public accountants work "diligently" on their clients' tax returns to avoid any penalties for a delinquent filing. Diligently most nearly means
   - A. procrastinate
   - B. slowly
   - C. assiduously
   - D. effortlessly
   - E. vainly

6. It was difficult to tell if he was "bluffing". Bluffing most nearly means
   - A. cheating
   - B. showing deception
   - C. in control
   - D. contradict
   - E. relaxed

7. The youngster was "unaccustomed" to taking his shoes off before he entered the house. Unaccustomed most nearly means
   - A. aware
   - B. partial
   - C. contemplate
   - D. content
   - E. unfamiliar

8. Legislation passed by a "marginal" vote. Marginal most nearly means
   A. majority
   B. overwhelming
   C. sensational
   D. borderline
   E. partisan

9. The Canadian geese seeemed "hesitant" to fly in close to the hunter's decoys. Hesitant most nearly means
   A. confident
   B. certain
   C. inclined
   D. unsure
   E. attentive

10. Cloud formations developing on the western horizon looked "ominous". Ominous most nearly means
    A. dull
    B. menacing
    C. pretty
    D. odd
    E. spectacular

11. Congressional incumbents tend to be "evasive" on controversial matters at election ime. Evasive most nearly means
    A. elusive
    B. understanding
    C. strongly opinionated
    D. receptive
    E. responsive

12. Pine trees have a very pleasant "odor". Odor most nearly means
    A. bark
    B. resin
    C. scent
    D. perspective
    E. shade

13. Sports fans are usually "optimistic" that their team will be victorious. Optimistic most nearly means
    A. doubtful
    B. surprised
    C. pessimistic
    D. opposed
    E. hopeful

14. When someone is thinking about purchasing a used car, "durability" should be a foremost consideration. Durability most nearly means
    A. longevity
    B. four wheel drive
    C. low price
    D. comfort
    E. tires

15. "Disagreement" most nearly means
    A. acceptance
    B. belief
    C. dispute
    D. happiness
    E. fanciful

16. "Inhale" most nearly means
    A. stand on your head
    B. breathe
    C. exercise
    D. jog
    E. perspire

17. The engineer displayed an acute sense of "ingenuity". Ingenuity most nearly means
    A. awkwardness
    B. laziness
    C. inventiveness
    D. flattery
    E. nearsightedness

18. Bank loans are made with the understanding that the borrower is legally "obligated" to repay the loan and any accrued interest to the lender. Obligated most nearly means
    A. responsible
    B. unaccountable
    C. relieved
    D. unbound
    E. indolent

19. "Trespass" most nearly means
    A. having permission
    B. intrude
    C. pass with care
    D. notify
    E. contentedness

20. "Contradict" most nearly means
    A. refute
    B. bewilder
    C. compliment
    D. in agreement
    E. satisfied

21. The lake seemed "placid" enough to go boating. Placid most nearly means
    A. turbulant
    B. calm
    C. rough
    D. bright
    E. agitated

22. Even doctors admit that it is healthy to drink liquor in "moderate" amounts. Moderate most nearly means
    A. overdose
    B. indulge until you cannot remember how many you have had
    C. reasonable
    D. excessive
    E. unreasonable

23. The young man driving the Corvette seemed "aggravated" when the police officer handed him a ticket for an illegal turn. Aggravated most nearly means
    A. surprised
    B. enthusiastic
    C. irritated
    D. drunk
    E. sober

24. It was very clear that the geneticist that gave the seminar was an "authority" on gene (DNA) splicing and recombination. Authority most nearly means
    A. in command of
    B. lacking understanding
    C. boring
    D. less than knowledgeable
    E. oblivious to the subject matter

25. The referee "intervened" before the game erupted into a fight. Intervene most nearly means
    A. intimidated the players
    B. talked to the coaches
    C. departed
    D. interceded
    E. took a coffee break

26. The little boy was quite "precocious". Precocious most nearly means
    A. colder than usual
    B. late
    C. foreboding
    D. unfavorable
    E. early in mental development

27. Demolition of older buildings with explosives is a "precarious" occupation. Precarious most nearly means
    A. risky
    B. humble
    C. dynamic
    D. technically sophisticated
    E. exciting

28. Patient records are supposed to be "confidential". Confidential most nearly means
    A. made public
    B. scrutinized
    C. private
    D. catalogued
    E. examined periodically

29. A receiver in football displaying a good degree of "alacrity" is considered an invaluable player. Alacrity most nearly means
    A. conservatism
    B. sportsmanship
    C. responsiveness
    D. courtesy
    E. cleverness

30. To those of us that have not participated in many running competitions, running in the Boston Marathon would be a "formidable" venture. Formidable most nearly means
    A. difficult
    B. inconsequential
    C. easy
    D. fast
    E. simple

31. Viewer "discretion" is advised for movies that may contain too much violence. Discretion most nearly means
    A. acceptance
    B. blackout
    C. network censorship
    D. applause
    E. judgment

The Postal Exam Preparation Book 267

32. China dishes have to be handled with care because they are extremely "fragile". Fragile most nearly means
    A. durable
    B. indestructable
    C. slippery
    D. breakable
    E. rare

33. The president of the Small Business Administration was very "humble" about his own ventures, yet it was obvious he was a very successful businessman. Humble most nearly means
    A. flamboyant
    B. modest
    C. conceited
    D. egotistic
    E. vague

34. Grandmothers always seem to have the best "remedy" for colds. Remedy most nearly means
    A. chance
    B. tolerance
    C. latency
    D. success
    E. cure

35. Fresh boiled lobster dipped in melted butter is a "savory" meal appreciated by seafood lovers. Savory most nearly means
    A. bland
    B. terrible
    C. high calorie
    D. delectable
    E. expensive

-END OF TEST-

ANSWER SHEET TO WORD MEANING/TEST II

1.	Ⓐ Ⓑ Ⓒ Ⓓ Ⓔ	19.	Ⓐ Ⓑ Ⓒ Ⓓ Ⓔ
2.	Ⓐ Ⓑ Ⓒ Ⓓ Ⓔ	20.	Ⓐ Ⓑ Ⓒ Ⓓ Ⓔ
3.	Ⓐ Ⓑ Ⓒ Ⓓ Ⓔ	21.	Ⓐ Ⓑ Ⓒ Ⓓ Ⓔ
4.	Ⓐ Ⓑ Ⓒ Ⓓ Ⓔ	22.	Ⓐ Ⓑ Ⓒ Ⓓ Ⓔ
5.	Ⓐ Ⓑ Ⓒ Ⓓ Ⓔ	23.	Ⓐ Ⓑ Ⓒ Ⓓ Ⓔ
6.	Ⓐ Ⓑ Ⓒ Ⓓ Ⓔ	24.	Ⓐ Ⓑ Ⓒ Ⓓ Ⓔ
7.	Ⓐ Ⓑ Ⓒ Ⓓ Ⓔ	25.	Ⓐ Ⓑ Ⓒ Ⓓ Ⓔ
8.	Ⓐ Ⓑ Ⓒ Ⓓ Ⓔ	26.	Ⓐ Ⓑ Ⓒ Ⓓ Ⓔ
9.	Ⓐ Ⓑ Ⓒ Ⓓ Ⓔ	27.	Ⓐ Ⓑ Ⓒ Ⓓ Ⓔ
10.	Ⓐ Ⓑ Ⓒ Ⓓ Ⓔ	28.	Ⓐ Ⓑ Ⓒ Ⓓ Ⓔ
11.	Ⓐ Ⓑ Ⓒ Ⓓ Ⓔ	29.	Ⓐ Ⓑ Ⓒ Ⓓ Ⓔ
12.	Ⓐ Ⓑ Ⓒ Ⓓ Ⓔ	30.	Ⓐ Ⓑ Ⓒ Ⓓ Ⓔ
13.	Ⓐ Ⓑ Ⓒ Ⓓ Ⓔ	31.	Ⓐ Ⓑ Ⓒ Ⓓ Ⓔ
14.	Ⓐ Ⓑ Ⓒ Ⓓ Ⓔ	32.	Ⓐ Ⓑ Ⓒ Ⓓ Ⓔ
15.	Ⓐ Ⓑ Ⓒ Ⓓ Ⓔ	33.	Ⓐ Ⓑ Ⓒ Ⓓ Ⓔ
16.	Ⓐ Ⓑ Ⓒ Ⓓ Ⓔ	34.	Ⓐ Ⓑ Ⓒ Ⓓ Ⓔ
17.	Ⓐ Ⓑ Ⓒ Ⓓ Ⓔ	35.	Ⓐ Ⓑ Ⓒ Ⓓ Ⓔ
18.	Ⓐ Ⓑ Ⓒ Ⓓ Ⓔ		

(This page may be removed to mark answers.)

WORD MEANING / TEST II ANSWERS

1.	B	19.	B
2.	E	20.	A
3.	A	21.	B
4.	D	22.	C
5.	C	23.	C
6.	B	24.	A
7.	E	25.	D
8.	D	26.	E
9.	D	27.	A
10.	B	28.	C
11.	A	29.	C
12.	C	30.	A
13.	E	31.	E
14.	A	32.	D
15.	C	33.	B
16.	B	34.	E
17.	C	35.	D
18.	A		

If your score was:
- 31 or more correct, you have an excellent score
- 25 to 30 correct, you have a good score
- 24 or less correct, you should practice more.

WORD MEANING / TEST III

TIME: 20 MINUTES

1. It is frequently stressed by parents and educators that we should return to the "fundamentals" of reading, writing and arithmetic. Fundamentals most nearly means
   - A. basics
   - B. theories
   - C. recreation
   - D. reformation
   - E. business

2. The guest speaker seemed a little "nervous" before giving his presentation to the company's management team. Nervous most nearly means
   - A. confident
   - B. incompetent
   - C. uneasy
   - D. polite
   - E. new

3. Receptionists always seem to have a "radiant" smile when greeting people. Radiant most nearly means
   - A. forced
   - B. distorted
   - C. haphazard
   - D. glowing
   - E. tireless

4. Without knowing much about auto repair, it would be difficult to understand an auto mechanic's "jargon". Jargon most nearly means
   - A. inventory
   - B. health plan
   - C. intentions
   - D. tools
   - E. lingo

5. Farmers find that when there is a "surplus" of a particular crop the prices offered on the market for that crop are reduced..Surplus most nearly means
   - A. oversupply
   - B. production low
   - C. drought
   - D. pestilence
   - E. theft

6. Duck hunting is especially promising in a "marsh". Marsh most nearly means
   - A. restaurant
   - B. swamp
   - C. next door neighbor's swimming pool
   - D. cornfield
   - E. tree

7. Firemen are a "gallant" lot as they often put the safety of others ahead of their own. Gallant most nearly means
   - A. cowardice
   - B. frightened
   - C. brave
   - D. sympathetic
   - E. remorseful

272 The Postal Exam Preparation Book

8. "Frequently", people will wait until the week prior to Christmas before they start their shopping. Frequently most nearly means
   A. rarely
   B. always
   C. biannually
   D. annually
   E. often

9. The gravel road "tapered" as it ran its course deeper into the wilderness. Tapered most nearly means
   A. widened
   B. improved
   C. deteriorated
   D. narrowed
   E. ascended

10. It was the Spanish teacher's "goal" to have all of her students speaking basic Spanish before year's end. Goal most nearly means
    A. gamble
    B. ambition
    C. problem
    D. responsibility
    E. requirement

11. Certain types of plastics are extremely "pliable". Pliable most nearly means
    A. flexible
    B. stiff
    C. flammable
    D. expensive
    E. fragile

12. Businesses can use one of two "methods" to figure income tax. Methods most nearly means
    A. procedures
    B. publications
    C. factors
    D. investigations
    E. virtues

13. Grocery stores always "rotate" their stock to prevent spoilage and out-of-date losses on unsold goods. Rotate most nearly means
    A. hide
    B. stack
    C. damage
    D. sell
    E. turn

14. It was too windy to accurately "gauge" the amount of snow that had fallen overnight. Gauge most nearly means
    A. shovel
    B. melt
    C. measure
    D. plow
    E. garner

15. The "ultimate" experience for any actor or actress is to receive an Oscar or Emmy Award for their performance. Ultimate most nearly means
    A. beginning
    B. maximum
    C. uncertain
    D. definite
    E. painful

The Postal Exam Preparation Book 273

16. The new high school football coach "boasted" about how well his team performed in the first game of the year. Boasted most nearly means
    A. disliked
    B. bragged
    C. disappointed
    D. unhappy
    E. argued

17. It can be dangerous to drive on or across a highway "median" when there is oncoming traffic. Median most nearly means
    A. shoulder
    B. bridge
    C. middle
    D. turn off lane
    E. emergency lane

18. Even though Mr. Smith was an architectural engineer, he was also very "handy" at fixing broken electrical appliances. Handy most nearly means
    A. unskillful
    B. capable
    C. inept
    D. confused
    E. cognate

19. It would be nice if all "prejudice" was non-existent. Prejudice most nearly means
    A. bias
    B. tolerance
    C. starvation
    D. famine
    E. war

20. The scientist was "startled" by the results of his experiment. Startled most nearly means
    A. comforted
    B. unconcerned
    C. estatic
    D. surprised
    E. reassured

21. A lot of people steadfastly feel that a dog is man's best "friend". Friend most nearly means
    A. arch rival
    B. nuisance
    C. pleasure
    D. companion
    E. notability

22. Sometimes it is hard not to be "jealous" of other people's accomplishments. Jealous most nearly means
    A. envious
    B. disgust
    C. righteous
    D. nervous
    E. iridescent

23. In a child's mind, the easiest way to get their parents' attention is to have a "tantrum". Tantrum most nearly means
    A. outburst of temper
    B. smoke
    C. fasting
    D. good amount of sleep
    E. debate of current policy

24. The heavy rains were an "impediment" to volunteer workers who were sandbagging the river embankments. Impediment most nearly means
    A. aid
    B. limited help
    C. hinderance
    D. incentive
    E. important

25. Without the immune system, a person's health would become "vulnerable" to disease. Vulnerable most nearly means
    A. vulpine
    B. defenseless
    C. closed
    D. tolerable
    E. oblivious

26. "Astronomy" can be an interesting subject for students that have a fascination for science. Astronomy most nearly means
    A. chemistry
    B. biology
    C. statistical inference
    D. observation of the celestials
    E. study of plants

27. It was difficult to find where the "error" was made in the checkbook even using the current bank statement as a reference. Error most nearly means
    A. correction
    B. miscellaneous expense
    C. deduction
    D. payment
    E. mistake

28. A line drawn between two points on a plane is said to be "linear". Linear most nearly means
    A. crooked
    B. straight
    C. perpendicular
    D. crossed
    E. mathematically lost

29. It is not difficult to be "distracted" if what you are doing is boring. Distracted most nearly means
    A. deviated
    B. agonized
    C. involved
    D. consumed
    E. complacent

30. Most of the African continent is suffering from a severe "drought" that has been responsible for repeated crop failures and starvation. Drought most nearly means
    A. flooding
    B. typhoon
    C. earthquake
    D. tornado
    E. aridity

31. A storm of such intensity is a "quirk" of nature. Quirk most nearly means
    A. common place
    B. peculiarity
    C. shower
    D. fact
    E. concentration

32. It was "inevitable" that the initiative would pass with as much public support as there was. Inevitable most nearly means
    A. impossible
    B. hopeful
    C. certain
    D. doubtful
    E. incredible

33. The Board of Regents' proposal was not very "plausible". Plausible most nearly means
    A. reasonable
    B. considerate
    C. information
    D. vague
    E. uplifting

34. Some of the foreign imports were found to be "inferior". Inferior most nearly means
    A. superior
    B. high quality
    C. low quality
    D. dynamic
    E. unmarked

35. The investigation was conducted in a very "thorough" manner. Thorough most nearly means
    A. haphazard
    B. incomplete
    C. reckless
    D. sophisticated
    E. complete

-END OF TEST-

ANSWER SHEET TO WORD MEANING / TEST III

1. Ⓐ Ⓑ Ⓒ Ⓓ Ⓔ
2. Ⓐ Ⓑ Ⓒ Ⓓ Ⓔ
3. Ⓐ Ⓑ Ⓒ Ⓓ Ⓔ
4. Ⓐ Ⓑ Ⓒ Ⓓ Ⓔ
5. Ⓐ Ⓑ Ⓒ Ⓓ Ⓔ
6. Ⓐ Ⓑ Ⓒ Ⓓ Ⓔ
7. Ⓐ Ⓑ Ⓒ Ⓓ Ⓔ
8. Ⓐ Ⓑ Ⓒ Ⓓ Ⓔ
9. Ⓐ Ⓑ Ⓒ Ⓓ Ⓔ
10. Ⓐ Ⓑ Ⓒ Ⓓ Ⓔ
11. Ⓐ Ⓑ Ⓒ Ⓓ Ⓔ
12. Ⓐ Ⓑ Ⓒ Ⓓ Ⓔ
13. Ⓐ Ⓑ Ⓒ Ⓓ Ⓔ
14. Ⓐ Ⓑ Ⓒ Ⓓ Ⓔ
15. Ⓐ Ⓑ Ⓒ Ⓓ Ⓔ
16. Ⓐ Ⓑ Ⓒ Ⓓ Ⓔ
17. Ⓐ Ⓑ Ⓒ Ⓓ Ⓔ
18. Ⓐ Ⓑ Ⓒ Ⓓ Ⓔ

19. Ⓐ Ⓑ Ⓒ Ⓓ Ⓔ
20. Ⓐ Ⓑ Ⓒ Ⓓ Ⓔ
21. Ⓐ Ⓑ Ⓒ Ⓓ Ⓔ
22. Ⓐ Ⓑ Ⓒ Ⓓ Ⓔ
23. Ⓐ Ⓑ Ⓒ Ⓓ Ⓔ
24. Ⓐ Ⓑ Ⓒ Ⓓ Ⓔ
25. Ⓐ Ⓑ Ⓒ Ⓓ Ⓔ
26. Ⓐ Ⓑ Ⓒ Ⓓ Ⓔ
27. Ⓐ Ⓑ Ⓒ Ⓓ Ⓔ
28. Ⓐ Ⓑ Ⓒ Ⓓ Ⓔ
29. Ⓐ Ⓑ Ⓒ Ⓓ Ⓔ
30. Ⓐ Ⓑ Ⓒ Ⓓ Ⓔ
31. Ⓐ Ⓑ Ⓒ Ⓓ Ⓔ
32. Ⓐ Ⓑ Ⓒ Ⓓ Ⓔ
33. Ⓐ Ⓑ Ⓒ Ⓓ Ⓔ
34. Ⓐ Ⓑ Ⓒ Ⓓ Ⓔ
35. Ⓐ Ⓑ Ⓒ Ⓓ Ⓔ

(This page may be removed to mark answers.)

The Postal Exam Preparation Book

WORD MEANING / TEST III ANSWERS

1.	A	19.	A
2.	C	20.	D
3.	D	21.	D
4.	E	22.	A
5.	A	23.	A
6.	B	24.	C
7.	C	25.	B
8.	E	26.	D
9.	D	27.	E
10.	B	28.	B
11.	A	29.	A
12.	A	30.	E
13.	E	31.	B
14.	C	32.	C
15.	B	33.	A
16.	B	34.	C
17.	C	35.	E
18.	B		

If your score was:

— 31 or more correct, you have an excellent score
— 25 to 30 correct, you have a good score
— 24 or less correct, you should practice more.

WORD MEANING / TEST IV

1. The high school graduate had a lot of "gumption" to file as many job applications as she did. Gumption most nearly means
   - A. initiative
   - B. complaints
   - C. resentment
   - D. fun
   - E. inquiries

2. The town "thrived" after gold was found in a nearby mine. Thrived most nearly means
   - A. deteriorated
   - B. vigorously grew
   - C. stagnated
   - D. vacated
   - E. celebrated

3. Customs officers at the US-Mexican border will "seize" any fruit that tourists try to take home. Seize most nearly means
   - A. stamp
   - B. inventory
   - C. overlook
   - D. take
   - E. examine

4. Tom had an "excuse" from his doctor for his absence. Excuse most nearly means
   - A. justification
   - B. objection
   - C. argument
   - D. ultimatum
   - E. disagreement

5. Most plants become "dormant" during the winter. Dormant most nearly means
   - A. frozen
   - B. hard
   - C. mulch
   - D. inactive
   - E. sticky

6. In Japan, the trains are literally "crammed" with people. Crammed most nearly means
   - A. empty
   - B. partially full
   - C. stuffed
   - D. shunned
   - E. side tracked

7. The roads around here are "treacherous" when they are covered with ice. Treacherous most nearly means
   - A. safe
   - B. closed
   - C. sanded
   - D. patrolled
   - E. untrustworthy

8. The antelope were too "numerous" to count. Numerous most nearly means
   - A. sparse
   - B. many
   - C. depleted
   - D. few
   - E. ordinary

9. Most people are a little "tense" before taking an exam. Tense most nearly means
    A. relaxed
    B. docile
    C. confident
    D. sleepy
    E. strained

10. The electricity "momentarily" went out this morning. Momentarily most nearly means
    A. permanently
    B. for an instant
    C. all together
    D. without warning
    E. slowly

11. Jim tends to "exaggerate" about his accomplishments. Exaggerate most nearly means
    A. gloat
    B. brag
    C. stretch the truth
    D. argue
    E. exult

12. After the game of Scrabble fell on the floor, we really had a "jumble" of letters to pick up. Jumble most nearly means
    A. mix
    B. ordered arrangement
    C. spelling
    D. solution
    E. intemperance

13. It is important to be "careful" when doing the arithmetic on a tax return. Careful most nearly means
    A. carefree
    B. sober
    C. awake
    D. rash
    E. cautious

14. My wife is always telling our friends that I have a "voracious" appetite. Voracious most nearly means
    A. small
    B. moderate
    C. insatiable
    D. spontaneous
    E. finicky

15. Lifestyles back in the late 60's and early 70's were much more "liberal" than they are now. Liberal most nearly means
    A. conservative
    B. favoring reform
    C. unprogressive
    D. stable
    E. unchanging

16. She was a "petite" woman in her late forties. Petite most nearly means
    A. beautiful
    B. intelligent
    C. complacent
    D. small statured
    E. overweight

The Postal Exam Preparation Book 281

17. Certified public accountants are "shrewd" when it comes to figuring taxes. Shrewd most nearly means
    A. incapable
    B. slow
    C. hesitant
    D. sharp
    E. expensive

18. The party is going to be in a "ritzy" downtown hotel this weekend. Ritzy most nearly means
    A. fleabag
    B. cheap
    C. older
    D. rundown
    E. swank

19. There were alot of "miscellaneous" parts with no apparent use. Miscellaneous most nearly means
    A. various
    B. delapidated
    C. catalogued
    D. new
    E. inferior

20. Kids sometimes get into the "habit" of not closing the front door after coming in. Habit most nearly means
    A. customary practice
    B. irregularity
    C. intermittence
    D. caprice
    E. variablity

21. He did not want "pity" from his neighbors. Pity most nearly means
    A. money
    B. gifts
    C. sympathy
    D. advice
    E. help

22. Fossils are "vestiges" of organisms that lived during the prehistoric era. Vestiges most nearly means
    A. computations
    B. compromises
    C. impurities
    D. evidence
    E. prominance

23. The river "meandered" for miles before it reached the lake. Meandered most nearly means
    A. straight lined
    B. wound
    C. swilled
    D. narrowed
    E. widened

24. Marvin felt he could only do "mediocre" work in his Calculus class. Mediocre most nearly means
    A. average
    B. excellent
    C. poor
    D. supreme
    E. unsatisfactory

25. Her folks thought her date for the prom was an "impressive" lad. Impressive most nearly means
    A. boring
    B. lewd
    C. salacious
    D. lethargic
    E. striking

26. The detective was on the "brink" of solving the crime. Brink most nearly means
    A. bandwagon
    B. verge
    C. case
    D. record
    E. groundwork

27. Susan "abruptly" quit her piano lessons for no apparent reason. Abruptly most nearly means
    A. secretly
    B. evidently
    C. obviously
    D. suddenly
    E. solemnly

28. There were several dents in the "rear" of the car. Rear most nearly means
    A. anterior
    B. side
    C. posterior
    D. topside
    E. door

29. The jury was "sequestered" while determining the verdict. Sequestered most nearly means
    A. questioned
    B. bribed
    C. segregated from the public
    D. applauded
    E. watched

30. If the governor has his way, there are going to be a lot of "radical" changes on how the state funds are appropriated for public housing. Radical most nearly means
    A. minor
    B. extreme
    C. incomprehensible
    D. subtle
    E. foolish

31. There was a strong feeling of "solidarity" among company workers. Solidarity most nearly means
    A. resentment
    B. apathy
    C. uneasiness
    D. penitence
    E. fellowship

32. I was frequently told by my parents that I was a "glutton" for punishment. Glutton most nearly means
    A. sidestepper
    B. person with great desire
    C. suspect
    D. likely candidate
    E. fine example

33. The trapper's hands were completely "numb" from the cold by the time he returned to camp from his trapline. Numb most nearly means
    A. devoid of feeling
    B. covered
    C. cracked
    D. tingling
    E. sensitive

34. The scoutmaster "influenced" the kids to go on another winter campout even when most of them swore they would never go again. Influenced most nearly means
    A. forced
    B. insisted
    C. begged
    D. induced
    E. arbitrated

35. Too many times he spent money on "frivolous" items and now he is poor. Frivolous most nearly means
    A. necessary
    B. expensive
    C. unimportant
    D. extravagant
    E. elegant

-END OF TEST-

ANSWER SHEET TO WORD MEANING / TEST IV

1.	Ⓐ Ⓑ Ⓒ Ⓓ Ⓔ	19.	Ⓐ Ⓑ Ⓒ Ⓓ Ⓔ
2.	Ⓐ Ⓑ Ⓒ Ⓓ Ⓔ	20.	Ⓐ Ⓑ Ⓒ Ⓓ Ⓔ
3.	Ⓐ Ⓑ Ⓒ Ⓓ Ⓔ	21.	Ⓐ Ⓑ Ⓒ Ⓓ Ⓔ
4.	Ⓐ Ⓑ Ⓒ Ⓓ Ⓔ	22.	Ⓐ Ⓑ Ⓒ Ⓓ Ⓔ
5.	Ⓐ Ⓑ Ⓒ Ⓓ Ⓔ	23.	Ⓐ Ⓑ Ⓒ Ⓓ Ⓔ
6.	Ⓐ Ⓑ Ⓒ Ⓓ Ⓔ	24.	Ⓐ Ⓑ Ⓒ Ⓓ Ⓔ
7.	Ⓐ Ⓑ Ⓒ Ⓓ Ⓔ	25.	Ⓐ Ⓑ Ⓒ Ⓓ Ⓔ
8.	Ⓐ Ⓑ Ⓒ Ⓓ Ⓔ	26.	Ⓐ Ⓑ Ⓒ Ⓓ Ⓔ
9.	Ⓐ Ⓑ Ⓒ Ⓓ Ⓔ	27.	Ⓐ Ⓑ Ⓒ Ⓓ Ⓔ
10.	Ⓐ Ⓑ Ⓒ Ⓓ Ⓔ	28.	Ⓐ Ⓑ Ⓒ Ⓓ Ⓔ
11.	Ⓐ Ⓑ Ⓒ Ⓓ Ⓔ	29.	Ⓐ Ⓑ Ⓒ Ⓓ Ⓔ
12.	Ⓐ Ⓑ Ⓒ Ⓓ Ⓔ	30.	Ⓐ Ⓑ Ⓒ Ⓓ Ⓔ
13.	Ⓐ Ⓑ Ⓒ Ⓓ Ⓔ	31.	Ⓐ Ⓑ Ⓒ Ⓓ Ⓔ
14.	Ⓐ Ⓑ Ⓒ Ⓓ Ⓔ	32.	Ⓐ Ⓑ Ⓒ Ⓓ Ⓔ
15.	Ⓐ Ⓑ Ⓒ Ⓓ Ⓔ	33.	Ⓐ Ⓑ Ⓒ Ⓓ Ⓔ
16.	Ⓐ Ⓑ Ⓒ Ⓓ Ⓔ	34.	Ⓐ Ⓑ Ⓒ Ⓓ Ⓔ
17.	Ⓐ Ⓑ Ⓒ Ⓓ Ⓔ	35.	Ⓐ Ⓑ Ⓒ Ⓓ Ⓔ
18.	Ⓐ Ⓑ Ⓒ Ⓓ Ⓔ		

(This page may be removed to mark answers.)

WORD MEANING / TEST IV ANSWERS

1.	A	19.	A
2.	B	20.	A
3.	D	21.	C
4.	A	22.	D
5.	D	23.	B
6.	C	24.	A
7.	E	25.	E
8.	B	26.	B
9.	E	27.	D
10.	B	28.	C
11.	C	29.	C
12.	A	30.	B
13.	E	31.	E
14.	C	32.	B
15.	B	33.	A
16.	D	34.	D
17.	D	35.	C
18.	E		

If your score was:

—31 or more correct, you have an excellent score
—25 to 30 correct, you have a good score
—24 or less correct, you should practice more.

What Follows After The Examination?

Once you have taken the exam, it will be a few weeks before your test results are mailed back to you. If your score was 70 or better, your name will be placed on the federal register of the Post Office that submitted the test. Your score is not transferable to other post offices that apply the exam. As a consequence, it is to your advantage to take as many of these exams as possible. The more scores outstanding on other registers, the better are your chances for employment.

When you are among those to be considered for a postal position you will be notified via mail about the time and place of your interview. It is very important to convey the best impression possible of yourself to the interviewer. Dress well and be, if not early, prompt for your scheduled interview time. If you happen to have some references on hand from old or current jobs, it would not be a bad idea to bring them along too.

During the interview, if you can show an awareness of what the position you are interviewing for entails and have some general idea of how the Postal Service operates, you will be much further ahead of those who walk in unknowing and just want a job. Try to draw a parallel between your old job experiences and the job you are applying for. You do not want to paint an over-glorified picture of yourself, but if you are a hard worker, take pride in what you do, and put out that extra effort when needed, tell the person who is interviewing you. It gives the interviewer an overall optimistic picture of you and your potential work performance.

It may take a few weeks before you are notified about the outcome of your interview. At this point, it would only be in order to extend the author's best of luck wishes to you. You have gone to a lot of hard work and time to find placement within the Postal Service. Once you are employed with the Postal Service, the job satisfactions are great.

Refund Policy

In the unlikely event of dissatisfaction with your test results (i.e., scoring less than 90%) your money will be refunded.

However, the following conditions must be met before refunds will be made. All exercises within this guide must be completed to show that the applicant did make a valid attempt to practice and best prepare to score 90% or better. This policy is in effect until 120 days from the date of purchase shown on your sales receipt. Anything submitted beyond this 120 day period will be subject to publisher discretion on determining refunds.

When mailing this guide back for refund, please include your sales receipt, validated test results and a self-addressed, stamped envelope. Requests for refunds should be addressed to: Bob Adams, Inc. Postal Exams Division., 260 Center St., Holbrook, MA, 02343. Please allow approximately three weeks for processing.